Moss Bluff Rebel

NUMBER EIGHTEEN
*Sam Rayburn Series
on Rural Life*

Sponsored by
Texas A&M University–
Commerce

M. HUNTER HAYES,
General Editor

Texas A&M
University Press

Moss Bluff Rebel

A Texas Pioneer in the Civil War

Philip Caudill

TEXAS A&M UNIVERSITY PRESS
COLLEGE STATION

Library of Congress Cataloging-in-Publication Data

Caudill, Philip Robert, 1947–
    Moss Bluff rebel : a Texas pioneer in the Civil War / Philip
    Caudill. — 1st ed.
        p. cm. — (Sam Rayburn series on rural life ; no. 18)
    Originally presented as: Thesis (M.A.)—Sam Houston
    State University, 2007. Includes bibliographical references
    and index.
    ISBN-13: 978-1-60344-089-9 (cloth : alk. paper)
    ISBN-10: 1-60344-089-5 (cloth : alk. paper)
1. Duncan, William Berry, 1818–1867. 2. Confederate States
of America. Army—Officers—Biography. 3. Confederate
States of America. Army. Texas Cavalry Regiment, 11th.
4. Texas—History—Civil War, 1861–1865—Biography.
5. Texas—History—Civil War, 1861–1865—Cavalry
operations. 6. Pioneers—Texas—Biography. 7. Drovers—
Texas—Biography. 8. Frontier and pioneer life—Texas.
9. United States—History—Civil War, 1861–1865—Biography.
10. United States—History—Civil War, 1861–1865—Cavalry
operations. I. Title. II. Title: Reluctant rebel. III. Series.
    E467.1.D885C38 2009
    973.7'82092—dc22
    [B]

                                                    2008034068

To Nance
Christopher and Rachel
Patrick, Sarah, Declan, and Dylan
You are blessings

Come my tan-faced children,
Follow well in order, get your weapons ready,
Have you your pistols? have you your sharp-edged axes?
      Pioneers! O pioneers!

      For we cannot tarry here,
We must march my darlings, we must bear the brunt of danger,
We the youthful sinewy races, all the rest on us depend,
      Pioneers! O pioneers!

      O you youths, Western youths,
So impatient, full of action, full of manly pride and friendship,
Plain I see you Western youths, see you tramping with the foremost,
      Pioneers! O pioneers!

      We primeval forests felling,
We the rivers stemming, vexing we and piercing deep the mines within,
We the surface broad surveying, we the virgin soil upheaving,
      Pioneers! O pioneers!

      O resistless restless race!
O beloved race in all! O my breast aches with tender love for all!
O I mourn and yet exult, I am rapt with love for all,
      Pioneers! O pioneers!

See my children, resolute children,
By those swarms upon our rear we must never yield or falter,
Ages back in ghostly millions frowning there behind us urging,
        Pioneers! O pioneers!

        On and on the compact ranks,
With accessions ever waiting, with the places of the dead quickly fill'd,
Through the battle, through defeat, moving yet and never stopping,
        Pioneers! O pioneers!

        These are of us, they are with us,
All for primal needed work, while the followers there in embryo wait behind,
We to-day's procession heading, we the route for travel clearing,
        Pioneers! O pioneers!

        Till with sound of trumpet,
Far, far off the daybreak call—hark! how loud and clear I hear it wind,
Swift! to the head of the army!—swift! spring to your places,
        Pioneers! O pioneers!

                                    WALT WHITMAN, 1900

Table of Contents

Contents

List of Figures and Maps

Series Editor's Foreword

SINCE ITS INCEPTION, THE SAM RAYBURN SERIES on Rural Life has sought to present works that examine all facets of the communities in and around East Texas. Encompassing an expansive geographical area that stretches roughly from the Red River to the Gulf Coast, this region's history and ways of life coalesce around what might seem at first to be a paradox: adherence to traditions, particularly customs of the deep South, and an iconoclastic spirit akin to that found in nineteenth-century pioneers. It is appropriate, then, that Philip Caudill's engaging study of William Berry Duncan should be included in the Sam Rayburn Series on Rural Life.

In *Moss Bluff Rebel: A Texas Pioneer in the Civil War*, Caudill combines meticulous research and an adroit sense of narrative to portray Duncan's life in all its complexity. Caudill describes Duncan's evolution from "a pioneer Anglo-Texas Everyman," one equally skilled in wrangling cattle, managing finances, and acquiring real estate, through his service as a cavalry officer during the Civil War, to the hardships he faced during Reconstruction. By drawing from Duncan's diary among other sources, Caudill gives readers a critical and penetrating look at a man whose experiences reflect in part those of his region and of Texas. Additionally, Caudill examines those people around Duncan who had great impact on the life of this cattleman-turned-cavalry officer: Duncan's wife and children; Ashley Ward Spaight; his slaves (later freedmen), such as Sabine and Texas, all of whom figure prominently into the course of Duncan's life during and after the Civil War. Just as *Moss Bluff Rebel* reads at times like a historical novel with Duncan as its complicated protagonist, these other men and women resemble well-drawn characters that refuse to accept their roles as secondary figures. Their lives are, of course, more than fiction and legend, even while they remain inextricably linked to Duncan's, and Caudill is to be applauded for his deft handling of such profitable source material. Indeed, *Moss Bluff Rebel* is in many respects a composite story, as Caudill makes clear in his epilogue.

It is a pleasure to include both Caudill and *Moss Bluff Rebel* in the Rayburn Series. Founded at Texas A&M University–Commerce in collaboration with Texas A&M University Press, the Sam Rayburn Series on Rural Life has since 1997 intended to present works that challenge and augment the cultural history of a region that is in its own right a mosaic. Philip Caudill's skill as a writer—his astute command of historical detail as well as his gifts for engrossing readers in a compelling narrative—further expand our understanding of this tumultuous period and its impacts in and beyond East Texas.

M. Hunter Hayes
General Editor

Moss
Bluff
Rebel

Chapter 1 **Pioneer**

WILLIAM BERRY DUNCAN RODE INTO TOWN FROM his house on the east bank of the Trinity River south of Liberty, Texas, on March 1, 1862, to nominate officers for a unit of Texas Volunteers in the army of the Confederate States of America (C.S.A.). It was the day before his forty-fourth birthday, the same birthday he shared with the Republic of Texas, created in 1836, and its first president, Gen. Sam Houston, born March 2, 1793. Commanding officer Capt. Ashley Spaight swore Duncan and twenty-six other men into Spaight's unit a month later. It was two weeks short of a year *after* America's Civil War began at Fort Sumter in South Carolina. Duncan marked the event in his diary on the day he took the Confederate army oath, "I was not willing but finally agreed."[1]

The Provisional Congress of the C.S.A. authorized formation of a regular army on March 6, 1861. The same day, Confederate legislators called out C.S.A. state militias and authorized recruitment of 100,000 volunteers for a provisional army. Clearly hesitant to enlist twelve months after these bills became Confederate law, what finally prompted the middle-aged Duncan, shown in figure 1, to join Spaight's battalion? With northern lawmakers in mind, was he a Jacksonian Democrat who dreaded big government and shared Thomas Jefferson's sentiments written in the Declaration of Independence eighty-six years earlier, "We have warned our (British brethren) from time to time of attempts by their legislature to extend an unwarrantable jurisdiction over us"? Or was he simply one of many Southerners who reacted to war cries from secessionist politicians? Could Duncan's response have been more measured, prompted less about defending states' rights and preserving slavery, more by fear of an alien invasion? Was he in fact driven to secure his economic independence, concerned that Federal occupation might mean confiscation of the frontier land his father, father-in-law, and he had worked so hard to improve? What were his thoughts

FIG. I.
William Berry Duncan.
*Photo courtesy Miriam
Partlow Collection, SHRL,
Liberty, Texas.*

and how did life change for pioneer Texas cattleman, farmer, and public servant William B. Duncan when he served as a Confederate cavalryman in America's Civil War?[2]

The town of Liberty, Texas, was established in 1831, named after the county seat of Amite County, twenty miles west of McComb in the Natchez district of southern Mississippi and the former home of several immigrants to Mexico's Atascosito District in southeast Texas. To make the new town's name politically palatable in imperial Mexico City, land commissioner J. Francisco Madero advised his government he had "proceeded to the formal creation of a town in this [Atascosito] District on the east bank of the Trinity River and on the road that goes from Bexar towards the Opelousas and which I have named *Town of the Most Holy Trinity of Liberty*," or Villa de la Santissima Trinidad de la Libertad. From their point of view, Liberty's colonists might have approved the name as a veiled signal to Mexico of how they felt about foreign domination. That independent attitude became a core value of Liberty County[3] citizens as Texas won its freedom from Mexico in 1836, defended it against Mexico in 1848, and stiffened its neck with secession from the United States in 1861. The *defense* of liberty was an intrinsic aspect of William Duncan's character. The *town* of Liberty, Texas was his home.[4]

Ashley Ward Spaight lived in the Moss Bluff community less than five miles south of Liberty, a short ride from Duncan's house. Spaight was a lawyer born in Wilcox County, Alabama, in 1821 and educated at the University of North Carolina.[5] He moved to Liberty County in 1860 from Alabama, where he served one term in the state legislature and practiced law with Thomas J. Watts, later the attorney general of the Confederate States of America. Spaight, three-and-a-half years younger than Duncan, enlisted in the Texas Volunteers of the Confederate Army on July 4, 1861, five months after Texas voted to secede from the Union. Spaight spent the next nine months recruiting a volunteer company of eighty-four local men who were mustered into the C.S.A. infantry on April 17, 1862. Folks in southeast Texas called them the Moss Bluff Rebels.[6]

After being sworn to defend the Confederacy, Captain Spaight's new outfit was designated Company F of the Sixth Texas Infantry Battalion, itself an outgrowth of the Sabine Pass Guard that had been organized in 1861. It was officially reorganized on June 17, 1862 and named Spaight's Eleventh Battalion, Texas Volunteers. It consisted of six companies: cavalry Company A and artillery Company B were composed of men from Sabine Pass on the gulf coast in southern Jefferson County; companies C and D were infantry companies with men from Newton and Tyler counties, both of which are linked to Sabine Pass by rivers doing double duty as those counties' eastern borders, the Neches and Sabine, respectively; Company E was an infantry unit made up of soldiers from Beaumont, the county seat of Jefferson County; and Company F was a cavalry company, most of whose horsemen were from Liberty County.[7] The men of Company F elected William B. Duncan their First Lieutenant, replacing the promoted Spaight.[8] When Spaight persuaded the 5'11" black-haired, dark-eyed, dark-complexioned Duncan[9] to join his Confederate army unit three months earlier, he welcomed a pioneer Anglo-Texas Everyman to the Moss Bluff Rebels.

Immigrants from two cultures form the heritage of the Texas cattle industry. Spanish-Mexican cowboys arrived in the eighteenth century, establishing settlements and herds in today's southern and south-central Texas. Prompted by the end of the War of 1812 and the panic of 1819—America's first great depression that sparked acrimonious fights on state and federal levels over tariffs, paper money, and debtors' relief—Anglo-Americans from the deep southern states arrived in east Texas in the early nineteenth century.[10] They were looking for land to raise cotton and cattle that combined "princely abundance, accessibility, fertility, and cheapness that amounted to in effect a free gift."[11] Mexico had won its independence from Spain in 1821 and offered land incentives to new settlers who could help stabilize and secure its northeastern region. The immigrant Anglos brought with them cattle husbandry evolved from practices in two far more distant lands, Celtic Britain and Africa's Gambia region. They added aspects of a "creolized system" of livestock management learned on their migration to Texas.[12] French and Spanish riders they met along the gulf coast trail introduced them to longhorn cattle, "razorback" hogs, and Spanish-Mexican roping techniques to handle their herds from saddles on the backs of quick, scrubby horses.[13] William Berry Duncan, born in 1818 in St. Martinville,[14] the first Acadian settlement in Louisiana, was a southeast Texas immigrant from this Anglo-African-French-Spanish ethnic stew. Creoles and Cajuns, longhorns and razorbacks were all familiar residents of his gulf coast world.[15]

Duncan's South Carolinian father had paused in southern Louisiana on the migration that would reach its ultimate destination in southeast Texas. In 1823, he carried a letter of introduction from New Orleans empresario Green DeWitt to Stephen F. Austin, the Anglo administrator of Mexico's northeast region, informing Austin that Duncan was headed for either the San Marcos or the Guadalupe River to claim land for several families.[16] Patriarch Duncan reconsidered his destination and stopped short of the San Marcos and Guadalupe to settle in the lower Trinity River area of northeast Mexico, approximately twenty miles north of the Galveston Bay estuary system.

The forty-year-old Duncan brought his family to Liberty in 1824. It included his twenty-eight-year-old wife Jane Oden Duncan, his unmarried first son Meredith, twenty-one—a blacksmith born in South Carolina at the dawn of the century—and two other children, Sidney Pamelia, age six, and William Berry, age eight.[17] Jane Oden[18] Duncan was William B. Duncan's stepmother. She married his father on July 24, 1825, in St. Mary Parish, Louisiana, when William was seven.[19] Almost forty years later, Duncan spent several weeks as a Confederate officer in St. Mary Parish, whose seat is Franklin and where the Confederates and Federals fought frequently on the coast around Brashear City, today's Morgan City. No record survives in Texas to explain the fate of Duncan's natural mother. If she did not die in childbirth, an all-too-common end for women of the day, she could have been a victim of yellow fever, so prevalent in New Orleans in the first half of the nineteenth century that it was taken largely for granted. Duncan and the rest of his family who survived south Louisiana's yellow fever epidemics before moving to Texas probably acquired immunity from suffering mild cases of the disease. This would explain Duncan's lifelong reprieve from yellow fever despite decades of cattle wrangling across the mosquito-infested gulf coast plains.[20]

The Duncan family lived among 331 permanent residents of Mexico's Atascosito District in 1826. Seven other heads of families in the region came from South Carolina, like Duncan. Twelve others were from Virginia; nine from Louisiana; eight from North Carolina; seven each came from Pennsylvania, Kentucky, Georgia, and Tennessee; six from New York; two from Massachusetts and New Jersey; and one each from Connecticut, Florida, New Hampshire, and Rhode Island. Six heads of families were born outside the United States: three in Ireland and one each in England, Italy, and Mexico. Duncan the elder along with several other Atascosito District residents petitioned the Mexican government represented by colonial administrator Austin for recognition of their land claims in 1827.[21] Duncan claimed land on the west side of the lower Trinity River, not far south of the town of West Liberty, known today as Dayton, and approximately twenty miles north of Trinity Bay. He called his chosen plantation "Auborne," a word from the Old English given to reddish brown and blond colors. The elder Duncan might have borrowed the name from Oliver Goldsmith's eighteenth-century poem "The Deserted Village," which begins, "Sweet Auburn! / Loveliest village of the plain, / Where health and plenty cheered the labouring swain, / Where smiling spring its earliest visit paid, / And parting summer's lingering blooms delayed."[22]

When William Duncan turned thirteen in 1831, he and his parents were baptized Catholics by Irish missionary priest Father Michael Muldoon, self-described as the "pastor of Austin's Colony and Vicar General of all the foreign colonies of Texas."[23] Baptisms performed by Father Muldoon and, more important, the documents he signed attesting to them, fulfilled the Mexican government's requirement that Anglo families be Catholics if they were to receive land grants from the Mexican government.[24] Young Duncan's godfather was Col. John Davis Bradburn,[25] the Kentucky-born commander of the Mexican garrison at Anahuac, south of Liberty in Chambers County, whom Stephen F. Austin described as "half crazy part of the time." Bradburn's despotic administration on behalf of the Mexicans, including indiscriminate arrests of colonists and declaration of martial law over all land within ten leagues of the coast, is said to have hastened the Texas Revolution by several years. Within weeks after the family received baptismal certificates as "Muldoon Catholics," the Mexican government awarded Duncan's father title to his chosen land along the Trinity River as well as to a town lot across the street from the courthouse on the Liberty town square.[26]

The Duncans adjusted well to their new homeland. They built a plantation in the humid, subtropical climate like many others in the south Trinity watershed, raising cattle, cotton, sugarcane, tobacco, indigo, grains, and vegetables. Duncan's father may also have harvested timber and operated a sawmill, as did Dr. E. B. Gillard,[27] William B. Duncan's future father-in-law, who settled on a plantation in 1845 across the river along the east side of the Trinity, a few yards north of the Duncan land.[28] The Duncans, Gillards, and other Liberty-area settlers took advantage of the area's fertile soil, rich grasslands, and dense piney wood forests watered by the big rivers, slow-moving streams, and murky bayous of southeast Texas, but prosperity did not come easily.

A British geographer made several excursions in 1842 along the Texas coast from his base at Galveston and reported to the Royal Geographical Society in London that the shoreline from Galveston to the Sabine River is low "with a few houses and occasional clumps of trees. From the Sabine . . . on to the Mississippi the shores are lower than the Texan, composed of mud and sand islets, covered with drift-wood. . . . The decomposition of this driftwood is very rapid under the blistering summer sun of these regions and copious rains, forming in time soil for the reception of vegetation and the abode of man. . . . Alligators and sharks revel in these waters, and the myriads of mosquitoes of several species [the Galley-nippers, to wit] are anything but pleasant." Along with swarms of galley-nippers, tropical storms and occasional hurricanes rampaged across the coastal plains. Millions of migrating ducks, geese, raptors, snowy egrets, and great blue herons stopped to rest in the area. They grazed in the fields and along the bayous with eyes trained on black bears, feral hogs, wild cattle, Native Americans, and pioneer immigrants. Mammals and birds alike stepped carefully around alligators, copperheads, cottonmouths, and rattlers, all of which were common in the area. William Duncan's nineteenth-century gulf coast home in southeast Texas was a wild, exciting, and yes, dangerous land.[29]

The boy who would command Company F of Spaight's Sixth C.S.A. Infantry Battalion as a middle-aged man grew up on a multicultural and rugged frontier (see figure 2), where people matured quickly into providers, traders, and defenders—or perished in the process. The most dominant aspect of William Duncan's youth was his immersion in the family business where he grew commercially literate, learning to think, calculate, converse, and write in the language of business. He watched his father sell cattle and crops locally, ship them down the Trinity to the port in Galveston, or hire cowboys to drive cattle overland to Louisiana to take advantage of higher New Orleans prices driven by export demand. He learned to listen, laugh, spin yarns, and negotiate with buyers and sellers of different ethnicities so today's deal was not his last. He learned the commercial opportunities of the gulf coast marketplace: who raised and traded cattle, where he could find pasture for steers and fodder for horses, and the best places to ford more than thirty rivers draining the land from Victoria to New Orleans. His father's plantation ran along the west side of the lower Trinity River, a market highway of nineteenth-century southeast Texas commerce. Alabama-Coushatta Native Americans had long paddled south from the Livingston area to trade, and smoke-belching steamboats from Galveston chugged north past the Duncan farm as early as 1840. It was a transformative world for a bright, impressionable child. Duncan's youth shaped him into an entrepreneurial and personable businessman with skills highly attractive to Ashley Spaight in his search for officers to serve in his Confederate army unit.[30]

Duncan's father died on April 3, 1836, four weeks after Mexican troops under Gen. Antonio López de Santa Anna breached the walls at the Battle of the Alamo in San Antonio.[31] Three weeks after patriarch Duncan was buried, Gen. Sam Houston and nine hundred other Texas soldiers defeated Santa Anna's army at the Battle of San Jacinto, less than forty miles west of the Duncan plantation on the Trinity. Two months later, Duncan's son William Berry was drafted into the Texas army, ordered to report "armed and equipped as the law directs to march forthwith to headquarters to aid in repelling the invading

Mexican army." Santa Anna's defeat at San Jacinto soon drove the Mexicans back across the Rio Grande and won independence for Texas, reducing requirements for additional soldiers in the Republic's army, so Duncan served only three months of active duty. After his discharge, Duncan began his adult life as a farmer, rancher, cattle trader, and drover along the upper Texas and Louisiana coastal plains. He was eighteen.[32]

It did not take him long to become a local civic leader. Young Duncan's neighbors elected him clerk of the Liberty County court in 1841 when he was twenty-three. Texas Republic Pres. Mirabeau B. Lamar[33] and Secretary of State J. S. Mayfield ratified his election on March 15 in Austin. His four-year term as court clerk ended in 1845, the same year the United States admitted Texas to the Union as its twenty-eighth state. The next year, at age twenty-eight, Duncan was elected to a two-year term as Liberty County sheriff and was reelected to another two-year term in 1850. From 1852 to 1853 he served as Liberty County's tax assessor.[34] It was during his first term as sheriff that his neighbor, the first president of the Republic of Texas and then-U.S. Senator Sam Houston asked him for help. Houston received reports that people working for A. J. Yates were cutting timber on his Cedar Point property south of Liberty in Chambers County. Senator Houston asked Sheriff Duncan to help put a stop to the unauthorized harvest, explaining: "For years this miserable scoundrel Yates has been cutting my timber and selling it . . ."[35]

When not keeping the peace or tending to duties as a Liberty County public servant, Duncan was a shrewd, trail-toughened trader. Far from the comforts of a town office, he ran his cattle business from horseback in the scorching sun, tropical rainstorms, and mosquito clouds across southeast Texas and southern Louisiana. He formed herds as far west as Goliad and Refugio and headed them across the coastal plains toward New Orleans. He guided his cattle out of Texas along the Atascosito Road, established by the Spanish in the eighteenth century. It was known also as the Old Spanish Trail and people in Louisiana called it the Opelousas Trail (see figure 2). Its main route ran from El Paso to San Antonio, then through Houston, Liberty, and Beaumont to Lake Charles, Vermillionville—today's Lafayette—and New Orleans, following generally along today's Interstate 10 and U.S. Highway 90. Sucking mud from heavy rains, water depths and currents at river crossings and local Louisiana market prices dictated specific routes Duncan would follow. His drives lasted several days, occasionally for weeks, as he guided cattle along the trail, around, through, and across creeks, bayous, and swamps to fords on the Guadalupe, Colorado, Brazos, San Jacinto, and Trinity rivers before reaching the Neches at Beaumont and Sabine at Ballew's Ferry above Orange. Following the main road across Louisiana to Lake Charles, then across the Calcasieu River to Vermillionville, Duncan often stopped short of New Orleans to sell his herds to brokers in satellite market towns on Bayou Teche and the Atchafalaya River like Washington,

Opelousas, St. Martinville, New Iberia, and Franklin. They all were served by steamboats that carried his animals on to primary buyers like tanneries, meat processors, and cattle exporters in New Orleans. It was a busy trail out of Texas. One source claimed 32,400 steers swam the Sabine headed for New Orleans in 1856, and the *Galveston Weekly News* reported 15,000 eastbound cattle crossed the Neches in just two months late that year.[36]

Duncan put herds together from three sources: animals he raised on land he owned in five Texas counties, steers bought from other ranchers, and cattle owned by others who paid him commissions-plus-expenses for driving their assets-on-the-hoof to market. He sold animals to brokers and buyers near and in New Orleans, the largest city in the South in 1860 with a population of 168,675, where cattle prices were usually higher than those in Texas. Those higher prices were propped up by export demand from major population centers in North America, the Caribbean, and Europe and were supported by steam-boat transportation on the waters of the Atchafalaya River basin. Although he did not trade actively in slaves, he owned a few and was handy with pistol, shotgun, knife, and rope, indispensable tools of a nineteenth-century frontier Texas cowboy. His cattle-wrangling horsemanship and familiarity with local geography equipped him well to serve as a Confederate cavalry officer on the Texas and Louisiana coastal plains. As the Civil War intensified far to the east in the fall of 1861, Duncan remained a civilian, hard at work on a cattle drive along the gulf coast.[37]

He had ridden west from Liberty in October with two other drovers and their cowboys for a roundup near Goliad, ninety-five miles southeast of San Antonio and twenty-six miles southwest of Victoria.[38] Duncan's teaming up with two other drovers shows how he often cooperated with other cattlemen to share costs and spread risk to protect their investments. Captain Spaight was attracted by Duncan's experience in risk management; it would be valuable, per-haps even lifesaving, for the Moss Bluff Rebels. Goliad had been the site of a Spanish settlement called Santa Dorotea since the sixteenth century. It was where General Santa Anna's Mexican Army massacred Col. James W. Fannin Jr. and 342 Anglo soldiers on March 27, 1836 during the Texas Revolution. By 1861, Goliad was the center of a region where cattle drovers like Duncan formed herds to drive to market. As the sun set on October 9, Duncan took inventory. That day his team corralled another sixty head of his own cattle, twenty-nine owned by rancher Dutch Reuben, six carrying the brand of a third rancher, and four others belonging to a local farmer; the day's total was ninety-nine animals. The roundup brought his total herd to 375 cows and his partners' drove to 240. Duncan, his fellow drovers, their cowboys, and the cattle headed east, but an addition to Duncan's family caused them to pause outside Liberty.[39]

Duncan's second wife, Celima, was due to deliver a baby at any moment. Duncan arranged for his herd to graze on watered pasture near town, paying

Upper Texas – Louisiana Gulf Coast
ca. 1863

Atascosito/Opelousas Trail

⎯⎯⎯ Transport by road
⎯⎯⎯ Transport by steamboat
·········· Connecting trail route

FIG. 2.
The main transportation artery of William Duncan's homeland on the nineteenth-century upper Texas and Louisiana gulf coast was an eighteenth-century trail used by Spanish explorers. Called the Atascosito Trail in Texas and the Opelousas Trail in Louisiana, it was the antebellum commercial connection between Texas cattlemen and the New Orleans market as well as a gulf coast highway used by the Confederates and thus a strategic Federal target during the Civil War.

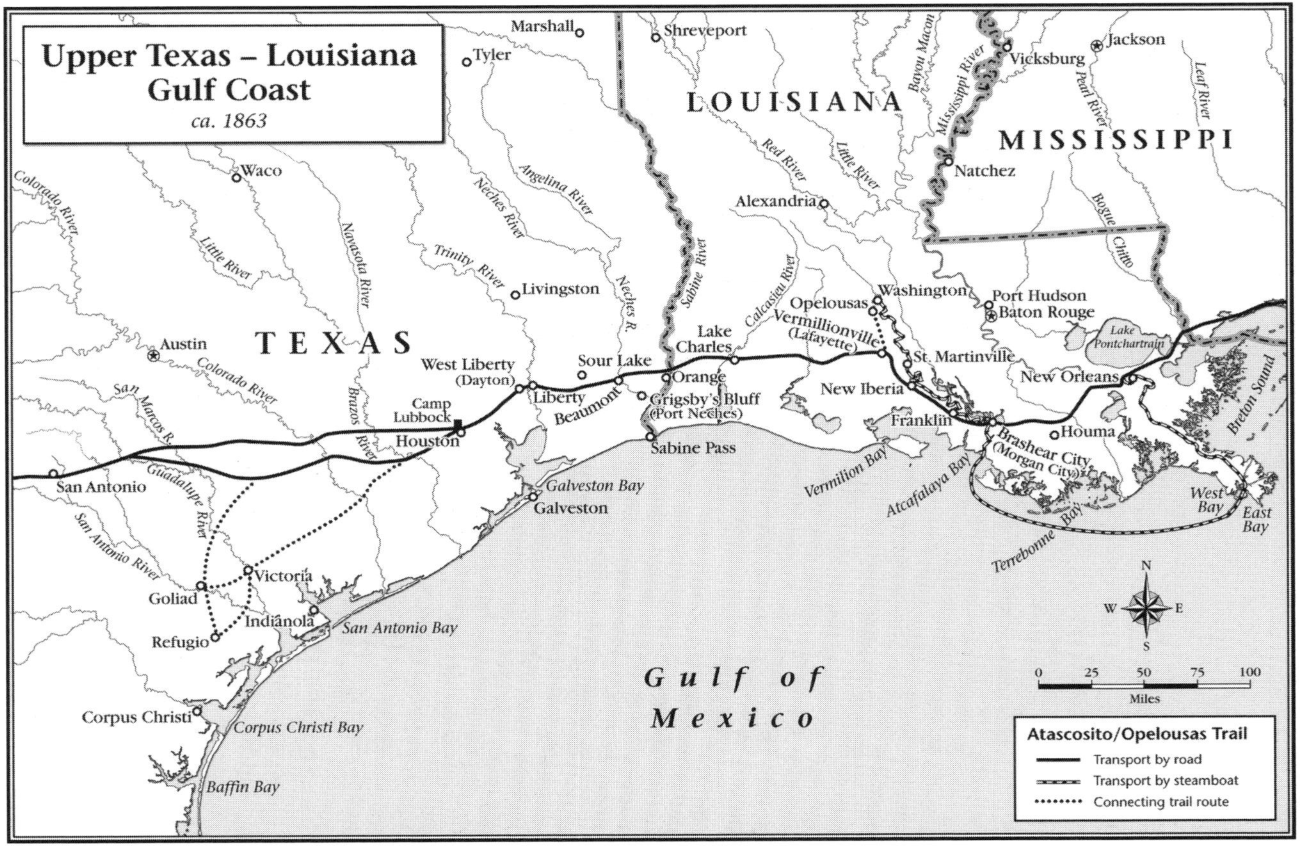

the landowner pennies per head if it was private land, or if not, enjoying the benefits of free range grasses. While he waited with Celima for the baby to arrive, his wranglers—a mixture of hired hands and slave cowboys—watched over the cattle. Duncan was in Liberty one day during the baby vigil and contributed $8 to buy blankets for Texas soldiers already serving in the Confederate Army. If Ashley Spaight learned of this donation, he will have considered it confirmation of Duncan's Confederate sympathies. With the help of a black slave midwife Duncan called old Fanny, "Celima gave birth to a fine daughter" on October 31.[40] Two days later when "Celima was in pain," her aunt and guardian—and Duncan's mother-in-law twice over—"Mrs. Gillard sent for Fanny who visited and left C. much better." Mother and child, whom the parents named Chessie,[41] were fine, and the proud husband and new father William Duncan paid Fanny $7 for her services.[42]

As Duncan prepared to resume the cattle drive three days after Chessie's birth, two speculators approached him in Liberty, wanting him to invest in a joint venture. Duncan was not interested in deals with people unwilling to put skin in the game, and furthermore, did business only with people he knew. With a tip of his hat to the two promoters, Duncan accepted $700 in gold from a Liberty County friend to buy 331 head of cattle from another local rancher—at an average cost of $2.11 per animal—and mingled them into his herd. He added cowboys and additional supplies to his wagons, organized the enlarged drove, and headed east on Sunday, November 10, paying $2 the next day for overnight pasture. Two days later he crossed the Sabine River into Louisiana, giving three cents per cow to hire special swimming steers to lead his herd across the river, paying $4 for wagon ferriage and complaining of especially bad mosquitoes. By November 15, Duncan found a buyer and made a deal to sell the cattle at $27.50 per head. This venture reveals much about William B. Duncan's appeal to Spaight: other men trusted Duncan with their money. Investors knew he had the skills to manage a complex project for significant profit. His integrity was a valuable, some would say indispensable, trait of a good leader. Spaight knew soldiers are more inclined to follow an officer they trust.[43]

The project illustrates the scope of Duncan's intellect and the depth of his abilities, all of which made him an even more attractive recruit for Spaight and his Moss Bluff Rebels. Duncan does not mention mishaps on the drive, so it is likely he made money on the venture. In fact, he probably made a handsome profit.[44] Duncan's operating income for the five-week drive could have totaled $8,568 in 1861 dollars, an estimated $165,042 in 2007 inflation-adjusted value.[45] Ashley Spaight would not have been privy to these numbers, but he knew William Duncan as a successful businessman who made a nice living trading cattle. Spaight wanted Duncan's experience and financial savvy, not to mention his purse, in his Confederate army unit.

Chapter 2 **Character**

ENTREPRENEUR WILLIAM B. DUNCAN BUILT A
respectable portfolio of assets centered in Liberty County on the southeast
Texas gulf coast during the quarter-century between formation of the Republic
of Texas and the beginning of America's Civil War in 1861. Cotton and cattle
anchored trade in the area, with harvested cotton hauled on wagons and river
barges to the port of Galveston and from there to markets as far away as New
York and Liverpool. That same British explorer who sketched the Gulf of Mexico shoreline used tax records to list Galveston's main exports in his 1843 report
back to London. "The exports from Galveston have principally been cotton,
buffalo-hides, ox-hides, buffalo-ropes, deer-skins, staves, moss, and sundries."[1]
No railroads rolled in Texas until the late 1850s and even then, they were inca-
pable of handling large cargos.[2] Southeast Texas ranchers moved their cattle to
market via barge from Galveston or in herds they drove east across the coastal
plains. William Duncan became a skilled cattle wrangler; he knew the lay of
the land along the gulf coast and traded profitably in the beef supply chain
across southeast Texas and southwest Louisiana.

Complementing his cattle business, Duncan was a real estate investor with
a healthy appetite for risk. Trading cattle generated more cash than he needed
for working capital to buy stock and finance expenses on his drives to market.
Rather than squirrel money away under his pillow or in gold bars locked in a
New Orleans bank, he put it to work in land. By 1860, Duncan owned 4,197
acres in five counties.[3] His personal property in Liberty that year included six
hundred head of cattle, eight horses, and three slaves, which when added to the
land for tax purposes totaled a twenty-first-century inflation-adjusted $184,944.[4]
Duncan also paid property tax in 1860 in Refugio County,[5] showing he spread
his economic pursuits along much of the Atascosito Trail. The Texas pioneer
cattleman practiced investment diversification long before modern financial
planners gave it a name.

FIG. 3.
William B. Duncan, his
first wife Eliza Gillard
Duncan and first child
Emma Cassandra, ca.
1852 when Duncan was
thirty-four years old and
heavily involved in his
professional life as a cattle
drover and public service
as a Liberty County
elected official. *Courtesy
Julia Duncan Welder
Collection, SHRL, Liberty,
Texas.*

When not at work, Duncan spent his days hunting along the lower Trinity River basin and the wildlife-rich coastal plain of southeast Texas. Hunting was good in the biologically diverse bottomland hardwood forests and other wetland habitats along the Trinity. They were home to a bountiful variety of fauna and flora, including more than six hundred plant species, four hundred species of vertebrates, two hundred species of birds, and seventy-plus species of butterflies.[6] He also enjoyed card games in town when he wasn't working. Gambling of all sorts was common entertainment in frontier Texas; in fact, one historian says, "A fever for gambling ran in the blood of the age."[7] Duncan clearly enjoyed it because he won more money than he lost most of his life. During the games, he and his cronies exchanged news, rumors, and fish stories amid acrid smoke from their pipes, cigars, and cigarettes and occasional sips of whiskey. From the frequency with which Duncan mentions the purchase of tobacco and spirits, he savored both on an almost daily basis.[8]

The handsome Duncan married twice before the Civil War. He wed his first wife, fifteen-year-old Eliza C. Gillard, on August 9, 1848 when he was thirty. Born of Irish immigrant parents, Eliza's birth name was Catherine Lamb. After her natural mother's death, infant Catherine's father returned to Ireland, leaving the baby in a New Orleans orphanage where Dr. Edward Joseph Gillard and his wife, Emma DeBlanc Gillard adopted her.[9] Before her death from pneumonia on November 11, 1856—the day after her twenty-fourth birthday—Eliza bore Duncan three children: Emma (see figure 3), born July 10,

FIG. 4.
Celima DeBlanc Duncan,
William B. Duncan's
second wife. *Courtesy
Miriam Partlow Collection,
SHRL, Liberty, Texas.*

1849; William, named for his deceased grandfather and father, died August 29, 1854 at the age of ten months; and Celima Catherine, born June 26, 1855. Her parents called Celima Catherine "Kate" and by the nickname "Tont"[10] to distinguish her from namesake Celima DeBlanc, Eliza's cousin by adoption.

Duncan married twenty-four-year-old Celima, Mrs. Gillard's niece and ward, on May 13, 1858, eighteen months after Eliza died (see figure 4).[11] William and Celima became parents of five children. Their first, Edward Joseph, named after Celima's uncle and guardian, Dr. Gillard, died January 9, 1861. Daughters Chessie and Julia[12] were born during the war on October 31, 1861, and January 30, 1863, respectively; son Emery Lee was born June 30, 1865, and Emery's brother and the youngest Duncan child, William, arrived February 22, 1867. Of Duncan's eight children, five survived to adulthood.

Edward Gillard was born ten years before Duncan in 1808. He and his wife Elizabeth, born in 1810,[13] were a Creole couple who lived in New Orleans before building a plantation in the Red River valley near Alexandria, Louisiana. They along with seven other Creole families, their slaves, and livestock emigrated from Louisiana across the Sabine River to Liberty County in 1845 in search of land on which they could build larger, more lucrative farms.[14] While camped on the banks of the Sabine River on their way to Liberty County, Peggy, one of the Gillards' favorite slaves, gave birth to a male child she named Sabine. A few days later, another slave woman gave birth to a second baby boy who was named Texas. Dr. and Mrs. Gillard's clan also included a Native American child called Ponce whom they raised as a slave after finding him ill and abandoned in the woods as a toddler. All three children were part of the Gillard extended family; Sabine in fact became Duncan's trusted manservant, accompanying him during much of his Civil War service. Both Sabine and Texas worked for Duncan after the war as emancipated freedmen.[15]

The Gillards shared a complex ethnicity as Creoles. Early in the nineteenth century, being Creole meant being part of the ancienne population of New Orleans, the indigenous people of French, Spanish, and African heritage. Creoles evolved in the years before the Civil War into an intermediate racial class lodged between white and black. They were free, educated, and affluent with multilingual skills, respect for learning, and an aptitude for trading that gave them the financial wherewithal to preserve their self-proclaimed social distinction. William Duncan's two wives, his in-laws, several neighbors in Liberty County, and many of the people to whom he sold cattle in southern Louisiana were Creoles. Their influence on Duncan, especially in commercial matters, was considerable.[16]

Creoles were not the only Franco-American people in Duncan's life. The twenty-two southwestern parishes of Louisiana known as Acadiana, through which Duncan drove most of his cattle herds, are home to descendants of an estimated 650 Acadian French immigrants who arrived in Louisiana from Nova Scotia in 1765. The Creoles welcomed the Roman Catholic Acadians to New Orleans, but Spanish rulers of the city at that time encouraged the French-speaking exiles to keep moving, so they continued their migration westward to the Atchafalaya River basin where they established their first community at St. Martinville.[17] William Duncan was born there in 1818. St. Martinville is located near today's Atchafalaya National Wildlife Refuge, whose 15,000 acres are part of the largest hardwood swamp in the country and home to bald eagle, black bears, white-tailed deer, wild turkey, the swallow-tailed kite, and many neotropical migratory birds.[18] The Acadians spread over southwest Louisiana's prairie from St. Martinville in the 1800s, north to Vermillionville, today's Lafayette, to Opelousas, northeast to Baton Rouge, and west to Lake Charles.[19] Cajun country—*Cajun* was originally an English mispronunciation of *Acadian* that became a disparaging term for the Acadians' descendants in the nineteenth and most of the twentieth centuries; it has since become a proud label of ethnic distinction and considerable commercial appeal—refers today to the land and towns in Louisiana west of New Orleans and south of Interstate 10. Cajun country was William Duncan's birthplace and his second home where he had many good friends and trading partners.

FIG. 5.
The Edward Gillard home, built ca. 1848 from lumber produced in the Gillard sawmill on Gillard's plantation on the east side of the Trinity River south of Liberty, Texas. Duncan lived in this home during his marriages to Eliza and Celima. *Photograph by author, taken on the grounds of the Sam Houston Regional Library and Research Center, Liberty, Texas, January 5, 2007.*

Duncan was a public servant, rancher, and cattle drover in the 1840s and 1850s when war clouds gathered first to the south, then later on his eastern horizon. He makes no mention in his diary of the Mexican-American War of 1846–48, suggesting the fighting along the Rio Grande and in Mexico had little relevance in his life. Duncan makes no comment twelve years later when South Carolina seceded from the Union on December 20, 1860. This is at least partially because his second son and first child with Celima, twenty-one-month-old Edward Joseph, was very ill at the time.[20] Three days into the New Year, as Duncan prepared to go hunting, he became especially worried about Edward because the big dog Duncan used to hunt bears would not leave Edward's side. Dog owners know how their pets can become protective if someone in the family is sick. When the ill person is an infant or toddler like Edward, it is not unusual for the animal to protect the baby, sometimes going so far as to warn away even the child's parents with a low growl.

Duncan left his bear dog at home with Edward under Celima's care on Friday, January 4 to join Celima's uncle, Jerome DeBlanc, two slave youths, and two Native American scouts on a hunt along the Trinity. One of the men shot a wild hog late Friday afternoon and the Indians killed four small bears over the next six days. Duncan was packing his gear to return home Wednesday, January 9, when he heard a horn in the distance. Duncan says it was a signal that "struck terror to my soul." As the hunters emerged from the trees along the river, they met Jerome's son Oscar who "told me my dear little boy was sick," Duncan says. "I left the others and started. Got home [at] 1. Horror of horrors, my dear angel [was] dying." Edward Joseph Duncan died that afternoon at 5 P.M. Duncan was grief stricken the next day when he wrote in his diary, "Today in the afternoon, they took my dear, dear little angel of a boy away to bury him."[21]

Edward was Duncan's second child to die as a toddler. His first son, conceived with wife Eliza and named William,[22] predeceased his stepbrother in August 1854. While the sorrowful father remained in mourning with his family at their home south of Liberty on February 1, 1861, Texas delegates to a special convention in Austin passed an ordinance of secession from the United States by a vote of 166 to eight. Seventy-five percent of eligible Texas voters ratified that decision in a statewide referendum on February 23.[23] The vote in Duncan's home county was an even bigger landslide in favor of secession. Ninety-eight percent of Liberty County voters—the vote was 422 to ten—marked their ballots for Texas to leave the Union. Duncan rode into Liberty that Saturday to vote with his friend, E. B. White, who would be elected Liberty County sheriff the next year.[24]

Heartbroken from Edward's death and wondering what secession might mean for him, his family, and neighbors, Duncan struggled to return to life's routine obligations. He harnessed a horse to the family buggy and drove eleven-year-old daughter Emma to Liberty the following Monday, delivering her to the convent boarding school. Their conversation into town must have been somber; Emma was mature beyond her years. Her first brother died when she was five, her mother died when she was seven, and her second brother had been dead less than two months. After hugging Emma good-bye, Duncan chatted with the convent's Mother Superior who would have extended her condolences. He climbed back onto his wagon and headed for the cemetery where Edward had been buried. He spent the afternoon alone, planting shrubbery around the grave.[25]

The Confederate States of America installed Jefferson Davis as their president in Montgomery, Alabama, on February 18, 1861, and the United States of America inaugurated Abraham Lincoln as its sixteenth president in Washington on March 4. At his inauguration, Lincoln declared the United States retained ownership of all Federal property, regardless of whether it was located in a secessionist state. In defiance of Lincoln's claim, President Davis ordered Confederate Gen. P. G. T. Beauregard to bomb Fort Sumter, located on an island near the mouth of Charleston Harbor in South Carolina on April 12. After thirty-four hours of Confederate shelling, Maj. Robert Anderson, Fort Sumter's Union commander, lowered the U.S. flag, surrendered the fort, and loaded his men on a steamship bound for New York. The Civil War had begun but William Duncan never said anything about Fort Sumter in his diary. Although Duncan does not mention political events or the beginning of the war, he was well aware of it. The omission is consistent with his focus on business transactions, expenses, and family matters. His habit to ignore politics in the nonnarrative diary suggests they did not interest him that much. While he certainly watched, listened, and chatted about matters political and military, his cryptic private thoughts reveal him primarily as a businessman, a family man, and ultimately, a reluctant Confederate volunteer.[26]

Duncan had been two hundred miles east of Liberty on July 2, 1861, about to close a sale after driving a herd of cattle through Cajun country toward New Iberia when the USS *South Carolina* arrived outside Galveston Bay to begin the Union blockade of Texas ports. He had no way to know the Civil War that began at Fort Sumter off Charleston in South Carolina on April 12, 1861, had arrived uncomfortably close to his Liberty County home forty-two miles east-northeast of Houston. The *South Carolina* soon captured ten Confederate vessels, three of which Commander James Alden transformed into Federal gunboats with sailors and weapons from his mother ship. Flying the Stars and Stripes and carrying remounted Union artillery, the *Dart,* the *Shark,* and the *Sam Houston* took up positions in the Gulf of Mexico outside Sabine Pass east of Galveston to block Confederate blockade runners from escaping through another important Texas access point to the Gulf of Mexico. Alden had taken very little time to quadruple his fleet of gunboats enforcing the nascent Union blockade of Texas.[27]

While the Federal blockade of the upper Texas coastline took shape near his home on the Trinity, William Duncan showed patience in south Louisiana when it looked like his customer might stiff him. He had sold his small herd in New Iberia to a man who promised his son-in-law would arrive soon with Duncan's cash. The fact Duncan agreed to his buyer's pledge that "My son-in-law will pay you later" suggests the cattle market at the time was soft. This particular buyer probably would have been Duncan's only option; it would have been far too expensive and time-consuming for Duncan to drive the herd back to Texas. Several days passed with no sign of the son-in-law, so Duncan settled into card games with other cattlemen and several New Iberia locals. When he finally got his money from the sale almost a month later, Duncan spent extra time counting the cash. Slow pay was an irritant in Duncan's early Civil War business world, but then as now, slow pay was better than none at all.

While he stewed in New Iberia's muggy heat, Duncan revealed more about the inner man who would soon relent to Spaight's pressure to join his Confederate battalion. Duncan saw a small herd of cows wandering unattended on the road. He climbed on his horse and rode out to count forty-six head carrying a brand he knew. He rounded up the strays and drove them into a secure corral, letting local cowboys know who their owner was. William Duncan did the right thing, even when no one was watching. Ashley Spaight would have admired that honesty. More evidence of Duncan's character surfaced when he arrived home from Louisiana after his extended cattle drive to learn a friend was in agony with Duncan's greatest fear. The friend's child was seriously ill, near death's door, and Duncan rode immediately to his house to offer support. When the doctor came to examine the child, Duncan excused himself and returned home. Realizing the gravity of the situation, Duncan traveled back to the family's place after sundown. "The child died at 11 1/2 o'clock pm," he writes and "I stayed all night." Two days after the death of his friend's child, William Duncan mentioned the war for the first time in his diary. He spent Saturday, August 31, 1861, at a meeting of the Moss Bluff Rebels in Liberty. After Sunday's day of rest, Duncan was back with the grieving family to mourn the child and talk about the war. [28]

Duncan and his wife Celima were prolific letter writers. Because he herded cattle on the trail for weeks at a time, Duncan kept Celima informed in advance of his route and estimated times of arrival at postal handling points so she could address letters to him that would arrive before he did. Duncan's primary themes in his correspondence were business related, while Celima focused on family matters, commercial news, and local gossip—and occasionally slapped his wrist. Celima was especially miffed at Duncan for embarrassing her in Liberty before he left on another cattle drive in mid-September 1861. She wished him good luck and good weather, then warned he was in for a scolding when he returned home. Instead of hitting the trail immediately, Duncan had ridden into Liberty and spent the day playing cards. The spouse of one of his fellow gamblers confronted Celima, accusing Duncan of being the cause of her husband's bender that day. Celima told Duncan she did not think the man needed much encouragement, but was embarrassed the woman blamed Duncan for leading her husband astray. [29]

Two weeks later, Duncan received another letter from Celima that must have grabbed his attention. "I said something to you in one of my letters about some men going to Joe Dark's house with the intention of killing him, his wife and children to get his money," Celima wrote. "After Dark killed one by the name of Chason [sic], the other two were hung last Friday. One of them was a lawyer in Hardin by the name of Willis and the other was Tom Magness. They were both hung close by old Mrs. Magness' house without no law." [30] News of the attempted robbery was exceptionally relevant for Duncan. Joe Dark, 6'4" tall and weighing 250 pounds, was a lawyer who lived in a big house north of Liberty near Moss Hill and later joined the Confederate Army like Duncan. Dark, the first county surveyor of Liberty and Hardin counties, plowed his garden behind two pet bears and always wore a gun belt with loaded revolvers on both hips. Talk had it that he kept a lot of cash at his house. [31] Like Dark, William

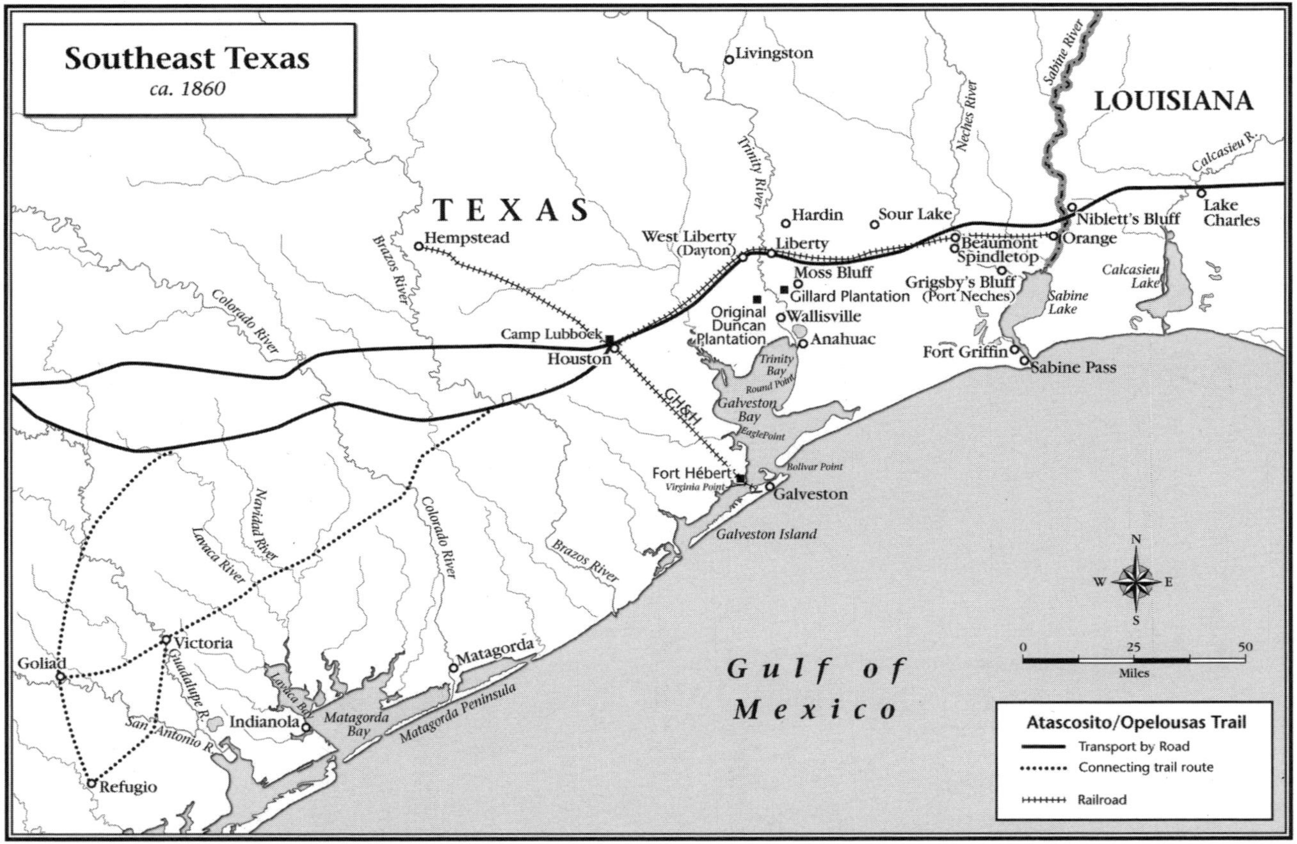

FIG. 6.

William Duncan grew up on his father's plantation on the west side of the Trinity River south of West Liberty. During his two marriages he lived with his wives and children in the home of his in-laws, Dr. and Mrs. Edward Gillard, on their plantation on the east side of the Trinity south of Liberty. Except for eight months' duty in southern Louisiana with the Second Cavalry Regiment, Arizona Brigade, Duncan's military duty was confined to southeast Texas in the coastal area bordered by Liberty, Beaumont–Grigsby's Bluff, Sabine Pass, Houston, and Galveston.

Southern Louisiana
ca. 1860

MISSISSIPPI

LOUISIANA

TEXAS

Gulf of Mexico

Natchez

Alexandria
Red River

Simmesport

Washington
Opelousas

Vermillionville
(Lafayette)

New Iberia
Jeanerette
Franklin
St. Martinville
Bayou Teche
Atchafalaya River

Port Hudson
Baton Rouge
Donaldsonville

New Orleans
Lake Pontchartrain
Lake Borgne

Lake Maurepas

Tangipahoa River
Bogue Chitto
Pearl River

Houma
Lake Salvador

Berwick Bay
Brashear City
(Morgan City)
Atchafalaya Bay

Terrebonne Bay
Timbalier Bay
Barataria Bay
Caillou Bay

Vermilion Bay
West Cote Blanche Bay
Marsh Island

White Lake
Grand Lake

Lake Charles
Calcasieu Lake

Niblett's Bluff
Orange
Sabine River
Neches River
Beaumont
Grigsby's Bluff
(Port Neches)
Sabine Lake
Fort Griffin
Sabine Pass

Calcasieu River

N E S W

Miles
0   25   50

Atascosito/Opelousas Trail
——— Transport by Road
- - - Transport by Steamboat
⋯⋯ Connecting trail route
+++++ Railroad

FIG. 7;
Duncan was born in 1818 in St. Martindale, the first Acadian settlement in Louisiana. His antebellum cattle drives took him primarily to buyers in Opelousas, Washington, and New Iberia who in turn moved his cattle by steamboat down Bayou Teche, the Atchafalaya River, and open gulf waters to the main New Orleans market. Duncan's eight months of service from May to December 1863 with Gen. Richard Taylor's Confederate forces in Louisiana occurred in the northwest-southeast corridor between Opelousas and Brashear City.

Duncan handled large sums of cash and gold and was a prime target for bandits. At all times, but especially when he was away from home on the trail, Duncan worried about outlaws harming Celima and the children.

Celima is accurate in her succinct report of the Dark episode. Dark shot and killed Austin Chessher after Chessher, Tom Magness, and G. H. Willis pulled guns to rob Dark on the night of September 16, 1861. Dark knew Willis and welcomed the trio into his home after Willis announced their arrival by sending his name into the house with a servant. Chessher took a seat on the floor, Magness sat on a chair, and Willis stood by a window. When Dark walked into the room, Chessher lifted his shotgun, aimed at Dark's chest, and pulled the trigger. The weapon misfired. Dark drew his pistol and killed Chessher with a single shot. Magness then shot and killed one of Dark's black servants before he and Willis ran from the house. As he fled, Magness fired another blast through Dark's front door, sprinkling his baby's crib with buckshot.[32] Magness and Willis jumped on their horses and galloped away. Dark spread the alarm and neighbors soon captured the pair. They were hanged the next morning after a street crowd outside the jail shouted a guilty verdict under nineteenth-century Texas vigilante justice. The crowd strung them up on a big tree next to the house where Magness's mother lived in Hardin.[33]

Celima moved from the gunfight to encouraging business and personal news in her letter. "Mr. Poter told me yesterday that the beeves [cattle] sell very high in New Orleans. He saw a man that came from there that told him that the beeves was scarce in Louisiana. . . . I hope the market will keep good till you get there. . . . I feel a great deal better since I think you are on your way home. I have not been sick. Every person that sees me says that I am very fat. I am almost ashamed to go out. Whenever my baby comes, I hope I will continue well till you come."[34]

Chapter 3 **Adjustment**

WHILE FEDERAL BLOCKADERS PATROLLED TO prevent Confederate states' exports, William Duncan remained true to his identity as a businessman. Early on Thursday, December 3, 1861, he agreed to a deal to build a telegraph line between Sabine City and New Iberia, spreading his risk with two other investors. One week later, he headed west with $5,000 in his saddlebags to buy cattle. This particular eighty-twenty investment included $4,000 of Duncan's money and $1,000 from a partner. He spent eight days forming the herd, then he and his cowboys moved it onto the trail headed for Louisiana.[1] Growing enlistments in both Federal and Confederate armies spiked demand for cattle, and buyers from both sides were active in the New Orleans market. Steers commonly sold in the $6 range in southeast Texas in 1860, but the next year the Confederate army bought cattle in southern Louisiana at $22 per head, and in April, 1862, the Union army paid "good Yankee gold $40 to $60 a head" for cattle. William Duncan aimed to earn those margins as long as he could. In the back of his mind he also wondered whether he could pursue his business if he joined the Confederate Army.[2]

Duncan's life changed little during the first quarter of 1862. On January 18, after selling the herd he assembled in December, he picked up his slaves and horses at Ralph Foreman's place in Louisiana and headed home to Texas. When he reached Beaumont, he found the train to Houston derailed, so he continued on horseback the forty-four miles to Liberty. On February 6, he "went ducking" and killed twelve birds. Five days later, Duncan went into Liberty to visit Emma.[3] She was enrolled at the Ursuline Convent boarding school that opened in 1859, staffed by four nuns from France and one from Quebec. The sisters came to Liberty from New Orleans by way of Galveston at the request of the local Creole families who wanted their children educated in the Catholic faith. In fact, Duncan's father-in-law, Dr. Edward J. Gillard, provided lumber for the school from his sawmill.[4] When Duncan stopped to see Emma that day, the Mother Superior, French Sister St. Ambrose, asked him about a calf he had promised her. The next day he arranged to pay a slave called ol' Abe $4 to haul wood to the convent. He settled up with Abe later, paying him $6, apparently adding a tip for a job well done. Duncan finally agreed to join the cavalry unit of Ashley Spaight's Moss Bluff Rebels in early March. After celebrating his birthday at home—his wife had a wild turkey prepared for the event—Duncan rode to Spaight's place in Moss Bluff for muster, but a sore foot prevented him from participating in the drill. On Monday, March 10, he went to town and found war excitement strong.[5]

Duncan was in Liberty the next Saturday and gave $50 to a collection for wives of Texas Confederate soldiers already at war. No records exist to reflect accurately the number of Texans who served in the Confederate war effort, but Texas Gov. Francis Lubbock said the number reached 90,000 at the end of 1863.[6] The state of Texas furnished those men to the Confederate army in 115 regiments, battalions, and batteries, including forty-five regiments of cavalry, twenty-three regiments of infantry, twelve battalions of cavalry, four battalions of infantry, one regiment of heavy artillery, and thirty batteries of light artillery.[7] Most people considered Ashley Spaight's battalion an infantry unit, despite its two cavalry companies. The day after Spaight told Duncan he was ready to mobilize his unit, Duncan stayed home to make a scabbard for his knife. He joined Captain Spaight a week after the swearing-in ceremony on a recruiting trip southwest of Liberty, looking to sign up more volunteers. The two men canvassed Wallisville on the east side of the Trinity River in northern Chambers County on April 5 and 6 and spent the 7th through 10th in Cedar Bayou, today part of Baytown in eastern Harris County. Duncan says he and Spaight "saw Amos Barrow and Sol Fisher [but] could not get them to join." Duncan and Spaight rode back to Liberty on Saturday, April 12, hearing a report at a unit meeting that seventy-three men had enlisted to date.[8]

They also heard that Union Gen. Ulysses S. Grant defeated the Confederates at the Battle of Shiloh in southwestern Tennessee six days earlier. Duncan might have noted Shiloh in his diary because Confederate Gen. Albert Sidney Johnston was killed there while rallying his soldiers on the front line. Like Duncan, Johnston served in the Republic of Texas Army. He was the only Confederate army commander to die in Civil War combat.[9] The *New York Times* reported Johnston's death on April 10, 1862, saying "he was considered by military men the ablest General, for command, in the rebel service and his loss will be a severe blow to the tottering rebellion."[10] When Duncan heard about Shiloh, it is conceivable the news caused him to second-guess his enlistment. However, a visit to his house in midmonth by the local dentist was more immediately relevant. He pulled four teeth for Duncan's children and Duncan paid him $1.50 per tooth. While the dentist worked, Duncan realized his commitment to the

Confederate army was irrevocable. He spent Wednesday, April 23 with Spaight, arranging to have tents made for the company. Four days later, Duncan called on a local man who had promised Duncan a camp stool. He was in Liberty again the next Wednesday to hear that thirteen Federal gunboats had anchored outside New Orleans.[11]

It was time for Confederate Lt. William Duncan to saddle up. His active duty army service began in early May 1862, but it took him awhile to gain traction. While his unit mobilized at a camp on the east side of Galveston Bay, he bought personal supplies and picked up a bugle in Liberty, then went home for the night. The next day, he traded his single-shot pistols for a revolver with the understanding he could get his pistols back at his pleasure. Single-shot pistols are either small derringers used for personal protection or long-barreled, often high-caliber weapons used for hunting. A fast-firing repeating revolver was much more valuable than a single-shot weapon to a Civil War cavalryman. After making the gun swap, Duncan rode out to his unit camped at Freeman Island on the bay south of Liberty. He was still struggling with his decision to join the army. "Stayed a while then went home," he says; "Tried to get ready." He left the house late the next morning, driving a small wagon through the rain, and caught up with his unit at Crackers Neck, today's town of Hankamer in Chambers County, east of Anahuac. He arrived cold and wet, unloaded the wagon, and sent it home with a man named Bob, probably one of his slaves. He wrote to Celima as the "men fiddled and danced 'til late."

Duncan's unit broke camp early the next morning. His men killed two deer that day along the tree line at the edge of the prairie where they stopped for dinner. They made camp at East Bay Bayou, east of Crackers Neck, on May 9. The next day they rode through a difficult marsh and made it to the beach where they camped "with brackish water to drink." The battalion had arrived at its first deployment near Sabine Pass on the Texas side of its border with Louisiana. First thing Monday morning, Captain Spaight presided over a confirmation election of battalion officers; Duncan was one of three men who were elected company commanders at the rank of lieutenant.

The new officers celebrated by pitching in to buy two gallons of whiskey for the men. Duncan's share of the hooch cost him $2.66. He wrote a short note to Celima with the news and sent it back to Liberty. The rest of the month saw Spaight's Battalion get down to the business of becoming a cohesive military unit through constant drilling, both on foot and horseback. Like soldiers of all armies, Duncan found drill boring and sleeping on the ground occasionally uncomfortable. One morning, he and another officer scrambled around the tent in their long-handles to keep high winds from blowing it into the gulf. Sand flies and stiff winds off the water became minor irritants two days later when a rider entered camp to report Federal soldiers had arrived in Galveston and demanded its surrender.[12]

Less than a month of active duty passed before Duncan noticed signs of the precarious economic condition of his unit and by extension, the Confederacy. He and his cavalry company were interrupted during drill one Saturday morning to have their horses appraised. When the process concluded that evening, Duncan reports, "my horses were val[ued] at $1.25 ea. Sad."[13] The Provisional Congress of the Confederate States of America had ruled that horses for Confederate artillery units and baggage trains were to be provided by the unit quartermaster who was also responsible for furnishing grain, hay, and fodder. However, each mounted Confederate volunteer was expected to furnish his own horse and tack in exchange for a forty-cent-a-day payment. Confederate politicians conceived this arrangement partly for reasons of economy and partly in the assumption men would furnish better horses than the government and would take better care of their own property. If a horse was killed in action, the government pledged to pay its owner, should he survive, the initial army-appraised value. It was this regulation that prompted Duncan's comment. His horse would have been worth much more than $1.25.[14]

Long hours of monotonous drill continued, with snippets of war news occasionally filtering into camp. One day an officer brought news from Beaumont that Galveston was all but abandoned. Three days later Duncan says there was no work in the morning to allow the men time to wash their clothes, but drill resumed in the afternoon. Despite almost a month of daily practice, the unit's marching ability was ragged. Duncan says they performed very badly that day.[15] Despite their sloppy formations, it was time for Spaight's Battalion to move north to its second duty station, approximately thirteen miles southeast of Beaumont at Grigsby's Bluff in the coastal watersheds of the Neches and Sabine rivers. The Texas Confederates called their Grigsby's Bluff location Camp Walker after Maj. Gen. John George Walker,[16] commander of Walker's Greyhounds; Grigsby's Bluff today is the town of Port Neches.[17]

The Neches and Sabine both flow into Sabine Lake approximately twenty miles southeast of Beaumont near the Texas-Louisiana border. The lake drains into the Gulf of Mexico through Sabine Pass, Spaight's Battalion's initial duty station. The Neches and Sabine carried relatively heavy commercial traffic in the mid-nineteenth century down their respective three-hundred-mile and four-hundred-mile routes from northeast Texas. Their shared point of entry to the gulf through Sabine Pass was a target of the Union blockade. Spaight ordered his infantry and unit supplies moved by boat and his mounted cavalry to ride and lead their spare horses north of the pass to the new camp. Duncan himself left at 7 A.M., Friday, June 6, reaching Taylor's Bayou—a tributary of the Neches in Jefferson County—at 11:00, finally crossing on the ferry by 1 P.M. He made it that night to Grigsby's Bluff, where another battalion company was already encamped. When he climbed down from his horse, the first words he heard were not good: "Mumps in camp."[18]

Spaight, Duncan, and Lt. B. W. Brown spent Saturday, June 7 looking for a suitable campground. They finally found an acceptable site about a mile north of another unit already in place at Grigsby's Bluff. Spaight's Battalion moved the next day—Duncan says it was very hot—and pitched their tents. Even though it was sweltering, Duncan did not complain to Celima. On the contrary, he told her, "I am very well and getting along firstrate [sic]. We have a very agreeable time. The Captain [Spaight], George Duncan [another lieutenant in the battalion from Liberty but not related to William Duncan] and myself occupy one tent, which gives us plenty of room. And the captain has one of the best negro men in the world for a servant, who does our cooking and housework."[19] As his men settled into their new camp, Captain Spaight called on Duncan to perform one of the roles Spaight had in mind for the Liberty cattleman when he prevailed on him to join his unit, that of supply master. Spaight asked Duncan to find some corn for the unit.[20]

The next morning, Duncan took a boat upriver to Beaumont, arriving at noon. He reached the train station in time to catch the Orange-originating Houston train that ran 110 miles through Beaumont and Liberty on its way to the Bayou City. Duncan had been using the train—people in Texas at the time referred to it as *the cars*[21]—since it began operating after its charter on September 1, 1856 as the Sabine and Galveston Bay railroad. Today the Orange to Houston via Liberty tracks are part of the modern Union Pacific system. In 1862, the locally owned, often undependable train was a strategically important tool for William Duncan, his commanding officer Ashley Spaight, and the rest of the Confederacy's local Texas Volunteers. Its value came not from the freight it carried but in the quicker-than-horses communication link it provided the southeast Texas Confederate command between headquarters in Houston and its border office in Beaumont.

The day after Duncan climbed down from the train in Liberty on his corn search, he bought a crib for $75. The next day, he found a man with five hundred bushels of corn to sell and made the deal. Duncan's problem at that point became bulk transportation, complaining he "could find no one to haul." Three days later, Duncan cracked the corn code, finding a teamster through word of mouth from another man he approached about the job. Duncan spent Sunday on personal business before shepherding Celima and the children into the family carriage for a visit to a friend's house where they "ate some fine watermelons and returned home, finished packing and went to bed tired."[22]

Spaight's order to Duncan to find a large store of corn—probably intended to feed horses rather than humans—sounds simple today, but Civil War southeast Texas was not dotted with feed stores, and Texas Confederates were part of a very poor organization. Its lack of resources was disappointing for Confederate leadership who in early days of the conflict expected the Trans-Mississippi territory—Texas, Louisiana, and Arkansas—to supply large volumes of salt, sugar, bacon, beef, wheat, wool, and cotton to the war effort. The three Trans-Mississippi states were also thought to be the route through which vital supplies from Europe and Mexico could find their way to Southern military forces.[23] These Confederate expectations never bore fruit. Brig. Gen. Paul Hébert, who assumed command of Confederate forces in Texas from Earl Van Dorn on September 16, 1861, was a beggar from the get-go. From his office in Galveston, Hébert informed C.S.A. Secretary of War Judah Benjamin his forces were destitute of arms, ammunition, provisions, and funds.[24] Nothing much had changed by March 1862, when Gov. Francis Lubbock wrote Secretary Benjamin to say Texas forces were "miserably inefficient."[25] So it was that Ashley Spaight and William Duncan resorted to the maxim that "God helps those who help themselves." Duncan took almost no time to locate an unusually large supply of corn, someone with the equipment to haul it, and a container in which to store it at camp. That was not the extent of Duncan's quartermaster talent; he also persuaded people to donate goods and labor or, failing that, negotiated prices down to lowest fair value. As the war progressed, he frequently paid for unit supplies out of his own pocket. When called to perform as an army supply officer, Duncan produced results well beyond expectations.

Chapter 4 **Duty**

DUNCAN WAS BACK IN CAMP AT GRIGSBY'S BLUFF ON Monday, June 30, when a thunderstorm arrived with the day's mail. It carried a letter from Celima telling Duncan that Chessie, their seven-month-old baby girl, was sick. Most Confederate officers would soldier on after receiving such news, but not Duncan. He requested and was granted leave and left the next day on horseback for Liberty. He rode hard and arrived home at 9:30 Thursday night, reporting he was "very tired but all was well." The next day was America's Fourth of July Independence Day and Duncan abruptly changed hats, transforming himself from a Confederate cavalry officer to an independent cattleman. He met a friend in Liberty and organized a cattle drive unlike any other in which he had ever invested.

A herd moved out of the Liberty area onto the eastbound Atascosito Trail on Monday, July 7, but Duncan did not ride with it. Instead he left the house at 7 A.M., rode to town where he loaded his horse on a rail car and took the train to Beaumont, arriving at 12:30 P.M. He unloaded his horse, climbed into the saddle, and rode to camp at Grigsby's Bluff where he talked with Captain Spaight until midnight. Four days later, Duncan stabled his horse at 11:30 P.M. in New Iberia, Louisiana, and went to bed hungry. The next morning, he rode to Camp Pratt, a Confederate training camp five miles north of New Iberia on Spanish Lake. There Duncan met the camp's namesake, Confederate Gen. John G. Pratt. After the two men exchanged greetings, the General excused himself because of illness. He apologized to Duncan, saying he wanted to see him again as soon as his health permitted. Duncan then walked to another area of Camp Pratt and "reported beeves." His brief meeting with the general and the subsequent transaction prove Duncan had resolved one of the major questions he had when he hesitated to join the Moss Bluff Rebels: could he fold his personal commercial interests into his military obligation? The answer was yes; Duncan had sold the herd making its way toward Louisiana to the Confederate army.

Duncan spent the next two weeks in Louisiana, losing $7 at cards in Alexandria on Friday, July 17 then winning it back plus an additional $2 the following Sunday. Between card games on Saturday, Duncan reports he "called on General Pratt, finding him well enough to talk." Duncan packed his things, paid his bills, and headed back to Texas on July 24, arriving in Sabine Pass on Wednesday, the 30th. He took tea with Spaight at the local tavern and stayed the night. Rising at 2:00 the next morning, he rode quickly to catch the northbound ferry and made it back to camp at Grigsby's Bluff for breakfast. The meeting with General Pratt in Alexandria on July 18 and his subsequent conference with Spaight at Sabine Pass when he returned to Texas are evidence Duncan interacted easily with senior C.S.A. field officers in Louisiana as well as Texas. His deal to sell cattle to the army while serving as an active duty officer would be considered a conflict of interest in the twenty-first century, but in Confederate Texas and Louisiana, it was a win-win deal. Armies move and fight on their stomachs and Lt. William B. Duncan had the contacts, cash, and know-how to help feed his fellow soldiers. More beggar than chooser, the army obviously did not object to buying supplies from one of its own. Once again Duncan proved his extraordinary value to Ashley Spaight and the Confederate army.

Duncan hung around camp at Grigsby's Bluff on Friday and Saturday that week and attended a religious service with the men on Sunday, August 3. A boat carrying Spaight and the five hundred bushels of corn Duncan bought in June arrived at the bluff on Monday. While Company F riders unloaded the corn, Spaight paid Duncan $4 he owed him for a bottle of whiskey bought "in Houston long ago."[1] While Duncan was on leave, Confederate brass promoted Captain Spaight two ranks to lieutenant colonel. At a dress formation on Wednesday, August 6, the colonel told the men that in light of his promotion, their lieutenants must be promoted or resign. Then and there, the men of Spaight's Battalion elected William Duncan and his fellow company commanders to the rank of captain. Duncan's men voted forty-three to six in favor of his promotion.[2] Lieutenant Colonel Spaight left camp at dawn the next morning, headed for Houston.

Three weeks passed uneventfully for Spaight's Battalion in the stifling August heat. A Beaumont woman came to camp two evenings to sing to the men. Duncan says one of her tunes was the ballad *Annie Laurie*.[3] The song celebrated the love of a beautiful girl and was a favorite of soldiers on both sides of the Mason-Dixon Line.[4] During the long summer days, gulf coast humidity made drill extraordinarily oppressive, no doubt contributing to Duncan's complaints that he suffered from a severe cold and could not sleep.[5]

Although Duncan was on duty in Texas near the Louisiana border, his ears were alert to news of Union blockade activity all along the gulf coast. He had special interest in developments around Corpus Christi at the mouth of the Nueces River, 250 miles southwest of Beaumont. He owned land and raised cattle in Refugio County where he built many of his herds for drives to New Orleans. Corpus Christi had been a part of Refugio County, one of thirteen original counties of the Republic of Texas, until Nueces County was carved out in 1846 and Corpus Christi became its county seat. Five Union warships under Lt. J. W. Kittredge sailed into Corpus Christi Bay in the second week of August 1862, and launched an artillery bombardment on the city.[6] Provoked by Union destruction of much of the town, local Confederate sympathizers took revenge by plundering businesses and destroying homes of known Union supporters. Later that autumn, two boys from New York were detained outside of town, brought into Corpus Christi, and hanged at the end of Mesquite Street. Confederate vigilantes decorated their bodies with signs that read, "Traitors Take Warning" and "Union Men Beware."[7] The Federal attack closed Corpus Christi's port, effectively eliminating its exports for the rest of the war.

Recovered from his head cold, Duncan climbed onto a wagon a week later at Grigsby's Bluff and headed down to Sabine Pass with nine other soldiers. Broken-down horses, deep mud, shifting sand, or a combination of all three meant they "could hardly move the car," says Duncan. "We worked and walked till we were nearly dead. Hottest sun. Got to Bayou and I gave three men $3.00 to do all the work to let us rest." Tough conditions finally won; they gave up and headed back to catch the ferry across Sabine Lake. The detail was back in camp before dark where Duncan learned his request for a week's furlough had been approved.[8]

Frequent visits home in the early days of his active-duty service were special benefits Duncan enjoyed as an officer in Spaight's unit. Duncan gradually reveals his close personal relationship with Spaight, which is easy to understand when both men are seen in their core civilian identities. Spaight was an attorney who wrote contracts, legal agreements that are not final until consideration—something of value—is exchanged. Spaight on the one hand made it clear in his work what his client expected to deliver, what he expected to receive from his customer, and what he, Spaight, expected as remuneration for his services. Duncan on the other hand was a trader. He made deals based on volume and value for the item to be exchanged and did not necessarily need a formal contract. For him, a man's word was sufficient. Their shared commercial ethic was binding: *everything* had an economic value. Duncan expected to arrange cattle deals for his own account, perform administrative chores, and enjoy frequent furloughs as part of his military service, thereby making that service more acceptable. Colonel Spaight in return counted on Duncan's popularity, leadership, horsemanship, local geographic knowledge, and his negotiating and management skills. Their quid pro quo relationship was modeled on their civilian lives as neighbors and businessmen on the nineteenth-century Texas coastal plains. They were not professional soldiers.

Duncan looked forward to getting home again. He rose the next day at 3:30 A.M. and cantered to Beaumont where he loaded his horse on the train at 9:30. The locomotive pulled out of the station at 10 A.M., arriving in Liberty at 2 P.M. He walked into his house at 2:30, relieved to find conditions normal. Duncan had dinner[9] the next day with his partner Gilbert, no doubt discussing the recent cattle drive to New Iberia and, more importantly, prospects for others. Duncan took advantage of the furlough to pay a blacksmith in Liberty $1.50 to shoe one of his horses. Business tasks of greater value were on Friday's agenda when he went into Liberty to collect what people owed him for the New Iberia cattle drive, including reimbursement for Duncan's costs and his share of the profit for arranging the deal and accompanying the herd for half the drive. After spending the weekend with Celima and the children, he caught the 11:30 A.M. Monday train back to Beaumont. When he climbed onto the passenger car, he found Colonel Spaight, who had boarded the train that morning in Houston. The two Confederate officers arrived back at camp late Monday night. When they woke the next morning, it was to a chilling report: a boat from Sabine Pass had docked overnight with news that "yellow fever was there."[10]

Yellow fever is a tropical disease spread to humans in the bite of an infected mosquito. Symptoms are high fever, chills, headache, muscle aches, vomiting, and backache.[11] The infection can lead to shock, bleeding, and kidney and liver failure. Liver failure causes jaundice—yellowing of the skin and the whites of the eyes—that gives yellow fever its name. Capt. George W. O'Brien, a Beaumont native and commander of infantry Company E of Spaight's Battalion, arrived in camp Thursday to tell Duncan he was in favor of giving the men a thirty-day furlough absent an order from Colonel Spaight to take other action in response to the threat. Later that day, a letter arrived from Spaight, who had left camp earlier in the week, giving permission to relocate but making no mention of a furlough. Duncan and O'Brien agreed they would move their two companies to Pine Island, twenty miles west of Beaumont. The Liberty cavalryman lent the Beaumont infantry officer a horse so O'Brien could ride to Beaumont to make arrangements.

O'Brien returned Saturday, reporting to Duncan he had run into a doctor in Beaumont who had been to Sabine Pass and "said it was real yellow fever and advised disbanding." Duncan says he and O'Brien reconsidered the plan to move camp and agreed to disperse the men, in effect ignoring Spaight's order. Duncan says his soldiers whooped with joy. He spent the next day writing seven-day furloughs to all except ten to whom he assigned guard duty. Duncan ordered tents struck, all equipment packed away, and the men to assemble at Dickinson's store in Liberty the next Saturday for further orders. Duncan and Sabine left camp for Beaumont Monday afternoon, unaware he and O'Brien had landed in Spaight's woodshed.

When he arrived in Beaumont to spend the night before catching the Tuesday morning train to Liberty, Duncan learned Captain O'Brien had received another letter from Spaight ordering them to move, not deactivate. Duncan and O'Brien discussed Spaight's second letter, concerned the colonel's orders had been made irrelevant by the furloughs he and O'Brien had issued. Duncan and Sabine went to the station as planned, loaded their horses on the livestock car, and left Beaumont at 10 A.M. They got home at 3:30 that afternoon. The colonel arrived in Liberty by train from Houston the next day and called Duncan to a come-to-Spaight meeting. The officers agreed to add a week to the already-issued furloughs, and the colonel told Duncan to meet him in Beaumont on Friday. When the chastened Duncan arrived in Beaumont two days later, he found Spaight and O'Brien waiting. The trio talked until 11 P.M. and agreed to look for a new campground. The last matter they discussed is an insight into Duncan's relationship with Ashley Spaight; he lent the colonel one dollar.[12] Colonel Spaight had chastised Duncan and O'Brien for disregarding his order. The two junior officers no doubt apologized for their well-intentioned mistake, then Duncan smoothed Spaight's feathers with a loan. Duncan knew it would be difficult for him to remain angry with his banker.

Duncan was home in Liberty on furlough one morning two weeks later when a courier woke him at 4 A.M. with a message that battalion sentries had sighted armed Union vessels heading toward Sabine Pass. Duncan dressed quickly, rode into town, and told all the men he could find to hurry back to camp. By noon, Friday, September 26, he and forty Liberty-area soldiers reached Pine Island to learn Union troops had burned Fort Griffin at Sabine Pass two days earlier.[13] Colonel Spaight ordered everyone to gather at their camp north of Grigsby's Bluff, where Duncan and his men arrived late Saturday. Spaight, who had been in Houston on court-martial duty when the Federals attacked,[14] showed up early the next morning, immediately sending fifty men to guard a nearby bridge. The next day, Spaight ordered Duncan to lead his company down to Sabine Pass. When he went to saddle up, Duncan found his string of horses missing. He sent his company ahead with a junior officer in charge, staying behind himself to look for his animals. Duncan finally found at least one mount and headed for the pass with two other men at 5 P.M. The trio joined the rest of the company around 10 P.M., shortly before sentries reported a boat was approaching. "All flew to arms," Duncan says. No shots were fired and "day light found us all under arms [with] no water for our horses [and] musketoes [sic] worse then I ever saw them."[15]

Spaight's Battalion had mobilized to counter the bombardment of Fort Griffin and Sabine City by Union mortar schooner *Henry James* and gunboat *Rachel Seaman* in the first Battle of Sabine Pass. Because of yellow fever furloughs, only small detachments of artillery Company B under Capt. Kosciusko Keith, a native of Sabine Pass, and Captain O'Brien's infantry Company E defended the fort. With Spaight away in Houston, Keith and O'Brien—and Duncan when he finally arrived—defended Fort Griffin under battalion executive officer and second-in-command, Maj. Josephus. S. Irvine, a Texas Republic–era veteran of the Battle of San Jacinto.[16] The Texas Confederates could do little more than shout and shake their fists at the Union gunners who lobbed shells at them beyond range of the fort's cannon.[17] Realizing the Federals would probably land soon after their artillery bombardment, Major Irvine ordered his men to remove all stores, spike cannon, and abandon the fort before Federal troops stepped ashore to press their attack.[18] By the time Duncan arrived, Union solders had landed, destroyed the fort, and withdrawn. The only battle he and his cavalrymen fought was against clouds of mosquitoes feeding on their necks. The Union attack on Fort Griffin at Sabine Pass elevated tensions dramatically for Spaight's Battalion. The men frequently linked actual observations of Union gunboats maneuvering offshore to what turned out to be false sightings of Federal soldiers landing near the fort. "We roused the men, saddled horses and got out arms and went on foot 300 yards and took position near the road in the mukeets to await the enemy," Duncan says. "After two hours and no appearance, we returned to camp. Stationed the men on two sides of the camp and sat up till day light. No attack."[19]

When he wasn't preparing to face invading Union soldiers, Captain Duncan was an army administrator, overseeing equipment repair, completing property and ammunition reports, submitting requisitions, and completing pay certificates—he himself received $230 for two months and nine days' service on October 6. He also continued his personal lending services to Colonel Spaight from whom he collected $19.60 on October 12. The colonel was proving to be a good borrower. He paid his debts, giving Duncan confidence to increase Spaight's credit limit the next time the colonel asked for a loan. Three days later, a messenger woke Duncan with news a Union boat had landed, firing on Capt. E. B. Pickett's Company of the Third Regiment, known also as Carter's Brigade, another Confederate unit formed in the Liberty County area.[20] Duncan ordered his bugler to sound the alarm as he and his men galloped off to the coastline. "Steamer came near and opened fire with shot and shell," Duncan says. "Shot flew thick around us. We come off. Yanks burnt bridge." End of the nonfight.[21]

A week later, the men of Spaight's Battalion became even more uncomfortable when a cold front blew in, bringing strong northerly winds. Clenching his pencil with numb fingers, Duncan recorded ice on standing water and "All of us freezing." Army boredom and frigid, wet weather were November's dual theme for Duncan and his men, except for a false alarm early in the month. A rider galloped into camp on Wednesday, November 5, saying a Union boat had entered coastal waters and fired on his detail. Duncan and a squad of cavalry started for the bayou but met infantry soldiers coming back the other way who said the Federals were gone. Duncan returned to camp and wrote a report to Colonel Spaight.

As November crept into December 1862, William Duncan's first six months of active duty slogged from slow to slower. He and Sabine took the train home to Liberty on Saturday, November 29 but headed back to Beaumont on Monday. Recalling his original reluctance to join the army, Duncan admits he was "unusually low spirited today." He stayed overnight at a local rooming house, paying $2.75 for the bed and breakfast, then rode through cold rain to arrive back at Grigsby's Bluff after dark on Tuesday. Duncan spent the rest of the week on make-work tasks, so bored one day he took time to write there was nothing worth writing about. At loose ends and lonely, he rode into Beaumont the next evening to find Colonel Spaight working at a table in a local tavern. The two talked until midnight. The next day, Duncan entered another transaction in his diary, this time another loan to Spaight in the handsome sum of $100. Duncan had raised Spaight's credit limit dramatically, probably because he wanted to insure that Spaight would grant him a Christmas furlough.

It was back to army tedium for Duncan the rest of the month, supervising occasional drills and performing ammunition and equipment inventories. The weather deteriorated further with freezing wind cutting through the men and playing havoc with the tents. One of Duncan's men rousted him Christmas morning with a bowl of stew. Duncan reciprocated by mixing up "a small nogg [*sic*] out [of] two bottles of liquor, gave the men a taste around." The next day while he was making a gun rack, he received an order to send an officer and twenty riders east to look for enemy invaders at Taylor's Bayou. No word on the outcome of the mission—except a note that it was raining.

Duncan's Christmas parcel from home arrived Sunday. It was a box of cakes from Celima that he shared with his men. That night, a lump of coal filled his stocking. Indicating Texas Confederates planned an action soon that would involve Spaight's Battalion, an order reached camp announcing no more furloughs were to be granted either to officers or enlisted men until further notice. Duncan spent the next day working on company rolls and received a supply of blankets he had ordered for seven soldiers. Tuesday was "too cold to do much work" and New Year's Eve dawned with more frost on the ground. Colonel Spaight rode in at noon, ate dinner with Duncan and the other officers, and inspected the company. Spaight pulled Duncan aside after chow and told him he had no power to let him go home. "I was deeply pained to hear it," Duncan says. "I wrote to Celima and sent it by the Col to Beaumont. Went to bed at 11."[22]

William Duncan considered the end of 1862 one of the lowest points of his life. Until then he controlled his destiny more than anyone could expect in nineteenth-century Civil War Texas. But this New Year's Eve his outlook was bleak. Expecting a Union attack at any moment, he shivered in a dirty Confederate army camp far from his warm, comfortable home and family in Liberty. He understood the isolation felt by many people in Texas and throughout the Trans-Mississippi Region.[23] Even though 75 percent of notoriously independent

Texans voted for secession,[24] they resented knee-jerk conformity to the policies of a generally unpopular Confederacy.[25] Duncan felt the doubt that plagued both the local civilian population and Texas Confederate soldiers deployed across the South, whose ranks were comparatively weak and ravaged by disease.[26] He knew also that former Texas Gov. Sam Houston, his neighbor until Houston moved from his farm in Chambers County north to Huntsville in Walker County late that year, supported slavery but opposed secession and resigned his office rather than swear allegiance to the Confederacy. "In the name of the constitution of Texas, which has been trampled upon," Houston had said, "I refuse to take this oath. I love Texas too well to bring civil strife and bloodshed upon her."

Duncan was not a professional politician; he was a businessman, a farmer-rancher, and a family man. He missed wheeling, dealing, and making money and hated being away from Celima and the children and his relatively comfortable antebellum life in Liberty County. As an older, middle-aged man, he was well aware of his own mortality after losing his mother, his father, his brother, his first wife, two children, and many friends. He understood life's frailty from years on the Atascosito Trail where cranky steers and mean horses, hurricane winds and virulent disease, sneaky alligators and venomous snakes—both reptilian and human—threatened survival.[27] Living on the mid-nineteenth-century southeast Texas frontier, Duncan knew war's dangers. Whether its protagonists were Mexican, American, Union, or Confederate, war had a way of catching civilians in the middle with disastrous results. His family, property and community were menaced by invasion when the USS *South Carolina* arrived outside Galveston Bay in July 1861 to enforce President Lincoln's maritime blockade of the South. When Union gunboats *Henry James* and *Rachel Seaman* bombarded Sabine City, burned Fort Griffin, and established patrols off Sabine Pass in September 1862, Duncan's cattle trail across the Neches and Sabine rivers to Louisiana markets was threatened by a potential Union roadblock.[28] When a Federal flotilla of armed former ferryboats occupied Galveston in October 1862,[29] the personal and financial pressure on Duncan rose considerably. By then, he was a Confederate cavalry captain in Lt. Col. Ashley Spaight's Battalion of Texas Volunteers, sparring with Union gunboats in their blockade of gulf coast ports and rivers. His reluctance to join Spaight's unit had evolved from shades of hesitant gray to no-turning-back black and white. Battles were brewing and William B. Duncan was at war.

Chapter 5 **Disgust**

FEDERAL GUNBOATS ON PATROL OUTSIDE CON-
federate river mouths and port cities numbered approximately three hundred
vessels by midsummer 1862. They had tightened the Union's economic grip on
southern ports to the choking point.[1] The Union blockade of Galveston had
been underway ten months when Southern forces surrendered New Orleans on
April 28 to forty-three enemy gunboats and mortar barges commanded by Flag
Officer David Glasgow Farragut.[2] The cantankerous Farragut, of the memo-
rable order bellowed later at the August 1864 Battle of Mobile Bay, "Damn
the torpedoes! Full speed ahead!" directed the Union's West Gulf Blockading
Squadron and was the first officer to rise to permanent flag rank in the Ameri-
can navy.[3] Spaight, Duncan, and the rest of the Texas Volunteers were fighting
Farragut on the Gulf of Mexico coast in the Civil War. In late September 1862,
Farragut's fleet made the Union gulf coast blockade complete when the *Henry
James* and *Rachel Seaman* destroyed Fort Griffin at Sabine Pass. When Virginia
native and West Point graduate Maj. Gen. John Magruder assumed command
of Confederate forces in Texas on November 29, 1862, his first goal was to break
Farragut's blockade of the upper Texas gulf coast.

John Magruder was a career army officer who became a favorite of Gen.
Winfield Scott as an artilleryman in the Mexican-American War. He resigned
his U.S. Army commission and joined the Confederacy in 1861. Gen. Robert E.
Lee exiled Magruder to the Trans-Mississippi Texas command after he earned
a reputation as "Prince John" for dramatic theater techniques he occasionally
employed as battlefield tactics.[4] Magruder was arrogant and ostentatious with
a lisp made worse by frequent drafts of whiskey.[5] South Carolina–born dia-
rist Mary Chestnut, a confidante of Mrs. Varina [Jefferson] Davis, remembers
how an acquaintance ridiculed Magruder's manner and speech impediment in a
comical picture of the general exhorting an army on the battlefield: "Chawge,"

said the mimic, "and chawge fuwiously."[6] Magruder's flamboyance dressed in
a general's uniform made him a clown in the eyes of many Texas Volunteers.
They were ordinary frontier citizen soldiers like Ashley Spaight and William
Duncan who probably sneered at the self-absorbed regular army general from
Virginia.

Wrapped in his bedroll inside a tent at Grigsby's Bluff southeast of Beaumont, Capt. William Duncan opened his eyes shortly after 3 A.M. on New Year's
Day, 1863. His sleep was interrupted by the low rumble of artillery fire erupting
112 miles away at the south end of Galveston Bay. Duncan's wife Celima and
her neighbors heard the cannon much more clearly from their homes less than
thirty miles north of the bay along the Trinity River in Liberty County.[7] Two
Texas Confederate cottonclads, the *Bayou City* and the *Neptune* under command of Capt. Leon Smith, had crept under cover of darkness down the bay
to attack six Federal gunboats at anchor near Galveston's docks as well as 264
men in three companies of the 42nd Massachusetts Volunteer Infantry Regiment bivouacked at Kuhn's Wharf at the end of 18th Street. General Magruder
chose the predawn hours of New Year's Day for the attack, hoping to catch
the Federals semiconscious after their late night New Year's Eve celebrations.
Texas Confederate artillery, cavalry, and infantry units followed their barge-
borne brethren in an extension of the surprise attack that captured or killed all
the Union soldiers and seized their substantial store of supplies. The Confederates also commandeered four Union vessels, including the USS *Harriet Lane.*
Federal sailors scuttled their commander's flagship, the USS *Westfield,* before
Confederate boarders could take it. The offshore Union blockade would throttle
the Oleander City's trade for the rest of the Civil War, but after New Year's
Day, 1863, Galveston was back in Texas Confederate hands.[8]

Before the victors were certain the battle was a clear-cut Confederate victory, Colonel Spaight sent Duncan an order by courier to load men and horses
onto the steamer *Sunflower* and head for Houston "with all dispatch." It took
Duncan and sixty men until 1:30 the next morning to load themselves, gear,
and horses on board the *Sunflower.* As they watched another of Spaight's companies cram themselves onto the boat, a rider brought a second letter from the
Colonel countermanding his original order. General Magruder and Colonel
Spaight determined there was no threat in Galveston from a Union counter-
attack, so Spaight's Battalion was ordered back to camp. Duncan was back in
bed by 3:30 A.M., only to rise again with the sun at 7:00. It was a day of celebration at Grigsby's Bluff for Spaight's Battalion, highlighted that afternoon when
a soldier rode into camp with firsthand details of the Galveston battle. Duncan
told his men, "We had gained a great victory." Celebrations continued into the
early hours of Saturday when Duncan decided sleep was not in the offing. He
left Grigsby's Bluff at 3 A.M. and rode to Beaumont for breakfast. No doubt
pleasantly surprised, he found several friends there from Liberty who shared

his passion for poker. The neighbors played cards all day and into the evening. Realizing limited resources sat around the table, Duncan "won some and gave it back, as I did not want their money."[9]

Federal forces stepped up patrol activity off Sabine Pass, undoubtedly irritated by their ouster from Galveston. Duncan rode to the Sabine Pass lighthouse on Friday, January 9, 1863, to watch two Union vessels maneuvering offshore as if they meant to land. He was so preoccupied with the enemy boats that he dropped his new $50 telescope into the water and lost it. Ten days later, Confederate steamers *Uncle Ben* and *Josiah H. Bell* entered Sabine Lake from their base at Orange on the west bank of the Sabine River east of Beaumont. They could have been one-man rowboats for all the firepower they carried; the *Ben* held two twelve-pound guns and the *Bell* carried only one. Rather than giving it a brawny name like Beauregard, the *Bell*'s crew called their single cannon "Annie" after Lt. Dick Dowling's wife. Nine months later Dowling would play a major role leading a small Texas Confederate artillery detachment against another attempted Union invasion through Sabine Pass.[10] The gentility of Annie the Cannon's nickname belied deadly firepower the *Bell* men knew they could deliver with their single small cannon. The *Ben* and *Bell* tied up for the night at the Grigsby's Bluff wharf. None of their crew was allowed to disembark.[11]

The two steamboats had chugged down to Grigsby's Bluff to transform three infantry companies of Spaight's Battalion into seaborne marines in a blockade-breaking attack ordered by General Magruder.[12] Captain Keith's infantry Company B boarded the *Uncle Ben* the next morning along with about seventy-five volunteer sharpshooters from Captain O'Brien's Company E. Another twenty-six volunteer riflemen and boarders from cavalry Company A commanded by Capt. O. M. Marsh of Sabine Pass scrambled aboard the *Josiah Bell*. Duncan's cavalry Company F stayed on shore. When the two Confederate steamers set course through the pass in pursuit of two Union ships patrolling offshore, Duncan jumped on his horse and galloped four miles south to watch as much of the action as he could see from the roof of a house near the beach.

The two Union boats tacking off Sabine Pass that morning were the *Morning Light* and *Velocity*, both sailing vessels and together armed with eleven cannon. *Ben* and *Bell* finally caught the Federals about twenty-seven miles offshore. The *Bell* opened fire on the *Morning Light* with Annie, scoring an estimated twelve hits. The *Ben* chased the *Velocity*, closing within range of Keith's and O'Brien's sharpshooters who sprayed the *Velocity*'s deck with rifle fire. From first round to last, the clash lasted only about forty-five minutes before the Federals surrendered.[13] The Confederate steamers towed the two captured Union boats back through the pass and across Sabine Lake to the Grigsby's Bluff wharf while Duncan rode beside them on the shoreline. On arrival, the victors removed one body, eight to ten wounded, and 110 prisoners from the two Union boats. There were no Confederate casualties. Duncan describes the chaos around the boats as "great rejoicing on our side [but] great delay in everything and bad management." Bad management was putting it mildly.[14]

In planning for the Sabine Pass action, General Magruder ordered Lieutenant Colonel Spaight to stand aside in deference to Maj. Oscar M. Watkins, a Magruder favorite from the general's Houston headquarters. Magruder's order replacing a senior officer with one of junior rank humiliated Colonel Spaight, who immediately submitted his resignation to Capt. William K. Foster, Magruder's adjutant. The general and Spaight must have exchanged strong words over Magruder's maneuver because an unsigned addendum was added to Spaight's letter of resignation before it was forwarded to Confederate headquarters in Richmond. The comment, certainly Magruder's words, read, "Respectfully forwarded and recommended with the remark that, in as much as this officer cannot understand and appreciate an order directing a *special expedition* under the command of an officer selected for the purpose, the service would be benefited by the acceptance of his resignation." When Spaight's resignation carrying Magruder's black ball recommendation arrived at President Davis's office, it was summarily rejected and sent back to Texas. The order had not made it back to Houston when Major Watkins removed all doubt about Magruder's poor judgment.[15]

Like his mentor, Major Watkins fancied a drink or two. Or more accurately, several drinks.[16] Instead of taking charge of the situation when Spaight's three companies aboard the two steamers returned to Grigsby's Bluff with the two Union sailboats in tow, Watkins staggered onshore and led a chaotic celebration.[17] Duncan was disgusted. "Everything [was] managed in the worst way in the world," he says. "There has been the greatest stealing carried on that was ever known." A group of Duncan's men asked him to intercede on their behalf "to see that they were not swindled in the divide" of captured Union clothing and supplies. Duncan partially filled Watkins's leadership vacuum by overseeing the last stages of a lottery in which twenty men from his company finally "got $7.64 worth each at high prices."

Duncan returned next morning to the wharf to find ongoing pandemonium as munitions were being removed from both Union vessels. As he walked through the milling soldiers, Duncan discovered the body of the dead Union soldier. He quietly ordered one of his men to fetch a wagon to remove the body and haul it to the graveyard for burial. Duncan would have been pleased to know that 140 years later, local Texans with a proud Confederate legacy installed a marker in the Sabine Pass cemetery to honor the unknown Union soldier. Duncan's initiative was not his only humanitarian act amid the general disorder. He spent the next morning visiting Union prisoners, and two days later stopped at the field hospital to check on enemy wounded. He says he "found one improving, but the other will die." The prisoners and captured ammunition were finally loaded on two steamboats and sent north to Beaumont. At least half the provisions, all the cannon and the boats themselves were destroyed to prevent recapture by the enemy. It was another foolish aspect of the Watkins affair; the impoverished Texas Volunteers could have put the captured Union vessels, weapons, and supplies to good use.[18]

Most of the plain folks who fought on both sides in the Civil War had little education; their ignorance bred prejudice and provincialism. Fantastic rumors were routinely believed and soldiers ridiculed the unfamiliar simply because it was strange. Profanity, gambling, drinking, and obscenity were common in both Union and Confederate camps. Regional prejudice made things worse. Eastern soldiers on both sides thought westerners were culturally inferior and ineffective on the battlefield. Westerners in both camps denounced easterners as uppity snobs and "bandbox soldiers" who were more impressive on parade than on the firing line. When victorious Confederate soldiers under poor leaders like Major Watkins came face to face with Union enemies at Sabine Pass, it is no surprise their ignorance and prejudice rose to the surface. Captain Duncan's respect for a dead enemy soldier and compassion for Union prisoners were uncommon exceptions to the rule.[19]

Federal defeats in January 1863 at Galveston and Sabine Pass refocused Admiral Farragut's attention on the upper Texas gulf coast. He did not intend to lose another slow, hard-to-maneuver sailboat to Confederate gunners. Four *steam-powered* Union boats soon arrived off Sabine Pass.[20] Captains Duncan and Marsh, commanders of the two cavalry companies in Spaight's Battalion, climbed onto their horses with three lieutenants in mid-January and trotted down to the pass on what Duncan called a spying expedition. "We rode to a bayou that we could not cross with our horses so we took it afoot and walked about three miles down the beach. We had a tolerable good view of the Yankee vessels, four in number, laying about five or six miles from the mouth of the Pass in the Gulf. The weather was a little foggy which prevented us from seeing them as well as we otherwise would. There is one large vessel and three small ones. They are very shy and keep at a respectful distance from shore."[21] Duncan could see Union sailors on deck, reporting later to his men they looked very busy "like they intended something soon." Several armed Confederate boats arrived at Grigsby's Bluff the next day, and Duncan ordered a cow slaughtered and cooked for their men. While they ate, he heard news of a Confederate defeat in Arkansas. "I feel in low spirits," he sighed before blowing out his lantern at midnight.[22]

Chapter 6 **Morale**

EVEN THOUGH FARRAGUT'S REINFORCED UNION armada sailed close to Sabine Pass and posed an imminent threat of invasion, Duncan would ride a mile for music. Several miles, in fact. On Sunday, February 1, 1863, he and two junior officers rode from Grigsby's Bluff south to Sabine City to visit Captain John and Catherine Magill Dorman's Catfish Hotel for supper and "some tolerable good music."[1] Duncan recounted the outing to Celima in a letter the next day. "Yesterday evening I called on some ladies and I think it is the second time since I have been in the army. I enjoyed their company very much; it had been so long since I had heard a female voice. They sang and played for me the following songs—*Yes we miss you at home* [sic],[2] *Bonnie Eloise* and *Annie Laurie*. The ladies I called on were Mrs. Dorman and her sister and daughter. The young ladies are tolerably pretty but you need not get jealous for they lack a good deal of being as handsome as you are. Mrs. Dorman has a younger sister in the convent [school] at Liberty."[3]

Captain Dorman, master of the Neches River cotton steamer *Doctor Massie,* married the widowed Georgia native Kate Magill in 1860 after his friend and Kate's first husband, Arthur Magill, was killed November 2, 1859 in a boiler explosion on the *T. J. Smith,* a Neches River mail packet. Kate and Arthur, who had been the chief engineer on the *Smith,* built the Catfish Hotel in 1852 about three hundred yards north of Fort Griffin. By 1860, it was Jefferson County's best-known inn. The two-story hotel had its own wharf where steamer crews docked to enjoy a meal in the regionally famous dining room.[4] Irish American Kate Dorman was a favorite of Duncan and his fellow Spaight's Battalion Confederates because she was much more than a singing local hotelier; she also was their compassionate nurse and a spunky Confederate patriot. The 4'10" Kate turned the Catfish Hotel into a temporary hospital during the yellow fever epidemic eight months earlier when permanent tenants fled with the town's residents. She and two friends cared for many yellow fever patients, including several soldiers of Spaight's Battalion. What probably endeared Kate Dorman even more to Duncan was her feisty Confederate spirit. On their way to burn Fort Griffin, its fourteen barracks, and stables the preceding October, Federal soldiers confiscated her husband's horse and cart to haul their howitzer. The outraged Kate gave the Union invaders a Texas tongue-lashing, shouting she hoped "our boys" would kill every last one of them and if she had twenty-five men, she would take them herself. On their way back to their landing craft after destroying the fort, the Federals returned Captain Dorman's horse and cart and told him if he did not keep his wife's mouth shut, they would hang him. Kate shouted she would see them in hell before that happened. When spunky little Kate Dorman sang for William Duncan and other Texas Confederates in the Catfish Hotel at Sabine Pass, they listened with wide grins on their faces.[5]

Captain Duncan's turn as battalion duty officer came up again in February 1863, a month unusually full of administrative chores. He and Captain Marsh, the commanding officers of the two cavalry companies, were the only two officers in camp. Confederate gunboats had left the immediate Sabine Pass area and retreated to the upper reaches of Sabine Lake.[6] Duncan began most days in court-martial proceedings, sometimes hearing a case but more often adjourning for lack of one. He kept his eye on several men suffering from the mumps, admitting in what turned out to be a premonition he was afraid of catching them himself. His officer-of-the-day duties included some local police and community-relations work associated with the battalion's always-hungry soldiers. After a local woman complained that one of her hogs had been slaughtered, Duncan identified his men as the pig poachers and rode to her house to apologize. Two days later, he paid a similar call on an area farmer who had lost a yearling calf in comparable circumstances.[7] Although busy with administrative tasks, he composed letters to Celima as he worked, usually waiting until nightfall to write. "The Yankees are still lying off Sabine Pass, two steamer ships and a boat," he wrote on February 1. "I will not be able to go home for some time yet, as General Magruder has issued orders prohibiting officers from asking for leaves of absence. I sent you a Yankee envelope that came off the ship. I wrote one letter and put it in one of the Yankee envelopes but I fear you will not get the letter."[8] Duncan knew Confederate censors would spot, read, and destroy what looked to be Federal correspondence.

While on the lookout for enemy activity, Duncan managed another battalion relocation during this time. Colonel Spaight ordered the men to move back south from Grigsby's Bluff to Sabine Pass to be closer to the coast and the Federal gunboats patrolling offshore. While the men struck tents and schlepped equipment, weapons, and horses to the new camp, Duncan joined fellow officers on rides through gale-force winds and sheets of rain to the beach to check on Union steamers.[9] With hat pulled down and head buried in his coat against the rain, his thoughts were of home as his horse plodded through the sand. If his soldiers could have read his mind, they would have been surprised at what their tough, cattle-driving commanding officer was thinking. "I want to send home some rose cuttings some time soon which I want you to take great care of as they are extra fine roses," he told Celima. "I will write when I send them. [Also] Sabine is getting short of clothes and I cannot get any here. Have you any at house for him if I should get there?"[10]

Duncan returned to Sabine Pass after dark on February 17 following a weekend at home that he tacked onto an administrative trip to Texas Confederate headquarters in Houston. Before leaving camp the previous Wednesday, he completed the monthly report, attended an 11 A.M. staff meeting of battalion officers, and grabbed something to eat at the mess tent. His lunch was interrupted by the whistle of the boat he aimed to take up the Neches to Beaumont, so he sent Sabine ahead to ask the skipper to wait. Duncan made it to the wharf by 2 P.M. and boarded the boat. When it cast off, Duncan says he was happier than he had been in three months. The ferry made it to the river's mouth by dark, but fog prevented the captain from making further headway. The boat got underway before dawn the next morning in the dim light of a pelting rainstorm. It docked in Beaumont at 8 A.M. Duncan and Sabine sloshed through the mud to the station, arriving just in time for the train's departure. They need not have hurried. After three miles, the tracks shifted in their soggy bed and the train derailed. The engineer maneuvered the cars back onto the tracks and headed west once again, but another derailment occurred almost immediately, this one causing serious damage to the train bed. The locomotive kept to-ing and fro-ing all day over the flimsy tracks. When it finally reached the house of one of Duncan's friends east of Liberty around 4 P.M., Sabine and Duncan jumped off the train and Duncan persuaded one of his friend's daughters to drive them home in their family buggy. They pulled up to the house just before nightfall, relieved to shed soaked clothing and pleased to find everyone well inside.

It would be an all-too-short weekend for William Duncan. He spent Friday settling debts with in-laws, repaying his father-in-law Dr. Gillard $250, and giving him another $160 to pass on to Duncan's brother-in-law, Simeon, for a previously purchased pistol and horse. Celima handed Duncan a shopping list on Saturday so he rode into Liberty and bought twenty-two yards of diaper material, a bolt of silk, some silk thread, net caps, and a hose. He also indulged himself with two purchases from his own list, a bottle of brandy and a supply of tobacco. He dropped by the blacksmith's barn to have his horse shod but found it closed. On Sunday, Celima and the children treated Duncan to a deferred Christmas celebration, entertaining him and seven houseguests with a roast turkey dinner.

It was raining hard again Monday morning when Duncan and his daughter Emma climbed into the family buggy for the slow, slippery drive into Liberty.

As the house and outbuildings disappeared behind them in the rain, his original reluctance to join the Confederate army descended again. It had never been easy for Duncan to leave his family, and it was getting harder for him to return to his unit. He dropped Emma off at the convent and drove to the station, expecting the eastbound train to be waiting. It was nowhere to be seen. He left his baggage at Thompson's store and went for something to eat. No sooner had he taken a bite than the big locomotive from Houston pulled into the station. While he loaded his things onto the train, Colonel Spaight, who had quietly resumed command of the battalion, climbed down from the passenger car. Spaight told Duncan the journey across the San Jacinto River had been slow because the tracks were exceptionally unstable due to the wet weather. He asked Duncan if he could borrow a horse because he had to get to Sabine Pass that night. Duncan gave the colonel his buggy, told him to drive to his farm and take his prized paint horse. Spaight climbed into the carriage and reined its pony out of town toward Duncan's homestead just as the conductor told Duncan the train would not leave Liberty that night. He paid two men fifty cents to carry his bags to a local rooming house where he arranged to spend the night since his transportation home had just left with the colonel. "I am in low spirits at being so near my loved ones and not being able to see them," he groused.

As Duncan sipped hot coffee and ate biscuits the next morning, the conductor interrupted to tell him to load his gear onto the train's flatcar and cover up for an exposed, wet ride to Beaumont. The engineer had decided to leave the passenger and livestock cars behind to make it easier for the train to make safe headway on the wet roadbed. The tactic worked because the train made it to Beaumont by 11 A.M., giving the dripping Duncan just enough time to transfer to a ferry bound for Sabine Pass. He arrived at camp shortly after sundown. The uncomfortable journey gave Duncan time to consider how much he missed his civilian life. Each time he left home, it drained him emotionally and his depressions were deeper and lasted longer. He was so cranky when he returned to camp that night, he admits, "It is just ten months today that I have been in the Confederate States' service. I heartily [*sic*] sick and tired of it."[11]

Other termites were gnawing their way through Duncan's morale. Southern unity in support of the Confederacy was in widespread disintegration by 1863. Confederate leadership has since been blamed for failing to develop an effective propaganda organization to maintain an attractive ideal for the Southern public so it would make patriotic sacrifices in support of unpopular measures like conscription, government impressment of private property, and suspension of the writ of habeas corpus.[12] Insofar as consensus exists among Civil War historians on the subject of Confederate morale, its high point is generally agreed to have been the beginning of the war. From that apex, war support in the Confederacy diminished gradually until the disastrous summer of 1863 when it cratered in many areas of the South after Gettysburg and Vicksburg.[13] Minor Confederate victories appeared to renew southern resolve from February through May of 1864, but it is impossible to say whether the random optimism was wishful patriotism or the effects of Confederate politicians jawboning southern newspaper writers. Based on reported difficulties with Northern conscription efforts, for example, a newspaper in the C.S.A. capital of Richmond concluded, "The (Federal) war spirit is broken, is gone and indications of peace will soon crop out all over the surface of Northern society. Confederate victories this Spring will end war spirit and fully and completely develop the prospects of an early peace." Reality did not unfold according to that prediction, and an increasingly ominous mood crept over the South after the 1864 summer before Lee surrendered to Grant at Appomattox Court House in April 1865.[14]

It is also probable Duncan worried about his commanding general, "Prince" John Magruder. His poor judgment had been exposed when Magruder replaced Duncan's commanding officer, Lieutenant Colonel Spaight, with the lower-ranking Magruder sycophant, Major Watkins. Spaight's embarrassment returned to top-of-mind for Duncan four days after he returned from his Liberty furlough when Colonel Spaight announced to the battalion in parade formation he was resigning because of the incident. Rejection of Spaight's resignation by Confederate leadership had not yet made its way back to Texas. Spaight's announcement to the men that he was leaving probably caused Duncan to fret about whom Magruder might appoint to succeed Spaight. Duncan was sorely disappointed by the incident. Many of his own men participated in the chaos after capture of the two Federal vessels off Sabine Pass a month earlier.[15] Duncan shuddered to think how unit discipline would evaporate if Major Watkins was named to replace Spaight.

Duncan the businessman was also soured on the South as an investor. The Confederate Congress authorized the sale of $115 million in bonds and another $170 million in treasury notes in 1861[16] to finance its war effort, but most Southerners either had no cash to buy them or were not interested. When even European investors inclined to support the Confederacy realized this, they too boycotted C.S.A. debt. Who better than her own planters and cattlemen, they reasoned, could judge the South's ability to repay? Duncan was among the few who early on bought C.S.A. bonds and would have been disheartened by Confederate battlefield defeats not just from a military point of view but also as an investor. If his bonds dropped in value with each Confederate setback and the South could not attract European investment, could the war effort be worth Duncan's time? Illiquid Confederate bonds may have been worthless but his life certainly was not.[17]

Then there was Duncan's horse. Every day since the battalion arrived on station at Sabine Pass southeast of Beaumont, his string of horses reminded Duncan how incongruous he was in Spaight's unit. The battalion was composed of six companies, each with approximately one hundred men. Four were infantry and two were what Maj. Gen. Richard Taylor, Confederate commander in west Louisiana from 1862 to 1864, called "horse" or "mounted infantry."[18] Regardless of how General Taylor tried to spin it, Captain Duncan was a Texas cowboy cavalryman in a Confederate infantry company. Confusing his situation further, he and his men rode their horses along the Texas coast waiting for an attack by Union sailors scurrying across the decks of patrol boats that were often in sight but rarely in range. Every day Duncan felt more like a square peg in a round hole. As time passed, Duncan came to see Federal vessels steaming along the upper Texas gulf coast as what they *actually were* rather than what they originally *appeared to be;* they were blockaders, not invaders. Their primary mission at that time was to choke King Cotton, not occupy Texas. The men on those Union gunboats were sailors, not combat infantry. Duncan and his Company F riders were skilled frontier horsemen, experienced cowboys who could shoot the head off a cottonmouth moccasin from the back of a quick-cutting cow pony. They were not farm boys on plow horses like many riders in the Union cavalry.[19] As long as Union gunboats were more blockaders and less invaders, Duncan and his cavalrymen rode their horses in stalemate. They were skillful riders and good shots, but their maritime enemy was out of range and beyond their cavalry competence. The situation was so corrosive to company morale that Duncan began a discreet program of furloughs for his men, permitting individuals and small groups to slip away unnoticed for weekend visits home.[20]

He wished he could join them, especially when letters from Celima arrived with news that stirred his hunter's soul. "Uncle Jerome went bear hunting with his negroes," Celima reported. "He killed two young bears and came very near killing the old one. He sent some meat here. It was very fat but tasted fishay [*sic*]. He is gone again; he started this morning he says there are a great many bears."[21] If the vision of hunting fat, fishy-tasting bears made Duncan homesick, he was in sad shape. But it would not be long before low morale became the least of his worries.

Chapter 7 **Mumps**

DESPITE FEELING OUT OF SORTS, DUNCAN DID HIS best to celebrate his forty-fifth birthday on March 2, 1863. He asked seventeen-year-old Sabine to prepare a birthday meal and proclaimed it a very good dinner, but he skipped drill and a dress parade that afternoon. A second wind and his love of gambling took him to a birthday card game that lasted until 3:00 the next morning; he won $17. Hot cards and a poker face overcame physical discomfort for Duncan again the next night when he won $55 in another game in the adjutant's tent that lasted until dawn. Four days later, though, Duncan felt *very* bad; pain in his back was excruciating. He had the mumps and spent several hours on Monday, March 9, with one of his card-playing pals who also happened to be the battalion physician. Finding no relief, Duncan soon retreated to his tent.[1]

Mother Nature interrupted his convalescence. A Confederate gunboat was on patrol in the gulf outside Sabine Pass one morning when high winds blew it onto a sandbar. Water depth there at low tide is only seven-and-a-half feet; it rises less than eighteen inches at high tide,[2] making navigation risky for a steam-powered keelboat even in calm winds. Duncan dressed, saddled his horse, and rode through the surf to help tow the stranded vessel into clear water. Just as the men fastened lines to the beached craft, Union gunboats appeared and opened fire. The Confederates shot back but both sides' rounds fell short as the boat popped free. It headed back through the pass to flee the Federal vessels while Duncan and other soldiers watched from the sandbar. The Confederate gunboat escaped and Duncan and his men returned to camp. When he climbed off his horse, Duncan was exhausted and in great pain.[3]

Duncan's decision to leave his sickbed to ride to the aid of the beached gunboat reveals another reason why Ashley Spaight worked so hard to persuade the Liberty County cattle drover to join his unit: Duncan was a natural leader. He learned to set an example from his lifetime in the cattle business where tough cowboys held high standards for trail bosses. If the headman was incompetent, lazy, or a coward, his status would not inspire a cowboy's loyalty or encourage him to take risks to save a stray calf. If a boss is full of bluster, down-to-earth folks in the American West today say he is "all hat and no cattle." Authentic Texas cattleman William Duncan would have known what that meant. It was how he would have described General Magruder.

When they chose their officers, the men of Spaight's Battalion participated in a highly subjective process. Most of them looked for character, intelligence, sociability, persistence, expressiveness, and judgment.[4] Some added dependability, integrity, and humility to the list. Others might have considered traits like self-confidence, plain speaking, courtesy, initiative, loyalty, tactfulness, sincere, spontaneous cheerfulness, and the willingness to do one's duty while asking others to do theirs.[5] There were a few who had no clue as to what makes a leader, but they knew one when they saw him. Whatever their leadership criteria, the cavalrymen of Company F knew William Duncan was a leader. When that Confederate boat was in trouble, no one ordered him to help. Sick though he was, Duncan did not send a substitute; he went himself. Duncan does not talk specifically about leadership in his diary, either as a businessman or a Confederate cavalry officer. It is clear however that he *lived* it, even though his ride to the beach with mumps that morning knocked him back into his bedroll with a body blow.

He stayed in bed the next five days, taking salts, drinking tea, and drifting in and out of consciousness while fever and chills plagued him. As the vernal equinox brought sunnier skies, milder temperatures, and calmer winds, his physical health improved but his attitude did not keep pace. "The weather is beautiful," he writes. "I know the country [*sic*] beautiful now. How I long to be at home to enjoy the beauties of nature with 'friends the beloved of my bosom.' I am real homesick," he continues. "I am thoroughly tired of this kind of life. But I must have patience and hope there is a better day coming."[6]

Other than formal discharge due to incapacitating illness or debilitating wounds, death was the only honorable escape from service for enlisted men on both sides of the Civil War. Desertion was their illegal alternative and it eventually reached epidemic levels in the Confederate army. Thousands of Confederate enlisted men went AWOL because their families begged them to come home. They were starving and needed their breadwinners to help deal with the food shortages that plagued the South.[7] A private in the 58th Virginia explained another reason for widespread Confederate desertions. "Many have come to the belief that we will never whip the Yankees and it is only a question of time to bring us under. . . . Many are anxious for the war to stop and they don't care how [just] so they get out of the Army."[8]

Both Union and Confederate officers in contrast could resign their commissions. Most officers however felt that resigning while their enemy was still in the field would disgrace their reputations. Furthermore, if superiors accepted an officer's resignation, people saw it as a signal the officer was incompetent. General Magruder embarrassed Lieutenant Colonel Spaight when he replaced him with Major Watkins two months earlier, forcing Spaight to resign. When Confederate brass rejected Spaight's resignation, they preserved his honor and further damaged Magruder's reputation, already tarnished from his exile to Texas by General Lee. In the ranks, respect for Spaight was restored while his men focused or reemphasized their antagonism on Magruder. The Magruder-Spaight-Watkins affair may also have influenced Duncan to resign his commission. He was far from enthusiastic about life in the Confederate army, and the thought of his friend heading back to Liberty County as a civilian would have enticed Duncan to join him. Duncan did not yield to that temptation. He might have agreed with a Tennessee cavalry officer who wrote that if one gave up the Confederate cause, it could mean "Disgrace, dishonor and slavery forever." Duncan had sworn an oath to the Confederacy and like many soldiers on both sides in the Civil War, his commitment to that promise remained strong.[9]

When General Magruder surprised Union soldiers on New Year's Day to recapture Galveston, Admiral Farragut increased the number of Union gunboats on patrol outside Galveston Bay. Farragut did not have to occupy the city to make the blockade work, but the enlarged, clearly visible Federal fleet sailing along Galveston's gulf beaches knotted Magruder's stomach with visions of another Union invasion. Following a key principle of military strategy, the general decided to concentrate more resources to Galveston's defense. He told Spaight's Battalion to relocate there as soon as possible. Duncan's unit got the word on Thursday, March 19 when a Confederate steamer arrived at Sabine Pass with orders to establish a new camp near Fort Hébert at Virginia Point,[10] a coastal prairie railhead approximately seven miles west of the Galveston docks.

There is little doubt Magruder's orders were conveyed with a sense of urgency, but Duncan took time before leaving Sabine Pass to say goodbye to local civilian friends. He and four other soldiers rode to the home of William and Sarah Vosburg the next evening; they enjoyed Sarah's piano playing in the parlor. She was another Texas Confederate patriot who helped Kate Dorman nurse yellow fever victims of Spaight's Battalion at the Catfish Hotel the preceding autumn. Around 10 P.M., Duncan and his companions thanked the Vosburgs for their hospitality and withdrew to a local gambling den. They played cards until 4:00 the next morning; Duncan won $33.50.

Magruder followed his Galveston relocation command the following Monday morning with transformational orders for the two cavalry companies of Spaight's Battalion. Duncan and Marsh were ordered to dismount their units. That meant Magruder had adjusted strategy to mirror his evolving understanding of the enemy's objective and possible tactics. Magruder and his staff officers realized Spaight's Battalion did not need its cavalrymen to defend Galveston

Bay against a Union invasion. The mission called for boots on the ground, so the battalion's two mounted companies were reclassified as infantry units. Duncan ordered his men to tear down the Sabine Pass camp, pack equipment in wagons, and return their horses to the paddocks, pastures, and barns at home in Liberty County. He told them to reassemble a week later at Round Point on Trinity Bay south of Anahuac for a ferry crossing to Galveston. Like young children anxious to leave for grandma's house, Duncan's men "bothered him out of his senses about going home." After he paid a carpenter $5 to build a wooden box to hold his belongings on the move, Captain Duncan refocused his men's attention to packing and preparation for their new assignment.

A scout reported that high water around Taylor's Bayou south of Beaumont would make that route difficult for wagons, so Duncan plotted a longer, drier path from Sabine Pass along the coastline to the western boundary of Chambers County south of Liberty. Duncan let several riders leave first thing Thursday morning; he followed around 2 P.M. with thirty-eight horsemen and several wagons, covering twenty miles before sleeping that night on the beach. The group saddled up in predawn light the next morning, riding the remaining twenty-five miles of the journey before stopping for breakfast. After eating they headed for Round Point on the east shore of Galveston Bay where they made camp next to other companies of the battalion that had arrived earlier. Duncan dismissed the men at the end of the day but not before inviting them to gather Monday for a barbeque at his home on the Gillard plantation on the Trinity River south of Liberty. He told them to be back in their tents at their temporary camp at Round Point Monday night after the picnic. He made it home himself Friday night around 8:30.

Either Duncan-Gillard family barbeques were famous in Liberty County or Duncan's men were especially hungry; the newly transformed infantrymen of Company F began to arrive at the Gillard plantation early Monday morning. Lieutenant Colonel Spaight was one of the first to show up. The men enjoyed a big dinner, probably at least two freshly slaughtered, slowly smoked Duncan steers prepared by Sabine and other Duncan slaves. The guests began to disperse around 2 P.M. and Duncan rode into Liberty to play cards at his lodge. He made it back to the Round Point camp around 10:00 that night; it was very cold and he slept restlessly.

The transfer of Spaight's Battalion across Galveston Bay to Virginia Point should have been routine. The Confederates controlled the bay, a relatively calm, shallow body of water compared to the normal three-to-five-foot chop of the deeper open gulf. It was not a long ferry ride; Duncan could see the western shore on the horizon. But ferries failed to show up at Round Point the next four days, leaving Duncan and his men at loose ends. He went home Tuesday, returning that evening to find that several wagons from Sabine Pass had arrived with the rest of the battalion and some of his men were drunk. The next day,

Duncan played host to a group of women from area towns who visited camp to watch a battalion drill. Although tired from entertaining the ladies, he accepted an invitation from friends to join a card game that night. A few hours later, he wished his pals good night and left with $47 of their money.

Excitement spread through camp Saturday morning when two steamboats arrived to carry the battalion across Galveston Bay. Word spread they would depart at 10 A.M. Duncan gave his men loading orders, then jumped on his horse and galloped home for one last hug with Celima and the children. The family's good-bye was brief because Duncan hurried back to camp—unnecessarily, it turns out—to find one ferry loaded and the other broken down and out of service. Duncan's unit and Captain O'Brien's infantry company watched the operational boat with three other companies head off across the bay while they settled in for a prolonged wait at Round Point.[11] It is doubtful anyone heard Duncan complain; he rode home Sunday morning and attended Mass at Liberty's Immaculate Conception Church with Celima and the children.[12]

Nine days after their originally scheduled crossing, Duncan led his company aboard another steamboat ferry. Its skipper told him he intended to cast off at 7 A.M. but complications loading men and equipment pushed departure back to 10:00. Celima and the children arrived to see their husband and father off. The parting was emotional; Duncan told them good-bye three times before he finally climbed onto the boat. It steamed the short distance northwest to Wallisville where more men from Duncan's company boarded. Five other soldiers were left behind to accommodate "several pretty women" passengers whom Duncan admired from a distance as the boat chugged across the bay. The ferry docked at the Galveston wharf at 11:30 A.M. Company F disembarked and made its way to Virginia Point.

The next morning, Captain O'Brien was ordered to hold his infantrymen at Fort Hébert on Virginia Point while Duncan and his men were sent to establish a beachhead a few miles north-northeast at Eagle Point, a bayside promontory east of San Leon and north of today's Texas City. In a sober moment, General Magruder was following two other basic principles of military strategy: placing resources at decisive points to avoid surprise and eliminating the possibility of annihilation in the event of an overpowering attack. As the sun set that evening, Duncan dug in at Eagle Point, worn out and bothered by biting horseflies worse than any he had experienced on the Atascosito Trail.

Captain Duncan got his dander up on Monday when a letter arrived from a Spaight's battalion sergeant major at Virginia Point that contained what Duncan considered an insult. He climbed into a wagon and drove down to the point where he confronted the senior noncommissioned officer. By the time the conversation ended, the sergeant major "took it all back" and Duncan returned to Eagle Point where strong winds, threats of rain, and a fog of fleas welcomed him to camp.[13] Eagle Point juts into the western shallows of Galveston Bay east of San Leon at the latitude where most of the bay's twenty-first-century commercial fishery begins its reach eastward to Smith Point on the Chambers County coast. Eagle Point comes by its name naturally, since eagles, hawks, gulls, and plovers use it as launching ground for a strip of good fishing that includes often-bountiful oyster beds across Galveston Bay. When Captain Duncan and the men of Company F, Spaight's Battalion, pitched their tents on Eagle Point in mid-April 1863, they watched big birds sail low over the beds, landing frequently in shallow water to snatch an oyster prize, then fly back to nests onshore to share it with their chicks. The always-hungry Confederate soldiers took a cue from the majestic birds and put oysters Galveston on their own menu. They would have been better off sticking to salt beef and stale biscuits.

Chapter 8 Oysters

DURING HIS FIRST FIVE DAYS AT EAGLE POINT, Duncan ate oysters twice. After supper on the fifth day—the one on which he confronted the sergeant major—he felt the onset of their revenge. He went to bed that night with severe chills, headache, fever, and excruciating pain in his head, face, and jaws. He felt progressively worse over the next five days as soldiers dropped around him with identical symptoms. On the tenth day after arriving on Galveston Bay, Duncan attempted to work at Virginia Point headquarters but the pain and chills became so unbearable he had to lie down. He sent a courier back to Eagle Point to ask one of his men to come to headquarters to stay with him. He also sent word to Captain O'Brien asking for assistance. O'Brien knew Duncan well enough to realize if Duncan asked for help, he was in trouble. O'Brien arrived soon with several officers in tow.[1] His fellow officers, including the battalion doctor, stayed with Duncan until midnight. While they sat by his bed, they must have worried that this would not be a good time for Union gunboats to reenter Galveston Bay. One of the battalion's six companies was flat on its back, incapacitated by virulent food poisoning from infected oysters.

Galveston Bay waters are warm enough for oysters to spawn year-round, but spawning is heaviest from late April to late September. Contemporary biologists have found a wide variety of less-than-delectable material in an oyster's stomach: larvae of insects, mollusks and worms like leeches, parasitic fungi, algae, silt, and fragments of rocks.[2] People who eat raw oysters are sometimes exposed to human pathogens like *Cryptosporidium* and *Vibrio vulnificus* that excrete toxins causing diarrhea, abdominal cramps, nausea, vomiting, headache, fever, and chills. If infected oysters were the culprit—and Company F's universal simultaneous misery with similar symptoms suggests they were—William Duncan was probably near death from the infection. His immune system had already been compromised by his serious bout with the mumps and his forty-five-year-old liver and kidneys were weak from regular drinking. Duncan was critically ill, making him wish Admiral Farragut had steamed into Galveston Bay with cannon blazing instead of hordes of *vibrio* assaulting his colon. At least he would have seen Farragut coming.

Duncan took to bed at Virginia Point headquarters, too sick to return to his men who suffered their symptoms at Eagle Point. He slipped into critical condition with high fever, severe head and abdominal pain, and dehydration caused by diarrhea and nausea. A slave was assigned to act as his nurse in place of Captain O'Brien and the other men who attended him on the first night.[3] It was accepted practice in the Confederacy for slave women to be loaned to Confederate hospitals and field units to provide nursing services. The loan arrangement was a form of indentured servitude where the slave nurse earned a daily stipend paid to her owner. Civil War nurses in both Union and Confederate armies had limited responsibilities. They were expected to keep their patients clean, wash and replace their clothes and bedding, prepare and serve food, administer medicine according to doctors' orders, and, if literate, write letters for the patient. If the nurse worked in a battlefield unit rather than a hospital, she could also be ordered to drive an ambulance wagon, clean weapons, and care for livestock.[4] Duncan must have been uncomfortable with the slave nurse because he soon sent a courier home to Liberty County with instructions to bring Sabine back to care for him.

Stabbing pain intensified in his head, jaw, ear, and shoulders. Duncan was so desperate for relief from an earache that he poured hot oil into his ear. After not eating for almost two weeks, he finally sipped some soup. He tried to write a letter to Celima but could not finish it. Feeling somewhat better after several days, he paid Old Billy Smith one dollar for a chicken, heard that B. F. Spinks's wife died, then looked out over Galveston Bay toward his customers and friends east of the Sabine River. "News reached here," he writes, "that the Feds were giving our men fits in Louisiana."[5]

Most Louisiana war news made its way back to southeast Texas just like William Duncan did when he rode home from New Orleans after one of his cattle drives: it traveled on horseback or in a wagon west along the Atascosito Trail. Although Duncan subscribed to several newspapers and magazines,[6] including the *Liberty State Gazetta*, the *Galveston Weekly News*, the *New Orleans Weekly Delta*, and before the war to *Sartain's Union Magazine*,[7] his primary news source during the war was the Confederate network. Military news reached him mainly through his close friend and commanding officer, Lieutenant Colonel Spaight. Spaight reported to General Magruder who was a peer of Maj. Gen. Richard Taylor, Jefferson Davis's brother-in-law and the commander of Confederate forces in Louisiana.[8] Magruder and Taylor, along with Little Rock–based Lt. Gen. T. H. Holmes, commander in Arkansas, Missouri, and the Indian

Territory—later Oklahoma—reported to Gen. Edmund Kirby Smith, head of the Trans-Mississippi Region, headquartered in Shreveport.[9] Spaight maintained his battalion headquarters in Beaumont close to the Louisiana border, but when not in that office or with his unit in the field, he rode the Beaumont-Liberty-Houston train regularly to spend time at Magruder's headquarters in Houston. Magruder and Taylor both wrestled with the Federal blockade in the gulf offshore Texas and Louisiana directed by Admiral Farragut. Sharing the same enemy with similar objectives—break the blockade if possible and prepare to respond to a Union invasion—Magruder and Taylor also shared courier-borne enemy intelligence. Spaight picked up the latest Louisiana war news on his frequent visits to Houston and passed it along to Duncan.

Duncan's second source of Louisiana news was the cattle market, and its grapevine could easily have been more efficient than the military. Duncan's business associates across the coastal plains continued to travel through Texas during the Civil War, with many stepping up the frequency of their visits through Liberty in response to war-related opportunities. These civilians kept a close eye on military developments with close-knit human intelligence networks in the Anglo, Acadian, and Creole ranching, farming, and trading communities that were probably the envy of Confederate and Union generals alike. Duncan's frequent furloughs home and proximity to Liberty when on duty gave him ample opportunity to reinsert himself into his commercial news pipeline. If he did not actually talk to his contacts, they talked to him through his third and most intimate source of news, his family. Duncan's wife was acquainted with his associates in Texas and with many in Louisiana, and they all knew Celima and Dr. and Mrs. Gillard. As established, multilingual trader Creoles, the Gillards and Celima could interact with Anglos, Africans, Creoles, Cajuns, and Native Americans with easy social license. Duncan's business colleagues trusted Celima with information they would not have shared with an ordinary workingman's spouse. Gillard-Duncan household slaves, always alert to overheard conversations, carried news from errands into town back to Celima. She and her aunt were also well established in the ladies' social network of Liberty County. What Celima heard, she told Duncan on his visits home or in her letters. Duncan probably knew more about the war in Louisiana than any soldier in Spaight's Battalion, often including Spaight himself.

When Duncan learned Union forces were giving the Confederates fits in Louisiana at the end of April 1863, he understood it was serious news for southeast Texas. Union Gen. N. P. "Nothing Positive" Banks[10] launched his Bayou Teche expedition in midmonth, attacking the Confederates in the heart of Duncan's Louisiana cattle markets. A prominent Texan whom Duncan and Spaight will have known, Col. James Reily, was killed fighting with the 4th Texas Cavalry at one of the clashes, the Battle of Irish Bend. Reily, whose home was in Houston, had been a member of the Diplomatic Corps of the Republic

FIG. 8.
William B. Duncan,
age forty-five, in 1863.
Courtesy Julia Duncan
Welder Collection, SHRL,
Liberty, Texas.

of Texas and subsequently served as U.S. Consul to Russia.[11] The Confederates slowed Banks's advance up Bayou Teche but did not stop it. With each Confederate defeat and retreat, Duncan realized a westbound Union invasion into southeast Texas grew more plausible. It was a threatening prospect for a Liberty County landowner and almost completely incapacitated Confederate cavalry officer suffering with food poisoning on the shores of Galveston Bay.

Duncan slipped in and out of consciousness for more than twelve weeks. The infection robbed him of his sense of taste and smell and he was unable to hear anything with his right ear. One morning he would feel strong enough to work, the next, he collapsed back into bed and fitful sleep. Some days, no matter how terrible he felt, the work came anyway. He handled burial arrangements after one of his men was run over by a freight car being added to a train at the Victoria Point railhead. Frank Spinks begged him for a pass home to attend his wife's funeral, but orders had been issued that no passes were to be granted to anyone. Reaching out to comfort Spinks, Duncan invited him to stay the night in his tent. Trying to remain in the loop of battalion business, Duncan updated muster rolls and clothing accounts, handled pay chores, oversaw drill, and talked with Lieutenant Colonel Spaight who called on him almost daily. Spaight was often Duncan's mailman during this time, delivering a letter one day from Duncan's daughter, Emma, in which she wrote she was worried about her father because it was public knowledge in Liberty that he was very sick. Duncan wrote back to Emma that night and to Celima the next morning, assuring them he had survived the worst of it and appeared to be on the mend.

The weather was not helping his recovery. Galveston lies in a mild, subtropical climate where hard winter rarely occurs and seasons come early. But instead of warm, springtime sunshine in late April 1863, the convalescing Confederate cavalry-turned-infantrymen of Company F, Spaight's Battalion, shuddered and sneezed in cold, wet, windy conditions at their exposed camp on Eagle Point. Duncan finally felt well enough to settle his debts at Virginia Point, paying gratuities to several slaves who helped tend him through his sickness. He finally rode a wagon back to camp and eased himself into administrative chores, overseeing drills, checking company roll calls and assigning sentry duties, always with one eye trained south on the mile-and-a-half-wide entrance to Galveston Bay between Bolivar Point and Galveston Island and the other focused on a vision of enemy soldiers marching toward Texas along the Atascosito Trail. That second image sharpened considerably when orders arrived from Houston on May 1 for the company to be ready to march at a moment's notice. Official word of several Confederate defeats in Louisiana and a request for help from General Taylor had reached General Magruder via Gen. Kirby Smith. Duncan spent the next week in meetings with Spaight and other officers. When not in conference, he issued clothing to several men, increased the pace of his correspondence to Celima, and struggled with deafness in his right ear. He tested his physical stamina on an exceptionally cold May 7 by walking from Eagle Point to Virginia Point to collect pay for his junior officers and himself. He returned to camp after dark with pockets full of Confederate scrip, admitting he was very tired.[12]

Chapter 9 **Louisiana**

COLONEL SPAIGHT'S EXECUTIVE OFFICER ARRIVED at Eagle Point the next morning with orders to break camp and prepare to leave in two days for Louisiana. Hampered by a nasty headache, Duncan ordered his men to organize weapons and other equipment, pack personal belongings, and send anything they did not need home to Liberty County. His main concern was with men still suffering from food poisoning. He separated those he thought could travel from the ones who obviously could not. He expected one of them who had been transferred to an area hospital to die. As he worked through the sick-call head count, Duncan learned three companies of the battalion would leave Virginia Point that night by ferry for the crossing to Round Point on the east side of the bay. He was told a boat would arrive the next day to collect his and another company. He wrote a short note to Celima, bought a bottle of rum for $10, and nursed it until 11 P.M.[1]

Duncan enjoyed spirits frequently throughout his adult life but wartime mumps and food poisoning gave him new excuses to imbibe. Patients afflicted with chills and fever in the nineteenth century regularly turned to concoctions whose chief ingredient was brandy, rum, or whiskey. Conventional wisdom on the Texas frontier held that alcohol was a curative panacea, swallowed either straight or mixed in some homemade recipe. Although quinine was recognized as an appropriate remedy for malaria, shortages prompted substitution with various tonics made from the bark of dogwood, poplar, and willow trees, all mixed with whiskey. One of the greatest difficulties encountered by Confederate physicians caring for soldiers was maintenance of an adequate supply of alcoholic beverages for anesthetic purposes. The rank and file was convinced whiskey shortages were the fault of thirsty army doctors, and often they were right. One Confederate doctor admitted after the war that he and his fellow surgeons would go on a spree the night after delivery of a load of spirits and they usually succeeded in "drinking up every drop . . . before morning." Duncan did not worry about doctors draining the battalion liquor cabinet. He had money to buy his own.[2]

Sunday around 11 A.M., Duncan and his men spotted a ferry approaching Galveston and assumed it was for them. It was not. A courier showed up before the boat landed with orders that Duncan and his company forget boats and take the northbound train up to Houston and transfer there to the Beaumont cars. His men loaded themselves shortly after dinner and the train pulled out of Galveston around 2:30 P.M., arriving in Houston at sundown. The company jumped to the ground, unloaded its gear, and bedded down around the depot. They were told to be on the Beaumont train by 6:00 the next morning. Rousted out of their bedrolls at 3 A.M., Company F climbed onto the eastbound train in time for a 6:30 departure. The train made only a few miles down the tracks before the engine broke down; mechanics took two hours to fix the problem. Under way again, it was not long before several cars derailed, causing another delay of three hours. Before sunset, the train shuddered to a stop three miles short of West Liberty on the west side of the Trinity. It had taken thirteen hours for the train to travel forty miles, an average speed of just over three miles an hour. If Company F had still been a cavalry unit, it could have ridden there at an easy trot in less than half that time. Duncan borrowed a horse, left a junior officer in charge of the company, and rode downriver to spend the night with Celima and the children. He got home just as dark fell; the children were already asleep.

Duncan left the house the next morning around 10:00, driving a family wagon to the Liberty station where the train had finally arrived the night before. The men clambered back onto the cars and they left at 2 P.M. The journey was smoother this afternoon and the train pulled into Beaumont at dusk. The company camped in open space between the station and the Sabine River. There was little sleep for Duncan; he spent most of the night at the latrine. The next leg of the journey up the Sabine by riverboat would not be smooth. Their destination was Niblett's Bluff, a trading post and Confederate supply depot on the Sabine River ten miles northeast of Orange in Louisiana's Calcasieu Parish. It was raining hard that day and no one was surprised when their steamboat failed to show. Aimlessly passing time, one of the men managed to shoot off three fingers while mishandling his gun. Duncan, still weak from his bout with bad oysters, spent the night in a nearby house.

Another train derailed near camp the next morning, surprising an unwary soldier who fell under its wheels. He was lucky; it only broke both his legs. Two of Duncan's men, also still fighting food poisoning, relapsed into serious condition, so he arranged for them to check into a Beaumont hospital. He assigned two other soldiers to stay with them. The riverboat arrived in early afternoon, the company filed on board and the boat headed up the Sabine for Niblett's Bluff. It was raining hard when they arrived after nightfall and made camp for the first time in Louisiana. Everyone did his best to find a dry spot to sleep except Duncan, who stayed on the boat, too sick to disembark. His lingering stomach upset was more his fault than the last vestiges of food poisoning. Back in Houston on his predawn walk to board the Beaumont train, he bought a bottle of whiskey for $6. It was the second jug of alcohol Duncan had purchased in a week. He might have thought the mash therapeutic, but each sip poured into his food-poisoned stomach was like splashing kerosene on a burning barn.[3]

Niblett's Bluff sat on the east side of the Sabine, whose lower waters southwest of Shreveport and south of the thirty-second parallel act as the Texas-Louisiana border. William Duncan and other southeast Texas cattlemen liked to rest their herds and replenish supplies at the bluff after they crossed the Sabine into Louisiana. Although riverboats carried cotton, wheat, and other agricultural production down the Sabine from northeast Texas, their primary cargos were raw and rough-cut lumber from the forest belt of east Texas.[4] Niblett's Bluff was a transshipment point where boats occasionally unloaded their cargos onto horse- or ox-pulled wagons that hauled them into Louisiana or across Texas along the Trail. If Niblett's Bluff was not their final destination, boats tended to stop at its dock anyway to socialize and trade before continuing down the Sabine to deliver their loads to customers at Orange, Beaumont, or Sabine Pass. The Trans-Mississippi Confederates chose the bluff as a major supply point. Texas Confederates knew if the Federals won control of Niblett's Bluff, two crucial arteries in the economic and military heart of southeast Texas would be cut: the east-west Atascosito/Opelousas/Old Spanish Trail and the north-south Sabine River. The Union knew it too.

Duncan woke on his first morning at Niblett's Bluff and surrendered. Not to Federal soldiers but to food poisoning flux. Duncan had decided the only way he was going to recover was to go home and rest. He found his friend, the battalion doctor, and asked him to sign a document supporting a furlough due to illness. The doctor obliged and his application for sick leave was dispatched later that day to Brig. Gen. Jean Jacque Alfred Alexandre Mouton, the Acadian commanding officer of southwest Louisiana under General Taylor. Mouton would be killed the next April at the Battle of Mansfield in defense of Trans-Mississippi Confederate headquarters at Shreveport.[5] Duncan's furlough request to General Mouton was not the only paperwork he handled that day; he also received orders to remount his company for its service in Louisiana. Far from Galveston Bay and well north of Sabine Pass where coastal plains replace beaches, his cavalry unit once again made sense to the Confederates of the Trans-Mississippi. Duncan rounded up a sixteen-man detail and sent it back to Liberty County to collect everyone's horses.[6]

Reconstitution of Captain Duncan's Company F as a cavalry unit was a TDY order—a temporary duty assignment—to join the Second Cavalry Regiment, Arizona Brigade, commanded by Col. George W. Baylor under the umbrella command of General Taylor in Louisiana. Duncan's transfer from Magruder's Texas to Taylor's Louisiana within the Trans-Mississippi department was another effort by Confederate Gen. Edmund Kirby Smith in Shreveport to manage the resources of his region. Cavalry companies were faster and more flexible than infantry and artillery units. They could be redeployed quickly to new assignments where threats and opportunities were perceived to be greatest. Spaight's Battalion's cavalry Company A, commanded by Captain Marsh, as well as Captain Keith's artillery Company B, were part of the reassignment. Company B was ordered to remain on board the Confederate gunboat *Uncle Ben* in Sabine Lake to fortify its crew. Infantry companies C, D, and E remained attached to Spaight's Battalion.[7]

Duncan received his fifteen-day furlough one day after his request was sent to General Mouton. Duncan probably asked the rider who carried it to Mouton to wait for the general to sign it. Although Duncan admitted he felt better, his lower intestines continued to hamper his mobility. He slowly packed his clothing and gear, attended to a list of administrative issues related to his new assignment, and learned the riverboat he aimed to take down the Sabine to Beaumont on his way home to Liberty would not cast off until late in the day. It left Niblett's Bluff at sunset but made steam only as far as Orange where it tied up for the night. Duncan slept well as the boat rocked softly at its mooring at the Orange docks. Stevedores began unloading a cargo of wool from the boat at dawn. After sipping coffee brewed by Sabine, Duncan disembarked and found a tavern where he wolfed down a big breakfast, the first meal he had eaten in six days. After eating, he wandered around Orange and bought two needles, pins, a spool of thread, and two newspapers before returning to the boat for its noon departure.

The riverboat arrived in Beaumont at sundown and Duncan checked immediately on schedules of westbound trains. Told of derailment problems that would prevent cars from leaving until the next day, Duncan went back to the boat for an evening nap. When he woke, he learned a train had left while he slept. He was so irritated he could not get back to sleep until after midnight. Thinking another train would not leave until late the following afternoon, he stayed on the boat for a leisurely breakfast the next morning. When he arrived at the depot to check on schedules, he found an engine building steam, ready to roll. The conductor would not wait for him to retrieve his horse and baggage from the boat, and Duncan watched the train disappear into the western horizon, marooning him for at least another day in Beaumont. He spent it relocating to a boardinghouse closer to the station, then visited his men still suffering in the hospital. Checking the station that night before heading for his room, he learned that prospects of a train the next day were poor due to unstable track conditions from continued heavy rain. Duncan was stuck on high center in Beaumont in very low spirits. His leave was shrinking with only thirteen days left.

The train situation deteriorated from difficult to impossible the next day. By this time Duncan had worn a path from his boardinghouse to the depot. When he followed it this morning, station personnel told him a locomotive sent to haul replacement tracks had itself derailed. Duncan headed for the hospital to visit his men, finding one of them in worse condition but the other improved. He took his midday meal at the tavern, a nap back at his room, and returned to the station in late afternoon to check on trains. Back at the rooming house for supper, he turned in at 9:30, skeptical that a locomotive would be ready to go early the next morning. Furlough remaining: twelve days.

Although no locomotive was in sight the next morning, the stationmaster told him one would be there by noon. Duncan returned to the hospital to find no change in his men's conditions. After a noon meal at the tavern, he returned to the rooming house for a nap, then headed back to the depot hoping to find the promised locomotive. No surprise, it was not there. Once again he heard a pledge that a train would be in place that night for departure the next morning. Past the point of believing the stationmaster's promises, the skeptical Duncan walked back to the depot late that night to find an engine hissing on the siding. Cautiously optimistic, he stopped at the tavern for a nightcap before heading back to bed at the boardinghouse. Days remaining on his furlough: eleven.

Duncan was up early the next morning, ready to start for home on the fifth day after leaving Niblett's Bluff. He might have admitted, grudgingly to be sure, that he benefited from the daily naps and civilian food at the Beaumont rooming house and town tavern during the delay. Yes, he could have done without the whiskey, but that would not have entered his mind. After breakfast at the rooming house, he went to the hospital again to see his men. The most seriously ill soldier was a little better, the other still sick. Duncan bought a new pair of spurs at a tack shop then walked to the depot where workers struggled to position the locomotive properly on the tracks. They got things organized around 11:30 A.M. While the engine built steam, Duncan hurried back to the boardinghouse, ate dinner, settled his $18 bill, and returned to the station. He paid an $8 freight charge for his horse, loaded it onto the livestock car, and boarded the train in heavy rain. It finally pulled out of Beaumont at 3 P.M. but the going was slow. Large pools of water had formed on the tracks, causing them to shift with each turn of the engine's big iron wheels. Duncan paid the conductor his $4 fare to Liberty and watched the slowly passing landscape, hoping the train would not sink into the mud. It finally made it to Liberty at 2:30 A.M. Duncan unloaded and checked his baggage at the station, saddled his horse, and rode home. He walked in the front door at first light, finding Celima and the children in good health. "Thank kind heaven," he wrote that night in his diary.[8]

Chapter 10 **Insurance**

IT WAS RAINING WHEN THE WESTBOUND TRAIN
came through Liberty; there were only ten days left on Duncan's furlough. Several infantrymen from Spaight's Battalion climbed aboard, heading for Houston to guard Confederate prisoners, most of whom probably were deserters. In town on a shopping trip, Duncan watched the train pull out, then bought a new coat for $22, a bottle of rum for $3.50 and a loaf of bread for a dollar.[1] Next morning, he took his children and a slave into the fields to make a bee gum, a short section of a hollowed-out tree with a loose board for a roof. When set on a box not far from blossoming plants, pollinating bees transform the excavated log into their hive, and before long it becomes a honey factory.[2] Thinking he would fast-track Mother Nature, Duncan looked for a working hive to transplant into the new construction. He recalled seeing one on an earlier hunting trip but when the group arrived in the area he remembered, the tree with the beehive in it had been cut down. The children would have to wait for bees to make a hive the natural way before they could harvest honey for their bread. When they returned to the house, a man was waiting to buy a roan pony from Duncan. The two struck a deal and Duncan pocketed $100 as a down payment for the animal, making note of the $75 balance due.[3]

Since he received orders at Niblett's Bluff to remount his company under General Taylor's command, Duncan had been thinking about his new assignment. Union-occupied Louisiana was a far more dangerous place than he was used to in Texas. Odds were good he would come face to face with Federal soldiers whose minié balls were far more accurate than occasional artillery rounds fired from offshore gunboats. As a Confederate cavalryman, he knew his orders would often involve escorting slow-moving wagon trains. To improve his chances of survival, he decided to look for a fresh, fast new ride. The most valuable weapon other than a reliable firearm that a Civil War cavalryman could

own was a strong, healthy horse.[4] After his bouts with mumps and food poisoning, Duncan's new horse must be extra special: it had to move smoothly. He had
lost stamina during the two illnesses and his insides were perpetually painful,
so Duncan wanted a new horse that walked, trotted, cantered, and galloped
with an easy gait.

Captain Duncan had put out the word in Liberty County he was interested
in a new horse and agreed to buy one over the weekend. After spending three
days of his final week of leave helping Celima care for Emma and the baby,
both of whom had come down with measles, Duncan rode to W. J. Swilley's
place south of Liberty to pick up his new mount. Swilley was not home when
Duncan arrived, so he continued on to Colonel Spaight's house in Moss Bluff.
Spaight was away on business at Crackers Neck, today's town of Hankamer, but
Duncan decided to wait. The colonel arrived after a short interval and Duncan
chatted with him through the afternoon. On his way home, Duncan stopped
again at Swilley's place to pick up his new horse, but Swilley had not made it
back. Duncan rode home through the twilight on his old horse to find Emma
tossing with fever and Chessie itching with measles.[5]

Duncan went into town the next day where a local man gave him $40 for
a pair of beeves. The two men probably had a neighborly understanding: the
friend could take a Duncan cow or two occasionally and pay him later. Duncan
also settled the account for the coat he bought earlier from Celima's brother,
Simeon DeBlanc,[6] who worked in his Uncle Edward's dry goods store. As Duncan walked across the Liberty town square, he met the private from his company who buried the Union soldier killed in the Sabine Pass action in January.
Duncan thanked him again for helping handle the burying and quietly pressed
$2 into his hand in thanks.[7] Dyed-in-the-wool Confederate sympathizers in the
Liberty town square would not have looked kindly on Duncan's respect for the
body of a dead enemy soldier. His discretion with the gratuity was wise both for
him and his trooper.

One of Duncan's men showed up at his house the next morning, intending
to accompany the captain back to Niblett's Bluff. Duncan sent him home, asking that he wait until Monday when Duncan planned to leave. Then he went
into Liberty where he met Swilley and his horse. After riding it, he agreed to
pay Swilley $600 for the animal. It must have been a fine-looking specimen for
Duncan to pay that much, but the price was much more an indicator of the weak
Texas wartime economy than it was the quality of the horseflesh. Continuous
issues of Confederate paper money printed to meet growing war expenses had
rapidly deteriorated the value of Southern currency, propelling it on its way to
collapse.[8] Duncan's deal for Swilley's horse shows how inflation rode roughshod
over both the Confederate war effort and trade of ordinary folks. Duncan probably thought Swilley's price was highway robbery, but he had not seen anything
yet. A year later in the summer of 1864, the market value for good horses in Virginia and North Carolina ranged from $1,500 to $2,500 in Confederate currency.

The average military impressment price paid at that time by the Confederates was $500, except for one month in June 1864 when it reached $1,000. Gen. H. T. Holmes, General Lee's commander in North Carolina, complained he was obliged to pay $4,000 that summer for a very ordinary horse.[9]

Confederate commerce over the course of the war demonstrated how inflation makes a bad economy much worse. The state of war compounded by the Union blockade not only strangled Southern exports but also prevented the Confederacy from obtaining necessary imports from its natural markets. Conditions were so difficult the Confederate army itself had to buy commodities from Northern suppliers who took full advantage of circumstances to raise prices to rapacious levels. In the ranks, Confederate soldiers starved, wore rags, carried rifles without ammunition, and often personally financed their own fighting. It was a measure of Confederate resolve that they continued to dig into their own pockets for as long as they did. Duncan handed Swilley $400 in cash and the reins to his horse, loaning it to Swilley until Duncan came up with the other $200. He climbed onto the new horse and rode to a friend's funeral, then returned home.[10]

On Sunday, the last day of his furlough, his daughter Emma was so ill that Duncan postponed the trip back to Niblett's Bluff. He sent a slave into Liberty for newspapers and the week's train schedule, then spent the day inside with the children. Emma was very sick and Duncan felt uneasy. No doubt he recalled the afternoon in January 1861 when he returned from his hunting trip in time to watch his baby son die. Duncan would have shuddered at the prospect of losing another child, especially his eldest. Emma was better the next morning, but Duncan nevertheless told another man who intended to ride the train with him back to Louisiana he was not ready to go. Tending to Emma and Chessie, still sick with the measles, had left Duncan no time to repair his saddle, bridles, hobbles, and leads for his return to cavalry status. While he worked, Swilley showed up and told Duncan he had found him another good horse. Either Swilley had second thoughts about selling his horse or, more likely, Duncan was bothered by something about Swilley's animal. On his ride to the funeral and back home the previous day, Duncan could have found Swilley's horse to be an unruly, half-broken stallion, or it might have galloped so awkwardly that Duncan felt like he was riding a three-legged cow. Duncan told Swilley to ask Summers, the owner of the other horse, to bring it by Duncan's place the next morning.

Departure day dawned and two of Duncan's cavalrymen arrived at the house. He sent them into Liberty to wait for him, assuring them he would be there in time for the afternoon Beaumont train. Around 11 A.M., Duncan climbed on Swilley's horse and lifted Chessie onto the saddle in front of him. The baby obviously was feeling better, so he let her ride to the plantation gate where he handed her down to a slave who carried her back inside. Duncan rode into Liberty, met Summers, and made a deal that Duncan and Swilley must have concocted the previous day. Duncan agreed to buy Summers's horse for $500, $100 less than he had given Swilley for his. Duncan handed Summers $100 in Confederate currency and the two men switched saddles and bridles on the two horses. Duncan told Summers to take Swilley's horse back to him and ask for $400, then Duncan headed for the Liberty train depot. He had bought another fine piece of horseflesh, considering the $500 price he paid for it. Swilley and Summers presumably were satisfied and Duncan had solved his horse problem. He had bought the best horse he could find at the lowest price, saved $100, and apparently left his trading partners happy. He loaded his new life insurance policy onto the livestock car and climbed on the train with three of his men. He paid the $20 fare for all of them, plus $2 for papers as the train departed at 2 P.M. They arrived in Beaumont at sundown, looked to make sure a boat was not leaving for Niblett's Bluff, then checked into the same boardinghouse where Duncan stayed on his journey home to Liberty two weeks earlier.

There was no boat to the bluff the next day so Duncan spent it on errands in Beaumont. He tried to buy a pony to use as a packhorse but was unable to make a deal. He looked for a farrier to shoe his new horse, but had no luck. He wrote a quick note to Celima, went to a concert, and heard about a "great Confederate victory" at the Battle of Vicksburg, proving the Confederate grapevine was way ahead of itself. Vicksburg would not surrender to General Grant's siege for another month. A boat arrived at the Sabine River dock the next morning, announcing its estimated time of departure northbound as 1 P.M. Duncan tried again but failed to buy a packhorse yet found a way to part with some money anyway. He joined a poker game in town and lost $29. He returned to the boardinghouse, grabbed something to eat, paid his $15 bill, and went back to the boat. It left on time and Duncan slept most of the trip. He was awakened when the boat stopped a short time at Orange but fell back asleep when it made steam again for Niblett's Bluff. They arrived at 8 P.M. and Duncan saw that his new horse was unloaded safely, then returned to his bunk on the boat and slept badly.

The war in Louisiana had not waited for Duncan's return. While he was on furlough, the sixteen-man detail he sent back to Liberty returned to Niblett's Bluff with the company's horses. Company F, Spaight's Battalion, Texas Volunteers, remounted in Louisiana without him and made its way to Vermillionville. Duncan and the handful of soldiers with him were in catch-up mode. Blinking his eyes from lack of sleep, he left the boat at daylight the next morning, grabbed breakfast, and made his way to the Niblett's Bluff quartermaster's shack to claim rations—bacon and flour—and a sack of corn for the horses. Then he bought a mule and packsaddle for $110 to tote his things.

After loading his gear on the new mule, Duncan arranged to store his trunk at Swearingen's Tavern. He and three men finally left Niblett's Bluff in the sweltering heat around 3:30 Saturday afternoon, heading northeast into Louisiana along the Atascosito Trail. They made it to Gabe Andrews's place after dark. He was another of Duncan's many friends who lived along the trail not far east of the Sabine River. It was an oppressive, still night and after paying Andrews fifty cents each for the group's supper, Duncan thanked Andrews for letting him bunk on the porch where the cool night breeze helped him sleep. Up early the next morning, the group rode only a short distance before stopping at the house of another acquaintance where Duncan found one of his cavalry-men quite ill. Duncan asked the householder to let the man have up to $15 on credit and Duncan said he would be responsible.

Climbing back onto their horses, the quartet made it to the Calcasieu River above Lake Charles at noon. They crossed the river uneventfully and rested in the shade until the sun lost its vengeance later in the day. Back on the road, the foursome met a wagon train escorted by Captain Marsh's Company A, the other cavalry unit from Spaight's Battalion that had been temporarily assigned to the Louisiana command. One of Duncan's men was with them, so he joined Duncan's party, making it a quintet. They spent the night along the trail at Arsene LeBleu de Comarsac's log cabin "cattle stand" where they paid one dollar each for supper, twice the tariff of the night before. Duncan was not about to haggle over fifty cents with Cajun friends willing to feed a group of itinerant Texas Confederate soldiers. That night, the group slept in an abandoned house nearby.[11]

From Lake Charles to Vermillionville, the Atascosito Trail runs seventy-two miles due east to the capital of Cajun country. Duncan knew the route well, having driven thousands of head of cattle over it in the previous decades. He and his men spent the next four days riding during the morning, stopping to "noon it" with siestas in the shade, resuming their treks around 4:00 and camping beneath prairie pines at night. They bought bread and milk almost daily from local farmers whom Duncan knew along the trail. Their routine was broken June 9 when they lingered in warm hospitality at Judge Martel's place west of Vermillionville. Duncan said his group "received a great deal of kind attention from him [Martel] and his wife. He would not have any pay from me." Leaving Judge and Mrs. Martel's comfortable bed and breakfast, the group crossed the prairie and camped five miles west of Vermillionville. The next morning, they skipped breakfast and rode into the Confederate compound around 9:00. Union soldiers had scattered the Louisiana Confederates into the swamps to the south and Duncan found Vermillionville camp administration in chaos, matching the turmoil in his lower tract. The eight-day journey from Liberty to Vermillionville via train, riverboat, and horseback had weakened his immune system once again.

Sabine erected Duncan's tent while Duncan sloshed through heavy rain toward the latrine. Later, Duncan's new boss, Missouri Col. James Patrick Major, commanding officer of the Second Cavalry Regiment, Arizona Brigade, dropped by to welcome him back. Captain Marsh from cavalry Company A, Duncan's card-playing doctor, and two junior officers tagged along as members of Colonel Major's greeting party. The men made ordinary chitchat, catching up on the latest reports of Union troop movements. When his visitors left, Duncan hit the sack with fever. There was not much happening around Vermillionville on the second weekend of June 1863, but while Duncan slept fitfully, cannonballs whistled 161 crow-flying miles to the northeast on the banks of the Mississippi where General Grant continued his siege at Vicksburg.

Still quite ill the next morning, Duncan went into Vermillionville and bought a canteen for $2, eggs, onions, and grease for $1.65, and a bottle of liquor for $3. He rode back to camp and strafed his stomach—little wonder—with fried groceries and alcohol, complaining afterward he felt very bad. Colonel Major dropped by again to discuss transfer of one of Duncan's junior officers to another unit. His business with Major concluded, Duncan wrote a long letter to Celima and asked one of the Texans headed home to carry it to her.[12] Late in the afternoon he received orders to lead his company with other Vermillionville-based units to Washington between Bayou Courtableau and Bayou Carron in present-day St. Landry Parish, seven miles north of Opelousas. Washington is the third oldest settlement in Louisiana, founded as an Indian trading post in 1720 by French settlers. It was known as Church Landing before its name was changed to honor the first U.S. president. Washington became an important steamboat port in the nineteenth century, full of travelers, traders, warehouses, and cattle yards. It was the farthest inland Louisiana port that a ninety-foot steamboat from New Orleans could reach. Passengers headed west to Texas and beyond disembarked there to board stagecoaches and wagons for their overland journeys. Texas cattle drovers like Duncan knew Washington well; it was where they delivered herds to bargemen who hauled the cattle down Bayou Courtableau to the Mississippi River at Plaquemine below Baton Rouge, then on to New Orleans.[13]

Company F set off for Washington the next day. Duncan rode only a short distance before stopping at the home of another friend, Valery Martens, who gave him a sack of potatoes and eggs. After he took a dose of pills to calm his stomach, Duncan wrote in his diary that "people [are] exceedingly kind to us in this country." Duncan overtook his men at 1:30 P.M. and decided to make camp the rest of the day because of the heat. The next morning, they reached Opelousas about 10 A.M., rested through the midday meal, and after naps rode the short distance north to Washington where they joined a Confederate battalion already encamped. Duncan walked around to get a sense of the camp's layout and bought $2.50 worth of fodder—fifteen bundles, he says—for his horses and mule. Then he rode into Washington to call on the Andersons, finding only Miss Anderson at home. Her father had been taken prisoner by the Federals and her mother was away in Alexandria. Duncan was back in camp at dusk.

He passed the next week in Washington taking walks, listening to music, and winning money as usual in late night card games. General Taylor's army passed nearby on its way south, Spaight's infantry companies marched through town, and a wagon train arrived from Sabine City. The bustling activity hinted that something was brewing in Washington, Louisiana in June 1863, but Duncan does not address it in his diary. He planned to go to church on Sunday but it rained so hard he decided to pass. Instead he gave Sabine $10 and sent him to fetch a bottle of whiskey. Captain Marsh and his company left with a wagon train to buy supplies from a friendly Indian tribe camped to the west. Duncan's diary is routine when he writes on June 24, "no news nor any thing [*sic*] to record. Bought fodder $2.00. Rained hard." Duncan's indifferent entry suggests he might have been oblivious to what was going on in camp. A better bet would be that his diary is bland because Duncan knew the danger of documents falling into enemy hands. He was well aware that one of the best ways to squirrel a business deal was to talk, or in this case, write too much about it. The same need for secrecy applied to Civil War military missions. It is also likely Confederate censors knew Duncan kept a diary and cautioned him to refrain from noting future plans.[14]

Censorship was a fact of life in the Civil War. It was practiced in the South long before the war, feeding on a closed, rural society where communications were difficult at best.[15] Adhering to southern cultural norms, the Confederate army prohibited newspaper publication of troop movements, correspondents were ordinarily kept away from the lines, reports of military operations were submitted to the appropriate commanding officer before publication, and severe penalties were enforced against editors who published statements that could threaten confidence in Confederate leadership. Military commanders distributed confidential instructions and dire warnings to newspapers, occasionally even suggesting silence to be a desirable journalistic value. Duncan, a habitual record-keeping businessman long before he wore the Confederate uniform, understood the danger of loose lips yet never stopped keeping his diary during the war.[16]

Whether Duncan's comment stemmed from military blackout or personal discretion, much more was happening in Washington, Louisiana, than feeding horses and dodging raindrops. General Taylor had ordered a raid by the Second Cavalry Brigade under Colonel Major to break Union supply lines and try to force their withdrawal from the strategic gulf port town of Brashear City, seventy miles west-southwest of New Orleans on the Atchafalaya River. Leaving Duncan to recuperate in Washington—it is likely Colonel Major made this call when he realized how weak Duncan remained from effects of the food poisoning—Major fought his way south, hitting Federal camps, trading shells with Union gunboats, and capturing enemy weapons, ammo, and supplies wherever he could. Anticipating his approach, Union Lt. Col. Albert Stickney positioned just over eight hundred soldiers on June 20 to meet Major's Confederates at LaFourche Crossing, seven miles east of Thibodaux, the parish seat of LaFourche Parish. Major's troops attacked late that afternoon but the Federals drove them back. The Confederates engaged Stickney's soldiers twice again the next day before falling back toward Thibodaux as night fell. After suffering an estimated 219 casualties, Major chose to disappear into the swamps and work his way around Stickney rather than fight through him. Accepting his defeat at LaFourche Crossing, Major pressed on toward his original target at Brashear City.[17]

Colonel Major and his men, along with units under Texas cavalryman Brig. Gen. Tom Green, approached the Union garrison at Berwick Bay just north of Brashear City in the predawn darkness of June 23. Green was another Republic of Texas veteran of the victory over General Santa Anna at the Battle of San Jacinto and had fought in the recapture of Galveston on January 1, 1863.[18] From the opposite direction—the south—Confederate Maj. Sherod Hunter, a transplanted Texan from Tennessee, passed the word to his 325 men to muffle oars on their forty-eight rafts and paddle quietly for twelve miles through the darkness to the rear of the Union fortifications. As the sun brightened the morning sky, Colonel Major, General Green, and their men opened a frontal assault on the Federals, grabbing their undivided attention. Hiding in the bayou on the other side of the Federal garrison, Major Hunter explained what happened next. "Everything being in readiness," he wrote later in his report,

> the command was given, and the troops moved on with a yell. Being in full view, we were subjected to a heavy fire from the forts above and below, the gun at the sugar-house, and the gunboats below town, but, owing to the rapidity of our movements, it had but little effect. The forts made but a feeble resistance, and each column pressed on to the point of concentration, carrying everything before them. At the depot the fighting was severe, but of short duration, the enemy surrendering the town. My loss is three killed and eighteen wounded; that of the enemy, forty-six killed, forty wounded, and about 1,300 prisoners. We have captured eleven 24 and 32 pounder siege guns; 2500 stand of small-arms (Enfield and Burnside rifles), and immense quantities of quartermaster's, commissary, and ordnance stores, some 2,000 African slaves, and between 200 and 300 wagons and tents. I cannot speak too highly of the gallantry and good conduct of the officers and men under my command.

The battle of Berwick Bay at Brashear City was a Confederate success with mixed blessings for the victors. On the credit side, the Confederates grabbed what would turn out to be temporary control of Brashear City in the seesaw battle against the Union blockade. They also captured a valuable cache of enemy arms and ammunition. On the downside, the Confederates inherited 1,300 difficult-to-handle Federal prisoners and 2,000 newly emancipated, hungry, and high-maintenance slaves who had attached themselves to the Union garrison. Yet in spite of the Brashear City Confederate victory, the Mississippi and Atchafalaya rivers, their networks of tributaries and bayous, and the always strategically essential port of New Orleans remained firmly in Union control.[19]

Chapter 11 **Escape**

THE DAY AFTER COLONEL MAJOR, GENERAL GREEN, and Major Hunter overpowered Brashear City, Captain Duncan organized a detail of twenty men in Washington to move 111 Union prisoners to Alexandria, sixty miles north of Opelousas. That night, he went into town with his doctor and two other officers for an evening of music and dancing. Duncan says he enjoyed the outing. He was very much at home with his Anglo, Creole, and Cajun friends in southwest Louisiana whom he described as "very clever people," including the five young ladies with whom he danced that night. He was up early next morning to supervise arrangements for the prisoners to go north and prepare a wagon train to head south to meet Colonel Major. Duncan did not yet know all the details of the Brashear City victory, but he did know Colonel Major needed wagons to haul the captured cache of Union weapons and ammunition to a more secure area away from New Orleans. Duncan's health had recovered sufficiently to let him conclude he could ride and fight, if need be.

The northbound prisoner detail left around 8:30 A.M., and Duncan rode out of camp with the wagon train headed south about the same time. After a few miles, he sent wagons and escorts ahead while he stopped to call on Mrs. Anderson who had returned home, then rode through Opelousas without stopping. Duncan's doctor was with him and the two overtook the wagon train at Bayou Carron Crow, camping there for the night. The next day, June 26, the wagons reached Vermillionville in the rain and Duncan wrote to Celima after they made camp beneath a bridge. He bought another bottle of whiskey for $5 and heard "news of a victory gained by our forces at Barwick [*sic*] City." The next day's ride took them to a spring one-and-a-half miles north of New Iberia, thirty-eight miles south of Opelousas. Sabine put up their tent while Duncan bathed and changed clothes before riding into town to spend the night at Alexander Hébert's place.

Duncan bid Mr. Hébert "Au revoir" the next morning around 11:00 after borrowing $100. His wagon train had already left New Iberia. Duncan stopped in town, buying a horse brush for $5, tobacco for $1.75, writing a short letter to Celima, and dropping by Mrs. Gravenberg's for dinner. That afternoon, he caught up with the wagon train between Jeanerette and Franklin, southeast of New Iberia. They had already made camp at Sorrel's plantation. Duncan rode into Franklin the next morning and made a beeline for Mrs. Hayes's place for dinner and conversation with her and two friends. No wonder Duncan wasted little time getting to Mrs. Hayes's house. She filled him with cakes and figs, the first of the season, and gave him a jar of orange preserves. Pleasantly stuffed with goodies, Duncan climbed back on his horse and rode slowly to join his men, in camp this time two miles south of Franklin on the Opelousas Trail.

After siesta to sleep off Mrs. Hayes's feast, Duncan went in search of the house of William Hayes, presumably a son or nephew of his dinnertime hostess. Duncan says Hayes "had married an old sweet heart of mine, Catharine Moss." He found the Hayes's house two miles from camp, knocked on the door, and introduced himself. Their surprise Texas visitor must have charmed Catharine and William Hayes because they invited Duncan to stay for supper. He left at 10 P.M. and rode back to camp. Reflecting on the evening and reunion with his former flame after twenty years, Duncan says it was the "First time I have met the woman since Aug., 1843. She has changed a great deal. But I reckon, not more than me."

Duncan had orders to load Brashear City's Federal rifles, cannon, and other bounty and move the captured arms and supplies to safer Confederate-populated territory out of range of patrolling Union gunboats. After Duncan's pleasant stay in Franklin, he joined his wagons as they rolled past Fort Bisland on the way to that night's campsite one mile south of Pattersonville. Duncan says he "saw the celebrated battle field [and] the bones of one Yankee who had been half covered. Houses and trees shot to pieces." He cooled off with a swim that night after dark. The wagons started early the next morning and arrived at the recently retaken Union garrison at Berwick Bay—Duncan calls it Berwick City—above Brashear City about 8:00. He sent a soldier across the bayou to check in with the newly appointed Confederate commander of the facility who sent word back to Duncan for his men and wagons to cross the water and enter the newly captured Confederate camp. Duncan ordered most of his riders across first while he and three others waited with the wagons. It took most of the day to get the company across the bayou and into camp. Duncan paints a rancid picture of the place: "Breashear [*sic*] City & Vicinity is a Yankee camp. Tents all standing. It is a stinking place. We are to stay here for the present."[1]

Duncan spent the next day loading captured enemy guns and ammunition into the wagons, making sure his company got its share. When the Civil War began, there were only a few arsenals in the South and all were poorly stocked.

Their paltry inventory was primarily weaponry and equipment for an infantry soldier. Few sabers, pistols, carbines, saddles, bridles, or horse blankets were on the shelves for cavalrymen. Confederate cavalrymen like Duncan were often forced to arm themselves, occasionally at the expense of their Union foes. The Brashear City victory was a welcomed windfall for the Louisiana Confederates but it did not mean their supply problems were solved. The Union cavalry was equipped with Chicopee sabers, Enfield rifles, Sharps carbines, Colt pistols, and, eventually, with Spencer repeating carbines. Because of successful raids on Union camps like Brashear City, it was not long before the Confederate cavalry was similarly armed. Complications arose for the confiscators when initial stores of ammunition for these small arms were exhausted. Enfield cartridges would not fit Sharps rifles or vice versa. Neither bullet would fit a Colt pistol.[2] Confederate Assistant Inspector Gen. Col. Alfred Roman described the practical impact of the weapon inventory mismatch in a report on the condition of a Tennessee cavalry corps toward the end of 1864:

> *The arms are of eight or nine different calibers, but mostly of calibers 57 and 54. The consequence is that, in many instances, ammunition for six or seven different calibers is required in the same company. This want of uniformity in the armament which impairs to a certain degree the efficiency of the command, is due to the fact that it consists largely of guns captured by the men; and it often happens that none but captured ammunition will fit those captured guns.*[3]

Duncan spent Saturday, America's Independence Day, wandering in awe around the Brashear City quartermaster's makeshift store. The Federal defeat had turned the former Union camp into a Confederate trading post. While soldiers swapped confiscated spoils of war, civilian vendors appeared with products and services to extract cash from the Confederates. "Never saw the like of stuff of all kinds, scattered through the House." He bought fifty pounds of coffee for $12.50, two pounds of ham for $7.50, two pounds of candles at $1.00 per pound, five pounds of starch for $1.00, and a slab of butter for fifty cents. Shopping was frenetic because scuttlebutt raced among the soldiers describing four Union gunboats circling below town in Atchafalaya Bay.[4]

The Federal boats did not approach, so four days after arrival, Duncan dressed in his finest uniform and rode to have his picture taken (see figure 9). The itinerant photographer employed the ambrotype process and Duncan used the technical term as his vernacular when he says he "went & had ambrotipe [*sic*] taken." The process used nitrocellulose in ether or acetone on one side of a clean, clear glass negative. After the wet glass was exposed in bright light to the subject of the photograph, the image formed in the chemicals dried and appeared as a positive when placed against a dark background. The photographer placed an identically sized clear plate of glass over the fragile emulsion side of the first piece to protect it and mounted both in a metal frame that in turn was

FIG. 9.
Capt. William B. Duncan,
Texas Volunteers, C.S.A.,
July 1863.
*Courtesy Julia Duncan
Welder Collection, SHRL,
Liberty, Texas.*

tucked into a protective case.[5] Like many people who have their picture taken,
Duncan did not like the photo: "[it] did not suit me." He tried another pose the
next morning after breakfast, but disliked the second one more than the first.
"First not good," he writes, "the other worse." He agreed to take the first one
and paid the photographer $5. He sent it back to Liberty with a soldier going
home on leave, including with it two pairs of shoes and a letter to Celima.[6]

Three days after Duncan had his photograph made at Brashear City, he
and Colonel Major shared a drink of captured Union whiskey from the stores
of the Berwick Bay garrison. It was the same day Duncan heard about Confederate surrenders at Vicksburg and Port Hudson almost three hundred miles
north of Brashear City on the Mississippi River. Their toast will have been one
of mixed emotions for the two Confederate officers. Union forces under Gen.
George Gordon Meade had defeated General Lee's Army of Northern Virginia
at the Battle of Gettysburg less than a week before the Confederate surrenders

at Vicksburg and Port Hudson. The three battles ended almost simultaneously over five days from July 3 to 8. The C.S.A. lost 24,000 men, almost a third of Lee's army, at Gettysburg; another 48,000 Confederates were killed, wounded, and captured at Vicksburg and Port Hudson. The Confederacy was critically wounded after the three mid-1863 Union victories and its Trans-Mississippi Region—Texas, Louisiana, and Arkansas—was severed from the rest of the South by the Union's capture of complete control over the Mississippi River. The Trans-Mississippi states now faced the most serious threat of Union invasion since the beginning of the war.

News of Vicksburg and Port Hudson made the Confederates at Brashear City nervous. Duncan says there was a "good deal of stir among our troops." Colonel Major asked Duncan to select an officer and eight men to guard a group of Union prisoners to Niblett's Bluff, and everyone in the command volunteered for the detail. While the men scrambled for duty that would take them away from Brashear City, the officers spread unrest. Duncan says, "Indications [are] that we are to fight or run." He was told to get his wagons loaded quickly and drive out of the garrison north-northwest back up the Atascosito Trail to Camp Bayou Boeuf, near Cheneyville, twenty miles south of Alexandria. One of General Green's units arrived at Brashear City after nightfall and began crossing Berwick Bay to reinforce another Confederate detachment to the north. Duncan says it took them all night to get across, shaking his head, "I cannot comprehend the movements of our troops. I know I am liable to loose [*sic*] all my baggage and clothing, for want of means to get it away, if we are attacked here."

He collected his personal effects the next day, Sunday, and ordered a wagon loaded with his trunk, book box, and mess chest and sent away. Working in the rain with a small squad of only five men, all of them on the sick list, Duncan supervised packing and loading of the company's tents and "extra equipage." The scene was hectic. Streams of troops hurried through the garrison on their way north across the bay. "Everything indicates a hasty retreat," Duncan says. With most of the wagons already departed, only a few remained in camp with Duncan and several of his men.

Amid the departure chaos, one of his Liberty friends arrived in camp carrying two letters from Celima, one dated June 24 and the other, June 30. Everything was okay at home. Around bedtime on Monday, July 20, Duncan received orders to move his remaining wagons and two companies of cavalry to the water's edge on Berwick Bay. Wagons and riders assembled at the appointed spot by 11 P.M. where they waited nervously in the mud. Exhausted and frightened, they finally crossed on a steam ferry the next morning, pausing to eat afterward in the hottest sun Duncan says he ever felt. "We just did away in time," Duncan says. As they rode away, they heard the cannon of approaching Union gunboats and watched flames from "the cars & Forts & every thing [*sic*] at Brashear City" after the last Confederates in camp put the torch to the place. Duncan and his group slept that night in the rain on the Fort Bisland battlegrounds.

The road was so crowded the next morning with retreating Confederate infantry that Duncan and Marsh's cavalrymen reined their horses aside to let the wagons lumber ahead. As they rode through Franklin, Duncan stopped to buy a bottle of rum for $2.50. The wagons and their cavalry escorts camped that night five miles above Franklin, south of Jeanerette. The next day the wagon train split up. One group with its cavalry escort headed to New Iberia while Duncan's men and wagons pushed on to Grand Lake, five miles west of New Iberia. Duncan says it was a very pretty place. His men occupied an abandoned sawmill and he moved into a small house. That evening, he and another officer rode down to the water's edge to enjoy views at the lake.

Instead of making haste for Camp Bayou Beouf the next morning, Duncan was ordered to pause at Grand Lake while the balance of Colonel Major's command moved ahead to reassemble in Vermillionville. General Taylor was spreading his forces to avoid giving the enemy a centralized target whose defeat could end it all for the Louisiana Confederates. While his soldiers fixed tables and otherwise made camp livable, Duncan grabbed two men and headed for New Iberia to stock up on provisions. On the way into town, he bought a fresh watermelon for one dollar from an Indian peddler along the road. The trio arrived in time for dinner at the home of "young and pretty" Mrs. Gravenberg, who fed the men for another dollar. Each. The group reached New Iberia late in the afternoon where Duncan mailed letters to Celima, then stopped at the commissary. He bought corn for his horses and mule and took a room for the night at Mrs. Humbles's for $3. He started on his shopping list first thing the next morning, buying coffee, three plugs of tobacco, liquor, and a barrel of flour. With his purchases loaded in a wagon by noon, Duncan headed back for camp but stopped on the way for another dollar supper with the comely Mrs. Gravenberg. Duncan arrived back at his tent by 11 P.M.

With immediate threat of Federal attack receding, Duncan relaxed along with his immune system. He complained of the colic and spent all but one of the next seven days in camp. The exception was a short ride one morning with one of his men back down the trail to Franklin where the two ate dinner at Mrs. Hayes's while one of her friends mended Duncan's coat. On his way out of town, Duncan bought some pills for one dollar and paid seventy-five cents for a spectacle case. When the two Confederates arrived back in camp at 10 P.M., Duncan found one of his men had arrived from Texas with a letter from Celima. He was relieved to read there were no serious problems back in Liberty.[7] It was payday on Sunday and Lt. B. W. Brown, the company paymaster and another original member of Spaight's Battalion, arrived Saturday afternoon.[8] Duncan promptly took $20 off him that night in a poker game. Somewhat lighter in his wallet, Brown spent the next day paying men out of his army satchel. Officer of the day

Captain Duncan received three months' wages of $420. Easing Brown's poker loss somewhat, Duncan repaid him $19.15, the amount Duncan had borrowed for his share of the mess account to date. While Lieutenant Brown finished paying the men, Duncan packed a hodgepodge of personal belongings in a bag to send home. The inventory included his Bibles, all of Celima's letters, a handful of captured enemy letters, a book of pictures, a pair of pants, and two pairs of socks. It was the second shipment of personal effects Duncan had sent home in three weeks, suggesting that he might have felt the chance of surviving his Louisiana duty was getting worse.[9]

Troop morale varies widely in different campaigns or phases of a war, but theorists suggest the *rate of losses* may be a special factor in a soldier's and a nation's continuing will to fight. At the time William Duncan sent his second package home, he was worn out after the helter-skelter retreat from Brashear City. He could not breathe easily, knowing Federal patrols moved freely across the land and waters of southern Louisiana. By now he was aware of the scope and devastation of Confederate losses at Vicksburg and Port Hudson and likely had heard too about Gettysburg. Many thousands of Confederate soldiers had died, some of whom were his friends and business associates. Compounding the weight of negative war news, Duncan's health was not good. Any optimism he might have found in his situation shrank with his strength. From his point of view, the Union was pressing the war with increasing fury against the Confederacy in Louisiana; Texas had to be next. It is not hard to imagine William Duncan daydreaming about a negotiated armistice that would permit him to return to his antebellum life. Neither is it difficult to picture him tossing with nightmares about an invasion of Texas, his capture and imprisonment in a Federal prison camp, or death from a Union bullet. If these were his dreams, the shipments home were their physical manifestations.

Chapter 12 Mission

DUNCAN'S INSIDES ERUPTED AGAIN, KEEPING HIM
close to camp the next three days. He had his horse saddled one morning to
go to Franklin but was too sick for the ride and stayed in bed cleaning his pistols instead. By Wednesday, he thought he felt well enough for the journey to
Franklin but it turned out to be quite unpleasant. It rained so hard he says he
"could hardly get about," but he eventually made it to Mrs. Hayes's place. While
looking for a farrier to shoe his horse, Duncan ran into Mannard Anderson,
who invited him to spend the night at his house. Duncan checked his horse into
a stable and enjoyed sleeping in a bed for a change. When he walked into the
barn the next morning, Duncan found his saddle blanket missing; he made the
attendant give him another one. He forked over the $2 stable fee and rode over
to Mrs. Hayes's in the rain for dinner. On the way back to camp, he bought a
fifty-cent protective guard for his watch, $2.50 worth of tobacco, a $15 bottle of
whiskey, and gave Sabine fifty cents.[1]

The next two weeks held peaks and valleys for Duncan. Some days were
exceedingly boring, others exciting and profitable. He pulled Officer of the Day
duty three times, breaking administrative work with four day trips into town.
One day he rode to New Iberia where he gave $3 to have his horse shod by Frére,
the blacksmith who afterward hosted him for dinner. He paid the ferryman
twenty-five cents the next day to cross the bayou with Captain Marsh for a
meeting and dinner with Colonel Major. Two others trips in the fortnight were
both to Franklin where he replenished his liquor supply with a $15 bottle and
stocked up at the local pharmacy with a container of pills for seventy-five cents
and a bottle of laudanum for one dollar.[2]

Laudanum is tincture of opium, a narcotic mixture of opium derivatives
and alcohol. An opiate like laudanum was a popular source of temporary relief
for a variety of ailments in the nineteenth century.[3] Duncan was interested in

laudanum's potential to cure diarrhea. It had plagued him for three months and he was at wit's end over how to end it. Despite laudanum's addictive danger, he decided to try it. It turned out Duncan may not have needed the narcotic to feel better. Eight straight days of profitable gambling left him in jovial spirits after he won a cumulative $460.50 at the poker table. If Duncan drew hot cards that often in Las Vegas today, the casino floor manager would invite him upstairs to a higher stakes game or ask him to leave. His biggest nightly purse was $88, followed by another of $80, two in which he won $70 each, and three from which he pocketed $60, $42.50, and $35. The game in which he won $15 was an anticlimax.

The war intruded around 10:30 the night after the streak ended when a bugle blared, marshalling a search party to track down a pack of deserters. Duncan saddled up with all the men he could muster. They rode all night through eight miles of dark swamp before finally calling off the search. The next week, senior officers asked Duncan to value the horses in his and Captain Marsh's cavalry companies. The Louisiana Confederate command evidently was updating records for its temporary duty Texas units. The job took three days and Duncan had help. A second inspector looked at three of Duncan's horses, giving one a $400 appraisal and the other two, setting values of $300 each. Duncan remembered the $1.25 Confederate valuation on his horse more than a year earlier back in Texas when his company was in its initial training. This time around, better horses and perhaps better judges of horseflesh came up with higher appraisals. But because of roaring inflation, they were not much better than the first. The job finished, Duncan went back to the card table that night and won $120.[4]

Confederate morale had dropped into an abyss by the end of August 1863. News of July disasters at Gettysburg, Vicksburg, Port Hudson, and loss of control of the Mississippi River worked its way through the South and almost everyone lost heart. General Lee offered President Davis his resignation after Gettysburg, regretting the defeat and blaming his health.[5] Davis rejected Lee's offer to quit but was powerless to do anything about the casualties, property losses, deprivation, conscription, impressments, taxes, and inflation that oppressed the southern states. Desertion became even more prevalent in the Confederate army and incidents of southerners trading with northerners or engaging in other acts of opportunistic speculation were routine. Military losses had severed the Trans-Mississippi states from the Confederate body and civilian sentiment had grown within them to separate politically as well.[6]

Lt. Gen. Edmund Kirby Smith, commander of Confederate forces in the Trans-Mississippi since March, knew all about separatist sentiment in the Trans-Mississippi. He described citizens and the state troops he commanded as "luke warm" and "disheartened" with little hope of success. Smith knew the only things that might spark a change of heart among the people were more soldiers, more weapons and ammunition, and fundamentally, more money. Instead

President Davis gave General Smith an ambitious list of assignments while admitting he could do little to help Smith accomplish them. "It grieves me to have enumerated so many and such difficult objects for your attention when I can give you so little aid in their achievement," Davis told Smith. Instead of coming up with weapons and cash for Confederate forces in the Trans-Mississippi states, Davis called a meeting in Marshall, Texas, in mid-August of their governors, members of Congress, and other prominent civilians. Aiming to reinvigorate public opinion in support of the Confederate cause, the politicians made patriotic speeches and the conference published documents proclaiming allegiance by the Trans-Mississippi to the Confederacy and confidence in ultimate Confederate victory. The political ritual was meaningless; nothing of substance came from the meeting.[7]

Captain Duncan will have heard reports from the Marshall meeting. He already realized what Gettysburg, Vicksburg, and Port Hudson meant in terms of a possible Federal invasion of Texas. Even with the Brashear City victory, the Confederates knew how freely Union gunboats moved about the Louisiana bayous and sailed uncontested at entrances to southern ports. Duncan, the longtime gulf coast cattle drover, was especially aware Federal soldiers could march across the Atascosito/Opelousas/Old Spanish Trail from Louisiana into Texas whenever it suited them. When they heard from home, Confederate soldiers from Texas, Louisiana, Arkansas, and Missouri felt the political winds blowing in their communities to abandon the Confederacy. For Texans like Duncan, it was nothing new. Leaving the Union without joining the Confederacy and reestablishing the Republic of Texas had been a prominent political attitude in the state before the war. It reemerged after the Marshall meeting because Texans saw more evidence the isolated, ragged Confederate army was struggling to survive.

Duncan and other Louisiana Confederate unit commanders around New Iberia were surprised on Friday, August 28 with orders to march southeast back into the teeth of Union strength to camp near Brashear City on Bayou Teche. It was an ominous command whose implied danger sent Duncan into a flurry of preparation and personal reflection. After advising a soldier to pay his debts, Duncan helped him send $70 to his mother back in Liberty. Duncan helped another man send $100 in wages home to his father and lent $50 to a third out of his own pocket. He paid one of his soldiers to make two gold and silver stars as souvenirs, ordered four others, and sent one of the finished stars home to Emma with one of his men. Unable to sleep, he labored until midnight by flickering candlelight on a letter home to Celima.[8]

The Confederate cavalrymen headed south out of the New Iberia area early the next morning. Duncan lagged behind his men in Franklin to buy whiskey, tobacco, and medicine. He overtook Captain Marsh who was already encamped at Fort Bisland and learned his own company had continued to its destination three miles north of Berwick Bay across the bayou from Brashear City. Duncan rode to the new camp and quickly decided he was not comfortable with the defensive arrangements. He checked to be sure sentries were posted properly—his term for sentry was "pickett"—and described the situation as "heavy duty." He was tired the next day, but nevertheless spent it riding the perimeter with another officer, lingering in a mill at its southernmost point on the water's edge. The next morning, a sentry galloped into camp to report an approaching Union gunboat. Duncan was angry, confessing "we were caught [a] good deal off our guard." Three days later, Duncan received a *big* surprise. New orders arrived, but this time, they were special and only for him. He was told to return to Texas as soon as possible on assignment to recruit AWOL Texas Confederate soldiers. He did not need to be told twice to get on with it.[9]

Duncan's new orders followed a proclamation by Pres. Jefferson Davis in early August promising amnesty and pardon to all Confederate soldiers who returned to "their proper posts of duty" within twenty days. Davis praised the courage of Confederates in more than two years of combat and railed against the Union's "design to incite servile insurrection and light the fires of incendiarism wherever they can reach your homes." Davis used fear to threaten AWOL Confederate soldiers back into the ranks. He said the North gave the Confederacy "no alternative . . . but victory or subjugation, slavery, and the utter ruin of yourselves, your families, and your country." He predicted the Union would turn defeated Southerners into white slaves. He underlined his AWOL amnesty offer with an emotional appeal to southern women, inviting his "countrywomen, the wives, mothers, sisters and daughters of the Confederacy" to use "their all-powerful influence . . . and take care that none who owe service in the field shall be sheltered at home from the disgrace of having deserted their duty to their families, to their country and to their God." Davis beat the Confederate amnesty drum well into 1864. "The man who repents and goes back to his commander voluntarily, at once appeals strongly to Executive clemency," he said the next year when almost two-thirds of the Confederate army was missing. Still trying to frighten deserters into returning, Davis used psychological sticks along with clemency carrots to ask where those who stayed away would shield themselves after the war "when every man's history will be told . . . ?"[10]

Duncan immediately began to prepare for the journey back to Texas. He paid off personal loans from three soldiers as others asked him to carry letters and cash home to family and friends. One soldier gave him $105 to deliver to his wife, another $90 for his mother, and another, $50 for his wife. He arranged for his washing to be done and turned in early for the night. Up at dawn, Duncan packed lightly for the trip, leaving most of his remaining possessions in a mess chest with his unit. He swapped his mule to a Liberty soldier who was riding one of Duncan's horses and hitched it to the wagon he intended to use on the journey. He and Sabine pulled out of Berwick Bay around 7:30 and rode northwest along the trail. They met Captain Marsh traveling south and Duncan told him he was headed back to Texas. They drove on to Fort Bisland where Marsh's company and several of Duncan's men remained in camp. Duncan visited those who were sick, telling them he had been ordered home. He gave them some items he did not need and shoved off for Franklin where he stopped for the night. Early the next morning, he reflected on the date as he hit the road again: it was three months to the day since he left Texas for Louisiana.

Moving northeast along the trail, he and Sabine came upon a group of Confederate soldiers alongside the road and asked whether they knew the whereabouts of Colonel Spaight; no one did. After crossing a bayou at Mossie's plantation, Duncan stopped at a temporary Confederate field hospital where he found two of his men; a larger group of Texas soldiers had recently left. He made it to Mrs. Gravenberg's by 3:30 P.M. for another dollar dinner. Rather than stay and chat with his hostess whose company and culinary skills he obviously appreciated, Duncan pressed on before stopping at a friend's place for the night. He ate supper in the house but slept outside in the yard by his wagon.

Up at first light, Duncan and Sabine hitched their horse to the wagon and headed for New Iberia. After buying corn for the horse, Duncan ran into old Alex Hébert, to whom he promptly repaid the $100 he had borrowed in June. Hébert pledged to tear up Duncan's promissory note later in the presence of a mutual friend. Duncan drove on until about 1 P.M. when the duo stopped to eat a bite and feed the horse. A few more miles up the trail, they came upon the infantry companies of Spaight's Battalion. The colonel himself was inspecting a dress parade formation away from camp, so Duncan talked with five of his Liberty County soldier-neighbors. The conversation was tense; Duncan says they were distant, "cause, jealousy." Their coolness was obviously a reaction to Duncan's special orders. They wished they could go home too. Colonel Spaight returned and he and Duncan stayed up talking with Dr. Blanchard until midnight. Duncan says Spaight gave him all the information he had concerning Duncan's mission. The officers agreed it would not be an easy task.

As he prepared to leave the next morning, several more soldiers asked Duncan to carry letters home to their families. Lieutenant Brown gave him $100 to pay off a personal debt in Liberty, and Riley Smith asked him to take $150 to Mrs. Olford. Colonel Spaight then rode with Duncan in the wagon to brief General Mouton on his mission. The general wished Duncan luck and the Texans took their leave. Spaight then gave Duncan $400 to carry to his wife and wished him a safe journey after once again going over details of Duncan's assignment. He rolled on for five miles before stopping to eat and rest at the house of a cousin of Alex Hébert. After another nine miles he stopped again, this time at Jim Daily's place. Daily had a brother in Duncan's company. About a dozen local men arrived at the Daily house around dark, announcing they had invited several women to drop by that night for a dance. No ladies showed up but that did not stop the boys from drinking, dancing, and making noise until midnight. Duncan admits there was "no sleep for me."

Up at 4 A.M. Sunday, Duncan washed down a breakfast potato with coffee and started out again. After crossing another bayou, he arrived at Jim Myres's tanning yard, a business that processed cattle and other animal hides into leather. It was exceptionally hot and while Duncan watered his horse, a bugle sounded, warning of an approaching Union gunboat. Duncan told Sabine to "gear up" while he organized his books, papers, and clothing and led the horse to the wagon. They were still scrambling to get things together when several men shouted, "There she is." Duncan ordered Sabine to drive the wagon into the trees and all the men to run away from the bayou. They broke several fences making their escape into the brush.

Rather than open fire on the tannery, the Union boat approached peacefully under a flag of truce. Its commander disembarked carrying a white flag, accompanied by a lady passenger he introduced to Duncan as Mrs. Stafford. Duncan walked over and talked with them, describing the enemy officer as "very polite." Despite his cordiality, Duncan did not trust the Union officer. Duncan expected him to return after dark with guns blazing instead of truce flags flying, so after the Federal boat left, Duncan rode the tannery's perimeter after sundown "on scout."[11] He woke at 2 A.M., unable to get back to sleep; he got up and made coffee, cooked some meat for breakfast, fed and hitched the horse, and made ready to depart at first light. He and Sabine made good progress across the Opelousas Trail that day, reaching English Bayou, the headwaters of the Calcasieu River, where they spent the night at the ferryman's camp. The Calcasieu River basin borders the Sabine basin and Duncan knew well he was almost back in Texas.[12] His supper that evening cost him one dollar.[13]

Duncan tossed and turned that night, waking the next morning again at 2:00. He nodded off for another two hours, but woke again at 4:00. He rolled out, made coffee, ate a bite, and fed the horse. The first ferry of the day carried him, Sabine, the wagon, and their horse across the Calcasieu after which they proceeded to A. B. Lyons's farm. Lyons was another Confederate soldier serving back in deep southern Louisiana. Duncan gave Mrs. Lyons a letter and $50 from her husband and said hello to Mrs. John Weed. Mrs. Weed was married to one of Duncan's men and she asked Duncan if she could travel back to Texas with him. Of course she could, he told her, and asked her to meet him at the Andrews place where he planned to stop for dinner. He drove on to Andrews's where he ate a meal and started up again at 3 P.M. with Mrs. Weed seated prominently in the wagon. The trio arrived at Niblett's Bluff after dark. Duncan treated Mrs. Weed to supper and arranged for her to stay in a tavern bedroom while he and Sabine camped out next to the wagon. Before turning in, he bought fodder for the horse from a black man outside the tavern, grumbling because there was neither corn to be had nor riverboat in sight.[14]

Chapter 13 **Amnesty**

UNDER COVER OF DARKNESS EARLY ON SEPTEM-
ber 8, 1863, four Federal gunboats and nineteen troop transports carrying an
estimated five thousand Union soldiers from New Orleans approached Sabine
Pass off the Texas coast.[1] Two hours after Duncan loaded his wagon onto the
first ferry of the day across the Calcasieu River east of Niblett's Bluff, the four
Union gunboats and seven troop carriers sailed through the pass at the bottom
of Sabine Lake. It was the second Federal attempt to conquer Sabine Pass since
Texas Confederates ended the eighteen-month Union occupation of Galveston
on January 1, 1863. Forty-four Confederate soldiers, most of whom were Irish
Texan longshoremen from Galveston and Houston, defended Fort Griffin. Sa-
loon keeper and Irish immigrant Lt. Richard W. Dowling, husband of cannon-
namesake Annie, commanded the tiny Confederate garrison that spent its days
in monotonous practice repeatedly firing six cannon at 1,200-foot range markers
on the lake.[2]

Practice must have made perfect because the Irish Texas Confederates
lobbed an estimated 135 shells at the Union gunboats, scoring several hits,
disabling two vessels, and forcing the Federal flotilla to retreat into the gulf.
Dowling's handful of artillerymen in the fort were backed up on Sabine Lake
by the *Uncle Ben*, with its two twelve-pound cannon manned by Spaight's Battalion Company B. The Federal force abandoned one of its gunboats, the *Clif-
ton*, which the *Ben* towed to shore along with two hundred Union soldiers whom
Dowling's men took prisoner. The Union fleet headed back to New Orleans, to
set sail later for Brownsville on the Texas-Mexican border where they hoped
Confederate defenders were less accurate with their cannon. William Duncan
picked up news of Dowling's defense of Sabine Pass the next day when he returned to Niblett's Bluff from shopping in the countryside where he bought a $10
bushel of corn and ten bundles of hay for his horse. Inaccurate bluff gossip had

it that "two boats had come into Sabine Pass and we had captured them, killing fifty and taking 150 prisoners." That evening, Sabine River steamboat *Grand Bay* arrived at Niblett's Bluff. Happy to carry Duncan, Mrs. Weed, and Sabine down to Beaumont, its skipper refused to load Duncan's wagon and horse.[3]

Duncan waited for another southbound boat at Niblett's Bluff the next day but none came. He was in a hurry, so that night he asked a swamp ferryman to come for him next morning. Instead of waiting for a steamboat to take him and his wagon downriver, he decided to ferry across the Sabine and travel overland to Beaumont. He spent that night teaming with another officer at the tavern in a poker game, and the pair managed to lose $80. Up early the next morning, he found the ferryman waiting. Duncan unhitched the horse, loaded the wagon with Mrs. Weed and Sabine inside onto the barge, then climbed on the horse and guided it slowly through the swamp. He met the ferry on the other side at 2 P.M., hitched the horse to the wagon, and the trio headed southwest. They stopped in late afternoon in the woods for a snack of beef, biscuits, and coffee, then pushed on to arrive after dark at a friend's house in northern Jefferson County. After supper, Duncan paid his host $1.25 for five bundles of fodder before turning in for the night.

The sun was up when Duncan woke the next morning. It was the latest he had slept in months, undoubtedly because he felt safer at his friend's house in Texas rather than camped in Union-occupied Louisiana. He fed the horse, ate breakfast, paid the bill for Mrs. Weed, Sabine, and himself, and started out at 7:30 A.M. They took the road to Collier's ferry but stopped short of the river when Sabine drove the wagon into deep mud. They had to lighten its load to get the wagon and horse out of the muck and onto the boat. After crossing and reloading the wagon, they made it to Patillo Higgins's place for dinner, and Duncan asked the cook to bake biscuits they could take with them. While they ate, it began to rain so hard that Duncan decided it would be wiser to stay the night.

The next day he was up at first light, fed the horse, made coffee, and ate breakfast. His early rising was to no avail, since he and Sabine had to wait for Mrs. Weed to finish her meal. Once on their way, they crossed the Neches on the ferry at 9 A.M. with Duncan paying the ferryman one dollar per person; there was no charge for the wagon and horse. They drove to Wilson Junker's house in Beaumont where Duncan explained his mission to Junker and asked for help. A lieutenant in a Jefferson County unit of the Texas Volunteers, Junker was also a local judge. His support could add significant credibility to Duncan's efforts because Junker knew plenty of people in Jefferson, Tyler, and Newton counties where many AWOL Confederate soldiers lived. Junker promised Duncan he could count on him. Duncan left copies of lists of absent soldiers with Junker and showed him a flyer Duncan planned to "send round through the upper counties calling in the men." Duncan told Junker he would be in touch, then drove the wagon to the local Confederate supply depot where the quartermaster "promised to furnish Junker with all the supplies he needed to subsist [the returning] men." Duncan and Sabine slept that night by the wagon while Mrs. Weed found accommodations elsewhere. When Duncan closed his eyes that night, he will have worried at the daunting odds he faced to persuade deserters to return to the ranks without fear of punishment. That punishment often meant death by firing squad.[4]

After Union victories at Vicksburg and Port Hudson, desertion rates in the Confederacy's Trans-Mississippi states climbed at an accelerated pace. Like many Confederate soldiers throughout the South, the Trans-Mississippi men were replacing wartime self-images as Southern nationalists with their prewar, local identities. Texas Confederates became Texans again and southeast Texas volunteers became local farmers again. Strong cultural currents flowed beneath this change of mindset. From the beginning, Confederate military policies exempted from service all farmers who owned more than twenty slaves. Favoritism of wealthier, slave-owning landowners created a class conflict in the South between the planter aristocracy and small yeoman farmers. The majority of Texas soldiers belonged to that lower class.

As prospects for Confederate victory deteriorated, the social divide created by this wealth exemption grew deeper. Tens of thousands of men from the small-farmer class had been wounded and killed while their families' standards of living declined precipitously. With each casualty and every hunger pain at home, bitterness against the Southern elite grew. Poor men did not want to die in a rich man's war, especially while rich men watched from the sidelines. As for slavery, with states' rights one of the two fundamental causes of the war, small holders and merchants in the South felt less passionate about it simply because most held no vested interest in it. Either they owned no slaves or they owned only a few. William Duncan was such an owner; he did not count his slaves by the score, did not buy and sell them, and trusted them as members of his extended family. If President Lincoln's idea for the Federal government to buy slaves' freedom rather than go to war had become reality, chances are Duncan and thousands of other small slave owners across the South would have taken him up on the offer. Instead the war exposed Southern class antagonism that eventually caused much public opinion to shift, undermining the initial excitement of secession. As the war progressed, a steady deterioration in Southern civilian morale matched an equivalent rise in Confederate army desertions.[5]

Duncan was a good choice to appeal to AWOL Confederate soldiers from southeast Texas to return to service. People knew him as dependable, honorable, smart, and strong. Most important, they knew him as *local:* a landowning, trail-tested cattleman, farmer, and former sheriff with pioneer roots in Liberty County. He shared original settlers' values with most Anglo and Francophone citizens of the region. He was *not* an imported career army officer or regional politician whose treasure lay elsewhere. He had done business for decades with

scores of farmers, ranchers, merchants, and hired hands in the region, earning a reputation for friendliness, honesty, and integrity. He was a credible in-
terlocutor between the privileged and the plain, an advocate for a remorseful
returning soldier if a by-the-book officer tried to pull rank or stiff-necked administrator tried to tear up a pardon. Duncan was a likeable man; had he been
bad-tempered or dishonest, he would not have walked away from so many card
games over his lifetime with pockets full of other men's money. He was not self-
righteous, nor did he harbor a political agenda. He was an ordinary workingman, defending family, home, and property. As a citizen-soldier, his judgment
was credible with the people of southeast Texas and southwestern Louisiana.
His goal was to defend Texas, not travel far away to guard someone else's home.
Local, honest, smarter-than-most, and tough enough, William Duncan was the
kind of person a southeast Texas AWOL Confederate soldier could trust. But
that did not make his assignment any easier.

He had breakfast the next day with Junker, then took the train to Liberty
after sending Sabine home with the wagon. On the way to the depot, Duncan
ran into two men he knew and explained why he was back in Texas. "They
want to join my company," he says. After making arrangements to swear them
in later, Duncan boarded the train that rolled out of Beaumont at 10 A.M. and
arrived in Liberty around 3:30 P.M. Word spread quickly that he was back in
town. The next day he left the house no less than six times to ride into town
but was stopped each time by surprise visitors. One man volunteered to ride
with him to Newton and Tyler counties to spread the word. Duncan thanked
him, explaining he was not ready to go.[6] Duncan finally made it to Liberty the
next day and headed straight for William Meyer's print shop to arrange for a
flyer to announce his mission. It ordered "all the men . . . left behind on the
march to Louisiana, sick in Hospital, on sick furlough, absent without leave,
and on detached service who have been relieved from such service, will report
forthwith to me at Liberty or to Lieut. Wilson A. Junker at Beaumont, Texas.
The men absent without leave and those who have been reported as *Deserters,*
[document's emphasis] will bear in mind that the 30th day of September is the
last day of grace. *All those who fail to comply with this order will be published as
deserters, and subjected to the penalties of military law.*"[7] As soon as the ink dried
on the circulars, Duncan handed a stack to two men and asked that they dis-
tribute them throughout the upper counties. He enclosed a note to Junker with
another package of flyers and sent it off to Beaumont, then capped off the day by
swearing two Liberty men into his unit. Duncan's magnetism as a commanding
officer was compelling, at least for these two. Perhaps in celebration or simply
to calm his nerves, he stopped on his way home and picked up a few plugs of
tobacco and a bottle of whiskey.

The next day, Duncan returned to the list of favors he promised his men
back in Louisiana. He rode into Liberty to give "old Lee's brother-in-law

$60 to take to Lee's wife," delivered a coat to Price's wife, and carried $100 to Mrs. Scales and $90 to Mrs. Hill that their husbands had sent home. Celima's brother, Simeon DeBlanc, asked Duncan if he could buy two of Emma's cows, so Duncan gave Simeon a brother-in-law price of $40 for the pair. Duncan sat in on that day's Liberty town square card game and won $64 before heading home after dark. The following Sunday, Duncan took Celima and the children to visit Mrs. Spaight at Moss Bluff. Duncan gave her the $400 from her husband but she straightaway handed half of it to Duncan to take back to Spaight.

Domestic chores filled Duncan's next three days, until a friend arrived at the house with troubling news. It was John Weed, Mrs. Weed's husband, returning from his ride through Newton and Tyler counties where Duncan had sent him to spread the word that AWOL soldiers were welcomed back without fear of punishment. Weed told Duncan there were "poor prospects for [the] men to come in." Duncan thanked Weed and paid him $17 in expenses. Weed's message was a prediction that applied not only in southeast Texas but also throughout the South. Jefferson Davis's amnesty appeal was falling on deaf ears.

Duncan felt he needed to rejoin his unit in Louisiana, so he went into town to pick up his wagon at the shop where Sabine had left it for repairs. His card-playing buddies saw him in the street and roped him into a game that afternoon. Duncan won $200 before the group broke up at dawn the next morning. Bleary-eyed and flush with cash, Duncan rode home, ate some breakfast, and took a two-hour nap. The rest of the day was lost to hangover; smoke, whiskey, and lack of sleep from the long card game caught up with him. Another penitent soldier dropped by the house the next day, along with Mrs. Spaight and Mrs. George Duncan, the wife of the lieutenant who had transferred out of Spaight's Battalion at the request of Colonel Major. Despite a nasty sore throat, Duncan welcomed and chatted with all three.

The Union's control over the Mississippi and its tributaries gave it virtual dominance over southern Louisiana. Thanks to Admiral Farragut's success offshore, the Confederate gulf coast ports remained closed, making exports by opportunistic blockade-runners possible but difficult. Union General Banks was smarting in New Orleans after Dick Dowling and his handful of Irish American cannoneers rebuffed Union invaders at Sabine Pass earlier in the month. These circumstances combined to put Texas in the Union bull's-eye for a planned invasion. Banks's idea was to transport troops, artillery, and wagons by boat from New Orleans up Bayou Teche, unload them at appropriate points on the Opelousas Trail, and march across southwest Louisiana into Texas. In support of the plan, General Grant sent Banks a division, commanded by Maj. Gen. Napoleon J. T. Dana, to garrison Morganza, a village on the Atchafalaya River in Point Coupee Parish thirty-six miles southeast of Baton Rouge to prevent the Confederates from using the river from either direction to harass Texas-bound Union soldiers.

Cajun General Mouton learned of these Union movements and warmed to the idea of attacking the Federals around Fordoche Bridge, ten miles south of Morganza. He chose Texas Brigadier General Green for the mission and provided him reinforcements to improve its chance of success. Green's cavalry skirmished with Union pickets at Fordoche Bridge for about thirty minutes before his other troops hit the full Union force around noon on September 29, forcing it to retreat. Colonel Major's unit, including riders from Duncan's Company F, were assigned to Green's command and patrolled the west bank of the Atchafalaya to protect the crossing.[8] Duncan obviously was still back in Texas on his recruiting assignment. The Battle of Stirling's Plantation—also called the Battle of Fordoche Bridge—was another hollow Confederate victory because it had no impact on Banks's planned march into Texas.[9]

But it did ramp up the rumor mill in Liberty. The day after his $200 dusk-to-dawn poker game, Duncan heard that the "Yankees were landing at Calcasieu [Parish]," whose western edge is the Sabine River and Texas border. Four days later, word had it the "Yanks [were] advancing from Berwicks [*sic*] Bay." Feeling pressure to get moving, Duncan decided to head for Beaumont to see how Judge Junker was coming with the amnesty appeal in Jefferson County, but rain had soaked the train's tracks, causing multiple derailments. Unable to use the train and unwilling to ride his horse forty miles through the mud, Duncan was at loose ends. He shopped and played cards in Liberty and visited his friend Pryor Bryan to watch while Bryan slaughtered cows. Duncan spent another day at home, repairing a harness and other tack. The train finally pulled into Liberty at 5 P.M. Saturday. Duncan climbed on board but the engine stayed put. While he waited for it to get underway, he paid a black man at the depot $2 to fetch his pistol that he had left at Simeon DeBlanc's during another card game the day before. Simeon's house rules wisely must have required gamblers to check guns at the door.

The eastbound locomotive finally chugged out of Liberty at 10 P.M. and made it four miles past the Sour Lake station, twelve miles northwest of Beaumont, before Duncan says it had "to stop because the dew had wet the rails. Spent [a] very disagreeable night." The train arrived in Beaumont at 10:00 that morning. He went immediately to Judge Junker's house where the two men talked all day. The Judge had names of only seven men on his list who had agreed to return to duty. Duncan thanked Junker for his help and hospitality and left for the depot to catch the train back to Liberty. It departed at 10 P.M., but ran off the tracks after only a mile with Duncan reporting it "killed young Hubert." Duncan slept in Beaumont that night. The train rolled an hour after dawn the next morning, taking almost all day to make it to Liberty at 3 P.M. While Duncan waited for his horse at the depot, he was invited to join another card game. After winning $45 and realizing his horse still was not outside, he borrowed one from Simeon and rode home. Both Julia and Chessie were sick.

With his deserter recruitment project stymied, Duncan sought help from General Magruder. Duncan left Liberty the next night on a train crowded with soldiers, arriving in downtown Houston at midnight, and checked into the Fannin Hotel. The next morning he walked to Magruder's office in the hotel but the general was not in. Duncan "went about forty times & finally had to go to his boarding house to see him. Said he was too busy to give my matters his attention [and] told me to wait." Duncan spoke to one of Magruder's staff officers, a Captain Turner "who promised to attend to it and write to [Duncan in] Liberty." Duncan then took advantage of big-city Houston shopping to buy several items for Celima, the children, and himself. He picked up forty yards of calico for $180, three yards of another, more expensive fabric for $36, a piece of leather for $20, pegs for $1.00 and a board for $12, a chain for $5, two decks of cards for $4, spelling books for $4, and liquor, coffee, and candy for $7.50. He bundled up his purchases and rode the train back to Liberty the next day, stopping at Pryor Bryan's house on the way home to dance.

Duncan killed time in Liberty the next two weeks, waiting for Magruder's help and talking up his mission around the Liberty town square. Nothing was happening. He sent a report to Colonel Spaight in Louisiana as well as a file of papers and letters to Texas Confederate headquarters in Houston. Magruder's office finally sent a response but its details were not worth noting in his diary. Duncan played in six card games in the fortnight, two in twenty-four hours in which he won $250 and $530, respectively. The second pot included $380 in cash and $150 in markers. He bought 428 bundles of hay from a neighbor for cattle and horses on his plantation and continued to settle personal matters for many of his men back in Louisiana. He spread the word to his new recruits that he planned to leave October 20 to return to Louisiana. October 20 arrived and they were ready but he was not. He spent the morning packing and drove a wagon-load of things to the Liberty train depot that afternoon. It was raining torrents the next day so he pushed his departure back again. He sent Sabine and two of the men off to Beaumont in the wagon on the 22nd, telling the trio he and two new soldiers would ride the train and meet them there. "After breakfast [I] bid my dear ones fare well again & started to town in buggy." He waited in Liberty forty-eight hours, losing $555 in an all-day poker game before a train finally arrived at night on the 24th. He climbed aboard but the train made it only to the Sour Lake station, fifteen miles southwest of Hardin in Hardin County, where the tracks were so loose the engine could not pull its cars any farther. Duncan pulled his coat up around his ears and slept fitfully in the crowded boxcar.

When Duncan and his two companions arrived in Beaumont about 11:00 Sunday morning, October 25, he found only a handful of men who had agreed to join his company. He also found his wagon much worse for wear after its trip from Liberty. Duncan told Sabine to drive it to a local repair shop and began to search for a replacement. Having no luck and unable to leave immediately for

Louisiana, he sent three men home to Liberty with orders to return on the 31st and two others "up country for shoes and men, to return 2nd Nov." Meanwhile Duncan sat down at a Beaumont poker table. He continued his winning streak through four games in six days, pocketing $360, $265, $485, and $145. He spent $25 on two pairs of shoes for Celima and Emma and sent them home with a friend. A local preacher, Parson Hinkle, gave Duncan $430 to take to the hospital surgeon of Spaight's Battalion. Duncan did not feel well on Sunday, November 1 but wrote a short note to Celima and sent it home with her uncle, Dr. Gillard, who was traveling through Beaumont to Liberty after a business trip by boat to Galveston. Whether a disgruntled gambler in one of the Beaumont card games pulled a gun on Duncan or his hangover made him wish one had, Duncan "resolved to quit card playing." Like most resolutions to give up a bad habit, it would not be long before Duncan broke this one.[10]

Chapter 14 **Disguise**

CAPTAIN DUNCAN MET A COLONEL FROM ANOTHER regiment on a Beaumont street who warned Duncan it would be next to impossible for him to make it across the Atascosito Trail in southern Louisiana. Too many Union troops occupied the region. Pondering the risks of the colonel's warning, Duncan modified his no-more-card-playing resolution after only two days with a bit of convenient self-deception. He rationalized joining a game by permitting four friends to finance his stake. Gambling with their money rather than his, he seemed to think, kept his resolution in tact. Duncan won $270, kept $170 as his fee, and distributed $25 each to his investors. After cashing chips, he sent a sack of potatoes home to Chessie with a friend and slept that night at Judge Junker's house.

A cold front arrived in Beaumont the next morning, prompting Duncan to buy himself two flannel shirts for $60. He decided to leave Beaumont for Niblett's Bluff the next day then changed his mind almost immediately. He would "not go to Bluff till I had transportation," and this time, transportation meant a horse and wagon. It was raining hard, slowing Beaumont business to a crawl and giving the fidgety Duncan time to think. He did not like his prospects for the journey back into Louisiana where he was likely to run into Federal troops. With no wagon to drive and no steamboat to take him to Niblett's Bluff, Duncan decided to go home. He caught the train at 3:30 P.M. Friday, got to Liberty at 8:30, borrowed a horse from brother-in-law Simeon, and arrived home by 10:00. The next morning, he ate breakfast with Celima and the children and left the house at noon. He picked up supplies in Liberty, boarded the train at 4:00, and got back to Beaumont at 7 P.M. The Niblett's Bluff steamboat arrived at midday Sunday and its captain said he planned to head back to the bluff Monday. Duncan resolved he was "going over on her tomorrow."

He wavered again the next morning, writing to Celima by lantern light before sunup then finally "went to work getting ready to start men off on [the] boat." One soldier was not cooperating. Duncan says Tucker was "still drunk and has been for three or four days," mourning the theft of two mules. Duncan ignored Tucker and turned his attention to the sober men. He helped ten get their gear onto the boat for its 3 P.M. departure. Duncan borrowed a horse to ride to the bluff and left by himself the next morning. He crossed the Neches River at 11 A.M. Tuesday and guided his horse carefully toward the Sabine River on a very bad trail. He camped near Higgins's that night, waking cold and uncomfortable to frost covering the ground. The next day, he stopped for dinner at Parish's before taking the ferry across the Sabine River, arriving at Niblett's Bluff in late afternoon. The steamboat with his men aboard docked the next day, suggesting it had been detained by mechanical trouble on the journey upriver. While the men disembarked, Duncan found an officer in camp who promised him a wagon and said the Union had taken Brownsville. The news from south Texas had taken ten days to reach Niblett's Bluff.

A cold front blew into the bluff the next day, encouraging soldiers there to step lively in preparation for an afternoon inspection. Duncan watched from the edge of the formation where he heard "news that Yanks are still in Vermillionville." The report increased Duncan's anxiety, causing him to reconsider the alternative routes he could follow on the journey back to his unit. As night fell, the temperature dropped and so did prospects for finding a wagon. Without one, he was marooned at Niblett's Bluff. The next four days held more of the same: cold, wet mornings, no good news, and no wagon. Duncan and his men took advantage of the wait to wash their clothes in the fresh water of the Sabine. Duncan also attended a ceremony where he "saw a soldier buried with military honors."

A wagon train hauling cotton to Opelousas pulled into Niblett's Bluff, and Duncan asked the head man whether he and his men might join it. The wagon master refused. Duncan understood how Union scouts would be suspicious of too many men riding with a wagon train. If the Federals stopped the train, inspected the wagons, and found the cotton, the wagon master and his men would be caught red-handed. They would be branded blockade-runners and at best, lose their cargo, horses, oxen, and wagons. If Duncan and his men were with them and exposed as Confederate soldiers, the teamsters could face imprisonment and possibly even a Federal firing squad.[1]

A second eastbound wagon train lumbered into Niblett's Bluff two days later. As cold, heavy rain fell, Duncan appealed to its boss to let him and his men ride with it into Louisiana. This time, the answer was a qualified yes. The wagon master said Duncan and his men could travel with his train only as far as Lake Charles, roughly thirty miles east of the bluff. Far from the solution Duncan sought, it was a step in the right direction. Duncan knew enough people in Lake Charles to help him find a wagon and he needed to get moving. If he stuck around much longer in boring, rainy Niblett's Bluff, Duncan knew his mission would be in jeopardy because his men's idle minds would become deserters' workshops all over again. They were getting too much time to think about their decision to return to duty. Duncan drew six days' rations, loaded his men and gear into the wagons, and left with the train late that afternoon.

They made only eight miles before darkness forced them to stop for the night. One of Duncan's recruits promptly justified Duncan's fears. While everyone slept, he slipped out of camp and disappeared, no doubt headed back to Texas. Two days later, the wagon train crossed the Calcasieu River near Lake Charles. Duncan rode to a friend's house in town, looking for a wagon, but once again, none was to be found. The householder was not home, but his family was. Always in the mood for music, Duncan "got the girls to play & sing for us." After the entertainment, he rode back to the wagon train and "made [a] bargain with Teamsters to take me to Opelousas at $12 wages." The wagon master had become comfortable with Duncan and his men in the short trip from Niblett's Bluff. He saw how Duncan conducted himself and how Duncan's men would pass as civilians to an inquiring Union soldier. Nasty weather also helped the wagon master make his decision. He knew Union soldiers would prefer to stay dry in their tents rather than slog through cold rain looking for Confederates. The dealmaker was Duncan's $12 offer, easy money for the wagon master assuming he did not have to take a Federal bullet to earn it. Once again, Duncan's comfortable manner, negotiating skills, and, ultimately, cash in his pocket came in handy.

It was still cold and rainy next morning, so the wagon master decided to postpone departure and avoid the mud of the Opelousas Trail another day. Even though heavy rain continued, the wagons headed out the next morning. They rolled east most of the day before making camp in late afternoon so the men could dry their clothes. The slow progress was getting to Duncan. Unable to sleep for several nights, he "had a dream tonight which made me feel quite melancholy." The wagon train made it to Opelousas around 1:00 the next afternoon. While the wagons pushed on the short distance to Washington to unload their contraband cargo, Duncan went in search of supplies but found "no provisions in Opelousas nor any chance of getting [a] wagon." Duncan told seven men to continue on foot to Carrion Crow, the most recent location he had for the rest of Spaight's Battalion. Then he reopened negotiations with the wagon master to see if he and the rest of his group could continue with the individual wagons as they made their way deeper into southern Louisiana.

Duncan felt he still needed cover to fool the Federals into thinking he and his men were innocent civilians instead of Confederate soldiers. The opportunistic Louisiana wagon train boss spotted a chance for extra money. He agreed to let the disguised Texas Confederates stay with him only if Duncan paid him twice the daily fee. Pushing his advantage, he also demanded the new rate be made retroactive to the first day. Duncan says he "had to agree to pay $12 per day out of my own money, pay them $24 per day for all the time I have been with them, swindling me out of $12 per day, which I agreed to give." Duncan agreed to the exorbitant new terms because he felt he had no other choice; they were easily more attractive than starvation in a Federal prisoner-of-war camp or death dangling on the end of a Union rope.

When he received orders to return to Texas on his special amnesty mission, Duncan knew it would be a dangerous trip. He would make it across Louisiana without capture only if he traveled in disguise. A white man riding a fine horse across southwest Louisiana in 1863 with a teenaged black companion would look too much like a Confederate officer in civilian disguise to a Federal soldier from New York. To escape detection, Duncan chose a slow wagon instead of a horse and dressed like a local farmer. That was why he gave away so many possessions and stored the rest in a trunk before leaving his unit. He left behind his quality clothing, newer footwear, and of course his uniforms in favor of an old shirt, threadbare pants, a worn coat, scruffy boots, and a soiled hat. Duncan could feign a local accent after years of doing business with Louisiana Creoles and Cajuns and being married to French-speaking Creole women. He knew the local geography and had many friends across the area. Driving a beat-up wagon pulled by an ordinary horse with a black servant in tow painted him seamlessly into the southwest Louisiana scene. When Mrs. Weed asked Duncan if she could ride with him back to Texas, he undoubtedly smiled at his good fortune. Yes, Mrs. Weed might slow him down but she also was another credible prop for his disguise. A middle-aged man in a creaking wagon with a shy wife and silent servant did not immediately conjure up a vision of a Confederate cavalry officer. When Duncan overslept on his first night back in Texas, it was from relief that his disguise had carried him unmolested past Union patrols. In stark contrast to General Magruder's ostentatious theatrics on the battlefield that General Lee had found so distasteful, William Duncan's late-1863 role-playing across southern Louisiana was unobtrusive.

Duncan's return trip was much riskier. If he was to infiltrate safely back into Union-controlled Louisiana with several secret soldiers in tow, his camouflage had to be enhanced. A group of armed horsemen riding east across the Opelousas Trail in 1863 looked either like an outlaw civilian gang or a disguised Confederate cavalry unit. It was likely to be stopped or maybe even attacked by suspicious Union soldiers. That is why Duncan would not move with his small group without at least one wagon. When the cotton wagon trains headed for Opelousas rolled into Niblett's Bluff, he knew they were imperfect but plausible screens for him and his men. Their cargo made them problematic but that obstacle was not insurmountable. If a Union patrol found the cotton, odds are they would either confiscate it or simply look the other way. Civilian blockade breakers moved frequently over coastal Louisiana and Texas in the Civil War, and it was not unusual for Union patrols to ignore them. The Federals did not want to slow themselves down by moving cotton themselves, thereby increasing their own risk of attack by Confederate cavalry. Duncan's men dressed in ordinary civilian work clothes would make them appear to be poor locals trying to earn a wage. Nevertheless the first wagon master turned him down because he was afraid a Union patrol might discover they were Confederate soldiers in disguise. The wagon master could have paid for that discovery with his freedom or even his life. Duncan understood.

The second wagon train's boss was a gambler. He sized up Duncan and his men, their mannerisms and accents, and judged them credible enough to pass Union inspection as civilians. Like many Southerners during the war, the second wagon master was a profiteer, willing to take risks to earn extra cash. When the train arrived at Washington's warehouses to unload the cotton and Duncan asked if he and his men could continue with the wagons, the canny head teamster recalculated his risk tolerance, adjusted his financial objective, and reopened negotiations. He had good reason. The farther south they went toward New Orleans, the more Federal patrols they were likely to encounter. A smart Union soldier would question why so many men were riding with empty wagons. If the wagon master was to face an increased hanging risk, he figured the favor to Duncan was worth a lot more money. The second-stage negotiations on price will have started much higher than where they finally settled because Duncan's instincts would never permit him to agree to double the original price. The wagon master probably asked for considerably more than twice the first fee. Duncan negotiated his way to the 100 percent surcharge because he considered it fair value. No doubt Duncan grumbled but he accepted the deal to stay off the business end of a Union rope.

Freezing temperatures and sucking mud played into Duncan's hands the rest of the journey. Rising before dawn, men and wagons moved slowly across ground white with frost. His soldiers killed a wild hog shortly after leaving camp on the first day of the second leg of the journey. They must have felt relatively safe or were ravenously hungry because they took time to dress and roast the pig for breakfast.[2] Duncan paid the Louisianans $90 the next day and he and his men left the wagon train. They pitched camp later around a schoolhouse on the Roberts plantation while Duncan "went to hunt a wagon." He found a local friend who agreed to "haul me to Simsport [sic]" the next morning. Simmesport was on the west bank of the Atchafalaya River fifty-five miles north-northeast of Vermillionville and the site of a temporary Confederate camp where Duncan thought Spaight's Battalion had relocated. Duncan's group made it to the edge of a bayou across from the encampment shortly after noon the next day, but no ferries were available for the crossing. That night, high winds accompanied a hard freeze that kept the bridge unusable, so Duncan and his men were forced to wait for a boat. They stamped their feet in place for five hours in the freezing cold before finally making it over the bayou after dark to Company F's camp. "Everybody came up and got their letters" and Duncan talked with his men until 10 P.M. The Texas soldiers had a lot of catching up to do with their commanding officer. He had been gone eighty-eight days.

Back with his men in the heart of Union-controlled southwest Louisiana, Duncan was somewhat relieved by a dubious sense of security from strength in friendly numbers. He "disposed of everything that I had brought to officers & men and spent the day with Col. and others. First resting spell I have had." He gave Dallas Bryan $100 that his father, Pryor, had asked Duncan to carry to him, along with $50 to Hail Johnson from his family. Duncan also delivered $150 to Billy Smither that Billy had sent home to Liberty's Dr. Alford for payment of a previous bill. The doctor forgave the debt, asking Duncan to take the money back to Billy with his compliments. Duncan handed Colonel Spaight the $430 contribution sent by Beaumont's Parson Hinkle for the battalion's hospital fund, along with the $200 Mrs. Spaight asked Duncan to return to her husband. He also gave the Colonel a bottle of "good brandy and some butter and lent him a cup of coffee in a large tin cup." Spaight gave the $200 from his wife right back to Duncan, telling him and Captain Marsh to use it for their units' hospital money. William Duncan, temporary recruiter of Confederate Texas deserters and Louisiana infiltrator in farmer's disguise, had reemerged as cavalry Capt. William Duncan, commander of Company F in Spaight's Battalion.

Rarely is there rest for the weary. A soldier woke Duncan at 4:00 the next morning "with orders for the army to move at 7." Duncan led his riders into Simmesport to join up with the battalion wagon train while Colonel Spaight continued south with his infantrymen on another patrol to the Brashear City area. Duncan submitted his expenses for the Texas trip to Lieutenant Brown who paid him "$81 for muleage and $116 for wagon hire and other expense." Brown needed a container in which to boil water, so Duncan "sold him my pot—$5.00." After two days spent waiting for orders with Brown, Duncan prepared to move his wagons north. He left Simmesport thirty minutes before the wagons at 11:30 A.M. to scout the route. He rode fifteen miles before turning east for another five miles to Faulkner's Ferry on Bayou Rouge. Faulkner lived another two-and-a-half miles down the road and sent word to Duncan "to come on and talk a while." He was another of Duncan's network of friends across southern Louisiana. As a Texas cattleman who regularly drove herds to New Orleans, he was a familiar customer of the ferry owner. Duncan accepted his invitation and spent the night, hearing Faulkner's daughters "play and sing my favorite song." He left his host's house late the next morning and paid the ferryman $7 to float him and his horse to the other side of Bayou Rouge. He stopped at another friend's house for breakfast and bought some dried beef and bread, but could find no corn for his horse. He crossed Bayou Boeuf and stayed the night near Mountville after buying forty ears of corn for one dollar from another area farmer.[3]

Duncan's careful itemization of purchases of bread, jerky, and corn for his horse was not simply mundane expense account management. It reveals the increasingly frequent obligation of a Confederate cavalry officer to forage and pay for food for himself, his soldiers, and their animals. Duncan and his Confederate brethren in the Trans-Mississippi struggled with scarcity and the inarguable fact the amount of forage and food available to a Civil War army in a given area was proportional to the density of its population. Primarily rural then as now, population density in the Confederate states was low. The population of the Confederacy excluding West Virginia and Texas was about seventeen persons per square mile—8,123,000 people living in 470,630 square miles. Assuming an army of 100,000 soldiers can sustain itself for fifteen days in an area raising food for 100,000 people, 5,800 square miles of Confederate land was required to feed an army that size for fifteen days. In comparison, the population of France in Napoleonic times was thirty million people who lived on 212,000 square miles. A Napoleonic army of 100,000 men could have been expected to sustain itself in an area of only 710 square miles. Confederate soldiers, especially in Louisiana and Texas where the population was even smaller, worked much harder to feed themselves and their animals, especially since they received little help from railroads or steam-powered boats. Population density and mechanized supply lines were major factors in the collection and transportation of adequate human food and animal forage. They helped determine the size, mobility, and tactics of fighting units on both sides in the Civil War. It meant supply lines could never be extended very far from the battle line.[4]

One of the major impacts of the Union blockade of Southern ports and its mastery over the Mississippi after Vicksburg and Port Hudson in mid-1863 was elimination of easy movement for Confederate supply boats in the Atchafalaya basin. Compounding the problem for the Confederates, the few railroads in the agrarian South came increasingly under Union army control as the war progressed. Louisiana and Texas where Captain Duncan, Colonel Spaight, and the Trans-Mississippi Confederates served under generals Taylor and Magruder offered clear examples of this railroad void. Between 1852 and 1857, the New Orleans, Opelousas and Great Western Railway Company built eighty miles of track between the west bank of the Mississippi River opposite New Orleans and the east bank of the Atchafalaya River at Brashear City. When the Union captured New Orleans at the end of April 1862, those tracks became useless to Confederate units operating in southern Louisiana.

Across the Sabine, the Texas and New Orleans Railroad Company built ninety miles of track from 1856 to 1861 between Houston and Beaumont, leaving a gap of approximately 185 miles across southwest Louisiana until 1873.[5] Although this stretch of trackless coastal plain guaranteed Duncan and his Texas cattle-driving brethren at least partial preservation of their civilian businesses after the war, it was crippling and downright dangerous for Confederate officer Duncan in 1863 because it meant he and his comrades in temporary service to General Taylor's army moved without logistical support from a nearby railhead.

Their only alternatives were to forage for their daily bread or carry sustenance with them in wagon trains. Neither was a good option. Wide expanses of forage areas made wagon trains even less efficient than usual and the larger the army, the more tons of supplies it needed. More tonnage required more wagons. When heavy rain turned trail dirt into knee-deep mud, the slower those wagons moved. Ponderous wagon trains were sitting ducks for enemy attack, causing commanders to reduce the risk radius of their unit's position. Their supply wagons were simultaneously their life source as well as potentially fatal millstones around their necks. The upshot? Their own wagon trains robbed commanders on both sides of surprise, deception, and the ability to pursue a defeated enemy.[6]

Duncan proceeded to Washington to call on three friends, but found none at home. Back on his horse, he rode to Opelousas where he found his chest and tent at the house of another friend, but decided to leave them, subject to receiving new orders. The command structure of his Louisiana unit had relocated to Vermillionville, so he decided to travel there the next day. Up before dawn that Sunday, Duncan stopped to call on Colonel Major, but found him still asleep. He dropped by Ursin Guidry's brother's house for breakfast, then visited Valery Martens during the midday hours. Duncan finally arrived "where our command were [*sic*] encamped, five miles below Vermillionville" and stayed up late talking to another officer. The next day, he ran into Captain Marsh who told him almost all of Duncan's men were out on special detail or on sick leave. Duncan gave Marsh $100, half the money Colonel Spaight donated to the two cavalry officers' hospital funds. It rained steadily that night but Duncan "kept tolerable dry under my little tent fly."[7]

Army politics reared its Medusa's head two days later. Duncan learned his fellow Spaight's Battalion cavalry commander Captain Marsh was trying to get his and Duncan's companies assigned permanently to General Taylor's Louisiana command. "I and other officers took steps to prevent it," Duncan says. The next morning, Duncan and a delegation of other officers called on Marsh to ask him to withdraw his application. Duncan says, "He promised to comply." The skies opened up again that night and made "everything look like a flood. Bayou Vermillion [was] out of its banks and running upstream." A small detachment of Marsh's men returned to camp with a report that General Mouton had taken Plaquemine "and brought news that we were all to go to Texas soon." While repatriation news raged through the Texans' camp, a court-martial of one of Duncan's men convened the next morning. Duncan says it was "the first of the kind [*sic*] that has ever taken place in the company." The accused soldier was convicted of disobedience of an order. Duncan failed to note the trial's outcome and later that afternoon, took time to "read [the] Bible some."[8]

Chapter 15 **Texas**

RUMORS THEY WERE HEADED HOME TO TEXAS prompted Colonel Spaight to call on General Taylor to inquire whether Spaight would be ordered to take his battalion back to Magruder's command. The tide of war had turned Union eyes westward and Texas Confederates could feel the threat. The rumors were true. Two days after the court-martial, Duncan got orders to prepare to leave Louisiana. With wind blowing sheets of rain from the north, he and his men spent the next day preparing the wagons for the trip home. Cold rain continued to fall on departure day when Duncan rose at 3 A.M., "got ready, ate and started [a] little after sun rise, off for Texas. Found the prairie almost entirely covered with water [and] so cold that I thought I would freeze. Stopped and put on another pair [of] flannel drawers and another pair of socks, which helped." Spaight's Battalion was not alone on its way back to Texas to prepare for an expected Union invasion. Duncan says he and his wagons paused the next morning to "lay still today for Green's Brigade to get farther ahead." Brig. Gen. Tom Green was leaving Louisiana as well.

The moisture drenched, then froze the soldiers' excitement as they made their way home for Christmas. Their going was rough as the ironclad wagon wheels cracked quarter-inch ice on the prairie, sinking the wagons up to their hubs in freezing mud. As horses and men struggled to free the trapped wagons from the goop, scouts fanned out, looking for signs of Union soldiers that might be on patrol in the area. The Texans reached Bayou Cane in Terrebonne Parish, three-and-a-half miles southeast of Houma and fifty-three miles southwest of New Orleans, on December 19. Duncan could not get to sleep and let his lantern burn until after 1 A.M.

Lower temperatures thickened the mud further next morning, paradoxically permitting the wagons to travel fifteen miles relatively quickly to the banks of Bayou LaFourche near Thibodaux. There they came upon several of General

Green's soldiers unable to cross because the bayou was out of its banks and covered the bridge. With no feed for the horses, Duncan sent Sabine and another black youth named Harry to forage for corn. They found "a little" and paid $3 for it. High water, exhausted horses, and tired, hungry men kept the wagon train in camp until late the next afternoon when they began to cross with only an hour left of sunlight. The last wagon reached dry ground on the other side around 10 P.M. Because they had been stationary almost two days, Union scouts had time to spot and report the Confederate location to their commanders, so the wagons kept moving another six miles before making camp as freezing rain again began to fall. Duncan says "all [were] worn out." Conditions grew tougher the next day. Duncan says the roads were horrible and supplies had disappeared. One of the men on foraging detail returned to the main column with a small amount of corn for the horses that he had found along Bayou Serpent that flows approximately thirty-one miles between Kinder and Lake Charles. The men slept hungry and cold that night in piney woods twenty miles from the Calcasieu River.

The wagon train was getting so close to Texas that soldiers from Jefferson and Tyler counties thought they could smell smoke from their home fires. Others wondered whether they would make it back to their hearths at all. Hands froze, stomachs growled, and eyes of emaciated horses begged for feed as they slipped and stumbled across the icy ground. If the enemy did not attack and they escaped death from exposure, the Texans' empty bellies reminded them that starvation loomed large. It rained "in torrents half the day" as the wagon train moved past Lake Charles where Duncan was lucky to find some oranges. The battalion reached the Calcasieu at dusk and began to ford the river immediately. Everyone was across by 11 P.M. Once again putting space between them and the guns of a pursuing Union patrol, they pressed on another four miles before making camp, "horses starving and nothing to eat. I [am] in same condition," Duncan said, "and everything [is] wet." He did not close his eyes until after 3:30 A.M.[1]

Christmas Eve brought a respite from hunger for the horses, but it was bad news for a local Louisiana farmer. The foraging Texas Confederates found his supply of corn and promptly confiscated it. The civilian would have considered the act grand larceny and been none too pleased with the Confederacy. The column of Texans moved on to make camp Christmas Eve seven miles east of Niblett's Bluff. The wagon train arrived at the bluff early Christmas morning and, along with several soldiers who had money in their pockets, Duncan bought two quarts of whiskey for the outrageous price of $60. He neither blinked nor stopped to drink, still wary that Federal soldiers could appear at their rear. He ordered all the cannon, other heavy equipment, and remaining supplies unloaded from the wagons and transferred to boats tied up at the Niblett's Bluff docks. He assigned one man from each company to accompany the cargo downriver to Beaumont and ordered the teamsters to move the empty wagons as fast as possible to the ferry. They completed their crossing at dusk and made camp in Texas before night fell. That is when the party began. "The Major and several other officers got tight and a good many men also," Duncan says. "[I] gave my company a drink round for their Christmas. I ate some of the little cakes I brought from home and gave some of the men a taste. That was our Christmas."

The threat of Union soldiers chasing them across the Sabine River was top-of-mind for Duncan and the returning Texas Confederates, so they rolled wagons shortly after first light with Duncan complaining he felt badly for want of sleep. The wagons bogged down frequently in the heavy mud on the western approaches to the river. The tired, hungry men, many of them hung over, struggled to free the wagons and tempers ran short. Two soldiers from another company "fell out and shot each other," Duncan says, "one mortally wounded." They made it across Cow Bayou near Bridge City in Orange County and made camp around 4 P.M. when the heavens opened again. "We were without tents," Duncan says and "had to take it. After midnight, [we] started fires and warmed and dried [*sic*] a little and slept some." The next day, Duncan says he "never saw the like of water. Wagons bogged all the time." Around noon a flooded creek stopped progress about ten miles from the Neches River ferry crossing, so they set to work to build a crude bridge. They cut trees until darkness forced them to lay down their axes for the night.

Sunny skies warmed their backs as they returned to work the next day. They finished the bridge and moved all the wagons across the flooded creek and pushed west. It was only a matter of hours and just ten miles when they reached another creek spilling over its banks. This time, men on horseback crossed while infantrymen clambered aboard the empty wagons whose drivers swam the teams and wagons across. The straggly procession made it by nightfall to Duncan's favorite Neches River crossing at Collier's Ferry, five miles north of Beaumont, and pitched camp nearby. Battling more bad roads in heavier rain, they made eighteen miles the next day and reached Pine Island near Sour Lake northwest of Beaumont. By this time, Duncan was exhausted and felt "very unwell with pain in [the] region of the liver." He asked permission to leave the slower main group to drive home alone to Liberty. He "started on with my little wagon at 2 1/2 o'clock [*sic*] [and] got home at dark. Still raining."

After welcomed rest in his own warm bed, he rose on New Year's Eve morning to celebrate his homecoming with family and friends who lived nearby. After dinner, he rode into Liberty in the "coldest weather I ever felt" and met three other officers of Spaight's Battalion who reported the company had not yet come in. He stopped to buy a bottle of rum for $10, dropped in on brother-in-law Simeon DeBlanc who welcomed him with an eggnog, then rode to Pryor Bryan's for supper. When he returned to the farm after sundown, "everything [was] hard frozen." Capt. William Duncan was relieved to be home but could not unwind. The threat of Federal invasion was as ominous as Liberty's freezing winter night.[2]

Duncan spent only two days at home before he hit the trail again, this time headed west along the Atascosito Trail toward Houston. As freezing rain pelted southeast Texas on January 2, 1864, he drove his small wagon to join six others at the San Jacinto River crossing the next evening. It had rained for several days, causing the wagons to bog frequently in the mud. The water level at the Atascosito Trail crossing was high, forcing the seven drivers to wait for a ferry rather than risk driving through the strong current. When all the wagons were across safely, Duncan sent them ahead while he, Sabine, and three other men took refuge from the weather in an abandoned slave cabin. "This morning it is freezing," he wrote Celima, "but we are very comfortable. We are in a negro cabin near old man Sims' and have plenty for ourselves and horses to eat and plenty of wood to burn . . . we are roasting potatoes, I have some of my turkey and Sabine and Jim Brown is [*sic*] cooking crackling bread."

After supper, Duncan loaned his saddle blankets to Sabine who had left his sleeping roll at Jerome DeBlanc's house on the east side of the Trinity on the first night of the journey. Duncan intended to send for Sabine's blankets as well as the lantern he forgot at home when they reached Houston. In a letter to Celima, he makes a special plea. "I want you to have my horses taken as good care of as you can and try to keep them from being stolen," he writes. "Get White and Randolph to keep a lookout all the time [to] prevent if possible some scamp [from] taking them off." Duncan's fear of horse thieves was evidence of the widespread lawlessness that plagued Texas when he returned from Louisiana at the end of 1863.[3]

Gov. Pendleton Murrah worried criminal behavior had become so prevalent across Texas in early 1864 that he called for creation of county-by-county militias. "Imperative duty requires of me to call your attention to the fearful demoralization and crimes prevailing throughout the State," Murrah wrote his fellow Texans. "In some sections society is almost disorganized, the voice of the law is hushed, and its authority seldom asserted. It is a dead letter, an unhonored thing upon the unread pages of the statutes. Murder, robbery, theft, outrages of every kind against property, against human life, against everything sacred to a civilized people, are frequent and general." Murrah said the militias would "aid in the execution of the laws, civil and military; would form an efficient police force to watch over and control the slave population, and prevent them from being tampered with; they would arrest deserters and break up their haunts, and root out disaffection, disloyalty, and treason to our cause; they would aid in protecting the community from violence, and from the horrid murders, robberies, and other outrages, which are daily being committed in many sections of the State . . . " As far as former Liberty County Sheriff William Duncan was concerned, no men were available to form an effective militia and protection of his property was up to him.[4]

Duncan, Sabine, and their three companions left the cozy, crackling-bread cabin the next morning for the short ride to Camp Lubbock, seven miles north of Houston. The county seat of Harris County, Houston was the headquarters of the Texas Confederacy's Second Military Sub-District that covered east Texas.[5] When they arrived at Camp Lubbock, finding fodder for the wagon teams was Duncan's first priority. Unable to locate any hay, he considered leading the horses to graze on grassland along the Brazos River west of Houston, but left them to eat corn in camp while he dealt with a more pressing problem: a recent order from General Magruder causing dissension in the ranks. "There has been a great deal of dissatisfaction among our two companies," Duncan says, "at an order of General Magruder attaching us permanently to Baylor's Regiment. Nearly all the officers and men of my company and Marsh's want to go back to Col. Spaight; I don't think we can ever get back to Spaight unless we give up our horses and go as infantry. I don't think the men will like to do that . . . walking would be too much like work to suit their notions."

Duncan and Marsh's cavalry companies had not officially been reassigned to a Texas unit after their Louisiana service. The debate over whether they would be designated cavalry rather than infantry was complicated by their preference for Spaight over Baylor as their new regimental commanding officer. According to Duncan, the men preferred to return to Spaight's Battalion the way it was originally organized in 1862 with four infantry companies and two cavalry companies. They clearly preferred Spaight over Baylor as their C.O. Duncan told the men he would support the wishes of the majority but quietly informed Spaight about the controversy so Spaight could lobby for his interests with Magruder and his staff officers. It was another occasion where Duncan quietly used his interpersonal skills to facilitate compromise while remaining loyal to his friend, neighbor, and commanding officer, Ashley Spaight.[6]

Duncan's confidential head's-up to Spaight helped the colonel negotiate a solution with General Magruder that pleased almost everyone—but only temporarily. On February 11, 1864, Magruder ordered Lt. Col. William H. Griffin's Infantry Battalion consolidated with Spaight's Eleventh Cavalry and Infantry Battalion[7] to form the 21st Texas Infantry Regiment with Colonel Spaight in command. Griffin was named executive officer and Maj. Felix McReynolds was made adjutant. Company F, Duncan's unit, was redesignated Company H and Duncan named its commanding officer.[8] Magruder ordered the new regiment of fourteen officers and 235 men to relocate from Camp Lubbock to Sabine Pass[9] as soon as possible. Duncan arrived at the pass on February 4, but Spaight did not show up until the evening of February 7 after breaking his journey at Beaumont. "Col. Spaight finds his favorite negro boy Tom at the point of death," Duncan tells Celima. "He has been sick with pneumonia for 8 or 10 days. I don't think there is any chance for him to recover. There has been a great deal of the disease about here."[10] His prediction was accurate; Tom died with Colonel Spaight at his bedside the day after Duncan left Beaumont for the pass.[11]

Duncan took a room in Kate Dorman's Catfish Hotel when the regiment arrived at Sabine Pass.[12] Kate was having trouble offering a complete menu in the dining room so Duncan wrote to Celima to ask her to help him stock a private larder. "I want you if you can to procure me some potatoes from Alfred," he writes. "I want some good bacon if you can get it as I will have to get everything from the country to live on. I can get nothing here to eat but beef and bread. I want you all to go to raising chickens as I want to have some chicken and eggs during the summer if I stay here." Duncan got even more specific with his grocery list, telling Celima that about fifty pounds of ham and bacon would be sufficient, along with three or four bushels of potatoes. He enclosed $200 in a letter to pay for the foodstuffs.[13] On his way to the pass from Houston, Duncan had left his bedding and lantern in Liberty again and blamed Celima for his forgetfulness. His tantrum obviously bothered him because he apologized at the end of another letter. "Don't think of the fret I got in about leaving my bedding any more. I was very much vexed at first and had to blame some body [sic]. But I have long since got over it and am very sorry I blamed you."[14]

The consolidation of Spaight's and Griffin's units into one regiment unraveled quickly, but not because of traditional enmity between cavalry and infantry. General Magruder revoked his February 11 order within hours after its issue and the news made it to Sabine Pass the same day. The general's change of mind was brought about by an urgent need to repair the railroad spur from Sabine Pass to Beaumont. Since Spaight's Battalion was already in place at the pass, Magruder ordered it to do the work. Duncan says, "We are Spaight's Battalion again and my company is F again. Everybody is very much pleased at the change."[15] Along with orders to repair the Sabine Pass-to-Beaumont tracks, Magruder authorized Spaight to recruit four new companies to his unit to maintain its designation as a regiment. Duncan wrote to Simeon DeBlanc, Celima's brother, suggesting he raise a company and "run for one of the company offices," or failing that, join another man to recruit enough soldiers to make a company-strength unit. There was pressure in early 1864 to force civilians who had not served to volunteer for the Confederate army to shore up Texas defensive forces in preparation for the anticipated Union invasion. Duncan says Simeon "will have to go into the service now and it will be much better for him to get into one of the new companies and get an office than to go in as a private. I hope he will do it."[16]

Spaight carved out Duncan's dismounted cavalry Company F and infantry Company D to work on the railroad. They established a staging area on the prairie about a mile south of Beaumont on February 24 and pitched tents along the tracks.[17] The rest of the battalion remained farther south on guard duty against a possible Union incursion through the pass. Plans called for the two companies to alternate crews on the rail bed until repairs were completed.[18] The detail moved its tents by March 7 to a site about four miles south of Beaumont,[19] indicating repair work was taking approximately four days per mile of track. Wily McGraw, a deserter from Company F, returned to camp that day and surrendered to Duncan,[20] adding another worker to the crew. Two days later, Duncan lost two other workers when privates Pleasant Hill and Hez Pruett went turkey hunting without permission.[21] Duncan had them arrested for being AWOL when they returned to camp. It was March 10, 1864, the same day President Lincoln named Ulysses Grant General-in-Chief of the Union armies and ordered him to focus his attention on General Lee's Confederate Army of Northern Virginia. A year later, Grant would accept Lee's surrender at Appomattox Court House.

After a six-day home leave in Liberty, Duncan returned to the railroad repair work south of Beaumont on March 21.[22] "I found on my arrival here that our command had been ordered to remain as it was, instead of going to Sabine Pass," says Duncan. "And the order sending Griffin's Battalion to La. [sic] had been countermanded. . . . Orders are so easily issued and countermanded that it would not surprise me to hear we were ordered to Louisiana or to any other place. So I must keep as well prepared for such an event as I can." For a Confederate officer in 1864 Texas, coping with a stream of scrambled orders intended to prepare for Federal invasions by both land and sea was maddening. "Everything seems to have went [sic] wrong while I was at home," Duncan says. "Twenty-three men had deserted from Company D and one from my Co. [sic], an old man named Pitman. He was a substitute and lived in Hardin County. His friends and acquaintances were in the other Co. and deserted and he went with them."[23] The departure-en-masse of the relatively large group of Hardin County volunteers reveals how local glue held many Confederate units together. When a soldier deserted, it often meant many of his neighbors did too.

The repair crew finished its work on the Beaumont–Sabine Pass rail spur at the end of March. Within a week, orders arrived from Houston directing Colonel Spaight to remount his cavalry companies. Duncan led Company F to the Beaumont depot where they boarded the train for Liberty, arriving there on the afternoon of April 7. At a station-side formation, Duncan ordered twenty-six men home to fetch their horses and sent four others home to do the same the next day.[24] In a frustrating reversal for Duncan and his men, General Magruder withdrew the order to remount Duncan's cavalry company on April 10 and instructed Spaight's Battalion to report to Burr's Ferry,[25] eighty miles northeast of Beaumont on the Sabine River.[26] Magruder's new order intended for Spaight's Battalion to help stop General Banks's army from crossing into Texas on the Old Beef Trail that ran from Alexandria to Huntsville, Texas. Magruder's idea had tactical defensive merit, but Banks never strayed from his retreat at the end of the Union's ill-fated Red River Campaign against Shreveport. Spaight's Battalion made it as far as Beaumont on its way to Burr's Ferry, but was ordered on April 21 to turn around and head back to Houston. They arrived at Camp Lubbock the following afternoon.[27]

Two days later, Duncan wrote a note to the Houston command's disbursing department acknowledging receipt of a promissory note for $1,413.50 in Confederate currency "to pay the enlisted men of Co's [sic] D and F of Spaight's Battalion for work on the Eastern Texas Railroad for the months of Feb. and March, 1864." The payment confirms the civilian manpower shortage in wartime southeast Texas and by extension, throughout the South. It also shows how the Confederate army occasionally provided military labor to build or repair civilian-owned infrastructure if the project was considered strategically important.[28]

Exasperated by a stream of orders that had it doing "About face!" almost weekly, Spaight's Battalion was ordered back to Beaumont late on April 26. Their ultimate destination once again was Niblett's Bluff.[29] Confederate scouts had been keeping an eye on General Banks's retreat, and General Magruder intended to be prepared if the Federals turned west when they reached Alexandria. When Duncan arrived at the bluff, he says "there is no news here of Yankees in this part of the state. I have no doubt it was a false alarm. I expect we will return in the course of eight or ten days to Beaumont. We may go out to Lake Charles and back before we return."[30] Duncan had it half right. The Battalion returned to Beaumont on May 2nd but stayed only three days.[31] Spaight ordered what was left of four of his six companies—A, C, D, and E—to rendezvous with Griffin's troops at Sabine City, forming a three-hundred-man force of infantry and light artillery. The combined unit under Griffin was dispatched to the Calcasieu River near Lake Charles while Spaight, Duncan, and the men of Company F left Beaumont in a wagon train for Lake Charles. Duncan explains, "there had been a gunboat at the mouth of the river and she sent one or two launches ashore and burnt down [an] old barracks, there being no soldiers there."[32]

Griffin left Sabine Pass while Spaight and Duncan headed for Lake Charles on May 5. The next morning, Griffin's troops attacked Federal gunboats *Granite City* and *Wave* at Calcasieu Pass, both of which surrendered after a brief exchange of artillery and rifle fire. The Confederates recovered fourteen cannon, the boats' ammunition and supplies, and captured 166 prisoners. They moved the two Union gunboats to a staging area where later they were converted into Confederate blockade-runners.[33] Griffin took charge of the prisoners while Duncan and Spaight loaded the captured material into the wagons and headed back to Beaumont on May 10, arriving two days later.[34] In the meantime, General Banks continued his retreat to New Orleans. Soon after arrival, he was relieved of field command and placed in charge of Federal military administration for southern Louisiana.[35] When Duncan's company reached Beaumont, the men pitched their tents on the same ground four miles south of town they occupied during the railroad repair assignment. That same day, Pvt. B. F. Brooks, one of Duncan's men, died at the Beaumont hospital. Duncan assigned privates Spinks and Hill to accompany the body back to Liberty.[36]

Chapter 16 **Spindletop**

DURING THE FLURRY OF ACTIVITY BACK AND forth to Beaumont and across the Sabine to Lake Charles, Duncan was thinking how best to pay his 1864 Texas state taxes. He told Celima, "I saw Charley Lund & spoke to him about my interest [from] Confederate notes and he told me they would not pay taxes."[1] Lund, a former Liberty County treasurer,[2] must have been aware the Texas legislature had passed laws that spring in an effort to protect its treasury from dramatic depreciation in the value of Confederate notes. The new law prohibited Texans from paying taxes with originally issued Confederate script except at a 33 percent discount off face value and declared that no Confederate interest-bearing bonds would be received in payment of taxes after June 30. The politicians were trying to recoup some semblance of purchasing power for the state despite rapid deterioration in the value of newly issued Confederate paper money. At the same time, Texas was having a terrible time collecting receipts from a specie tax, a tax payable in gold, to meet interest and principal repayment requirements of a $1 million bond issued in 1861. The special gold tax began to fail in early 1863 and for the year ending August 31, 1864, produced only $1,352.77 in government revenue.[3] With the Texas economy in shambles, Duncan respected Charley Lund's financial advice because as a West Liberty dry goods merchant, he had to know the value of currencies, gold, and bartered goods for commercial survival. If Lund thought the *original* Confederate currency was still worth something, Duncan was inclined to believe him. "He also told me," Duncan said, "they were the best money now in circulation. So I do not wish you to use them until further instructions."[4]

While Duncan fretted about how to pay taxes and Texas Confederates worried about Federal invasions, Union generals Ulysses Grant and William Sherman began campaigns in early May 1864 that would ultimately deliver coups des grâce to the Confederacy. Sherman left Chattanooga on May 4, followed the Western and Atlantic Railroad south to Atlanta, and from there burned his way across Georgia and South Carolina, then marched up through North Carolina to Virginia in the early months of 1865.[5] Grant focused the 115,000-man Union Army of the Potomac on the 64,000-strong Army of Northern Virginia commanded by Robert E. Lee. Grant told Gen. George Meade, "Lee's Army will be your objective point. Wherever Lee goes, there you will go also."[6] Grant's order reveals the Union's singular focus in May 1864: Robert E. Lee's Army of Northern Virginia. After their futile Red River Campaign, the Federals realized they could essentially ignore the Trans-Mississippi Region. Union control of the Mississippi; the war-long success of its blockade of southern ports; shrinkage of Confederate forces from battlefield defeats, disease, and desertions; and empty Confederate treasuries, arsenals, and warehouses meant the Trans-Mississippi could not affect the outcome of the war. William Duncan did not know these details, but it is reasonable to think he sensed their implications. His thoughts these days shifted from worries about the war to dreams about his future when it ended, predicated of course on his survival.

Before leaving Niblett's Bluff for Beaumont on the way to Lake Charles in early May, Duncan ran into French Sister St. Ambrose, mother superior of the Ursuline convent school in Liberty, on board a docked southbound riverboat. She was traveling with two laywomen from Liberty and Duncan had time only for a few words before the ship's bell rang and he had to disembark. "You and Emma will, I suppose, go to see them," he writes Celima "and get a history of their adventures. I hope the Superior will open her school again with plenty of good teachers, as I want Em and Kate to go to school if it is possible."[7] Duncan's wish for his two eldest children to continue their studies with the nuns makes clear his support of education for his daughters and concern he might not be around after the war to make it happen for them.

After its successful mission into western Louisiana in early May 1864, Spaight's Battalion was ordered to reestablish camp in Jefferson County to wait for invading Union soldiers either overland on the Atascosito Trail or by water through Sabine Pass. On May 19, the unit settled into a new camp on a hill surrounded by marshland four miles south of Beaumont.[8] They called it Camp Spindletop, named for the stumps of dead trees visible around the hill that reminded local people of a crop of spindles. Duncan wrinkled his nose when he pitched his tent at Spindletop. The stench he smelled came from sulfurous hydrocarbon gases seeping from petroleum trapped in salt domes about a thousand feet below the surface. For thousands of years, residents of the upper Texas gulf coast, including Native Americans, seventeenth-century French explorers and Spanish conquistadors, nineteenth-century cattlemen, and Confederate soldiers, were aware of natural oil seeps dripping out of creek banks and oozing into the bayous of Jefferson County and throughout southeast Texas. People

occasionally collected the gooey hydrocarbons to burn in lanterns or for inges-
tion as homeopathic pharmaceuticals. Thirty-seven years later in January 1901,
southeast Texas boomed when oil was discovered at Duncan's Camp Spindletop
on the western bank of the Neches River. Had William Duncan the entrepreneur been alive, there is no telling how many investments he would have made
in the turn-of-the-century black gold rush that transformed coastal Texas and
Louisiana after the Spindletop discovery.

But in May 1864, Duncan had no idea the odor he smelled at Spindletop hinted at the upcoming birth of the modern oil industry. He was a Texas
Confederate civilian soldier more concerned with what he might eat to survive
at his new camp southeast of Beaumont while waiting for a Union invasion.
Celima sent him a basket of vegetables and fruit that he shared with Colonel
and Mrs. Spaight, explaining that Spaight "did not want to take them but I
made him take them, telling him he could pay me back when he got some from
home." Duncan realized later he gave Spaight a cucumber he wished he had
kept. "When I opened the basket by moon light," he tells Celima, "I put the
piece of paper in my pocket until I got here without reading it. And as I do not
eat cucumbers, I gave it to the Colonel as he said his wife ate them. But had I
known it was my dear little Chessie that had sent it to me, I would have eaten it,
even if I had known it would have made me sick. I am almost tempted to send
back for it in the morning."

Duncan coached Celima on how to pay for household supplies in that same
letter. He told her he had seen a merchant from Liberty who offered him "a fine
calf skin for $6 in specie and white domestic [material] at sixty cents a yard in
specie and muslin at fifty cents and linen for shirt bosoms at a dollar. He said he
did not think he could sell any calico as he had promised it all." Duncan says,
"I want the calf skin and I want you to get what domestic and muslin you need
for yourself and the children. About the pay, tell Thompson that I will go over
[i.e., return to Liberty] in two or three weeks and will pay him myself in specie
or Louisiana money. But if he should want to settle before that time, tell him
to call on you and I want you to pay him part in La. money and part in gold."
Duncan told Celima how she should calculate the exchange. "If you should get
as much as $25 or $30 on $40 worth, let him have a $50 La. bill and pay the balance in gold. He takes La. money at two for one, except the Bank of America
and that he takes at par."[9] What Duncan does *not* say in his instructions to Celima is notable. He makes no reference to Confederate currency, implying it was
useless in this potential transaction.

Spaight's Battalion grew on May 26, 1864 with the addition of a new infantry company formed by Thomas Leonard of Newton County,[10] seventy miles
northeast of Beaumont on the Louisiana border. Undoubtedly motivated by
fear the Federals were heading their way, the new recruits of Company G had
waited almost to the end to enter the war. But things were quiet for Company G
and the rest of the regiment serving on the gulf coast throughout the summer,

except for an August assignment Duncan tried to avoid. "I received an order today to start [to] Sabine Pass in the morning with my company to witness the execution of two men sentenced to be shot on Friday," he says. "All the troops about here are to be present. I have tried my best to get the Col. [*sic*] [to] let me off but on account of only having junior lieutenants in the company, he would not agree for me to be absent. The men to be shot are Lt. Buck Allen . . . and a private of Griffin's Battalion, Norman Rogers."[11] Duncan does not mention why the two were sentenced to die, but chances are, it was for desertion. The day after the firing squad did its grisly duty at Sabine Pass, Union Adm. David Farragut and Maj. Gen. Gordon Granger began joint operations to close Mobile Bay on the Alabama coast to blockade running by the Confederates. Farragut forced Confederate gunboats in the bay to surrender on August 5, and Granger captured Fort Morgan on August 23.[12] Within ten months, General Granger would arrive in Galveston to play a historic role in postwar Texas life.

Trans-Mississippi Region Gen. Edmund Kirby Smith reassigned General Magruder to commanding general of Confederate troops in Arkansas on August 4 and replaced him with Gen. John George Walker as the new commander of the District of Texas, New Mexico, and Arizona. Walker commanded a column under Stonewall Jackson at Harper's Ferry and led a unit at the battle of Antietam a few days later. He took command of a new division on January 1, 1863, at Little Rock that later came to be known as Walker's Greyhounds. Walker led his division with distinction against Union forces in the Red River Campaign and was seriously wounded at the Battle of Pleasant Hill on April 9. He came to Houston from Louisiana where he had relieved Gen. Richard Taylor as commanding general in early June.[13]

Ashley Spaight's career prospects improved dramatically when Walker replaced Magruder. Enmity between Spaight and Magruder had smoldered nastily after President Davis rejected Spaight's resignation carrying Magruder's appended blackball during the Watkins debacle at Grigsby's Bluff. William Duncan himself was caught in the middle of the Magruder-Spaight feud when the vindictive Magruder sent a clear message to Spaight by refusing to see, let alone help, his friend and junior officer, Captain Duncan on Duncan's special AWOL amnesty mission fourteen months earlier. When General Walker ordered Spaight's Battalion to strike tents at Camp Spindletop and move south once again to Sabine Pass,[14] Spaight moved into Walker's inner circle. In fact, Walker promoted Spaight to full colonel the next month and made him commanding officer over four companies of Griffin's Battalion in addition to six of Spaight's own seven companies in the revitalized 21st Texas Infantry. Artillery Company B of Spaight's Battalion, most of whose men were from Sabine Pass, remained on duty aboard the gunboat *Uncle Ben* on patrol in Sabine Lake. Walker also made Spaight commanding officer of Houston district headquarters and ordered the 21st Texas Infantry to relocate to Camp Lubbock[15] outside Houston where it would spend all but the very last days of the war.

As Spaight's star rose in the Texas Confederate hierarchy, so did that of his friend, neighbor, and confidant Capt. William Duncan. Spaight relied heavily on Duncan in administrative matters related to the new regiment. "I have been so busy all day that I hardly had time to eat," Duncan wrote Celima on a cold night in early December. "I received a lot of clothing and blankets, which the men needed very much and have been hard at work all day issuing them out, except when I was called off on some other business. . . . There was [*sic*] four hundred Yankee prisoners sent here to be taken care of. They were from Camp Groce on their way to Galveston to be exchanged. They left here this morning. They must have suffered greatly with cold today as they were nearly naked."[16] Camp Groce, the first permanent Confederate military prison west of the Mississippi, was located close to the Houston and Central Texas rail line on Col. Leonard Groce's Liendo plantation two miles east of Hempstead in Waller County.[17] The poorly clad Federal prisoners on their way to Galveston were not the only ones suffering in the cold. Duncan told Celima he wanted to help Sabine keep warm by giving him his hunting jacket the next time he was home.[18] He did not think it would be in time for Christmas. "I am satisfied that an attack is expected somewhere on the coast," Duncan says, "and our regiment will be kept ready to move at once to any point that is attacked or threatened. I believe we will go to Sabine [Pass] if we move at all. I now have almost no hope at all of being able to get home before Christmas," he continues, "for if the enemy is expected, I know that no leaves of absence will be granted to officers or men."[19]

Chapter 17 Collapse

NEW YEAR'S DAY FELL ON SUNDAY IN 1865 AND Duncan spent it updating the unit's muster rolls at Camp Lubbock.[1] The latest war news to make it to Houston from across the Mississippi was personal for Duncan because it involved Celima's cousin and his daughter Emma's future fiancé. A month earlier, Gen. John Bell Hood, a Kentucky native who adopted Texas as his home state when he joined the Confederacy, had ordered 20,000 soldiers of his 39,000-man Army of Tennessee to attack Union troops in a frontal assault just south of Nashville at Franklin. Hood's army included the 3rd Texas cavalry regiment from east Texas, many of whose riders Duncan knew. Oscar DeBlanc, son of Duncan's hunting pal, Celima's uncle Jerome DeBlanc, was one of them. Hood's troops were hungry, poorly equipped, and dressed in rags. Thousands wore shoes so flimsy they in effect fought barefoot. Hood's corps commanders urged him to attack the Federals on the flanks, but the arrogant, impatient Hood refused that sound advice. When the shooting stopped that night, nearly 7,000 Confederate soldiers were dead, wounded, or missing. The Army of Tennessee was crushed beyond repair and two weeks later, on December 16, the rest of Hood's command was routed at Nashville. Hood resigned his command in January and his officers discharged their men as dozens more deserted daily. The first among them began to arrive in southeast Texas as Duncan packed his things to leave Camp Lubbock early the next day for a week's pass at home in Liberty.[2]

A sentry rousted Duncan in his Camp Lubbock hut at 2:00 the next morning. He grabbed his gear, climbed into a wagon with two other soldiers, and steered the team toward a local market where they bought mugs of hot coffee to counter the chill of Houston's predawn darkness. The early Beaumont train was scheduled to leave at first light but departure was delayed until 9:30, forced to wait for General Walker and Colonel Spaight. Duncan rode with the two senior officers as far as Liberty where the train arrived at 1:30 P.M. Celima and Chessie were waiting at the station for Duncan in the family buggy, and daughter, mother, and father arrived home in time for a late dinner. His family was glad to see him because deep anxiety filled the hearts of Confederate families and communities in Texas and throughout the South in early 1865. People realized Union victory was only a matter of time and worried what it would mean for them. Many Texans expected they would be among the last battlefield casualties of the war. Duncan rode into Liberty two days later to buy newspapers brought to town by the train. The "news [was] bad," he says.[3]

Living in Texas had become increasingly complicated by early 1865. With the state's economy a wreck and Confederate finances no better, Duncan began to record not just how much but also *how* he paid for things. He was careful to distinguish between Confederate paper money and specie, that is, gold coins. The regimental relocation to Houston forced Duncan to dig deeper into his stash of gold because Houston merchants would not accept Confederate script. "I shall need some more specie," he tells Celima, "as everything here now sells for specie."[4] He paid a local cobbler "in advance $5 in specie" to resole a pair of boots and "sent to Capt. Peacock's for gal. whiskey, $5 specie." The next day, he paid Dr. Breshear $13, also in gold.[5] Trading in new Confederate paper money had become rare in Texas at the beginning of 1865, although it was issued almost a year earlier. Posted quotes for the new script remained substantially lower in Houston from quoted values for the same new currency in eastern Confederate states because of illiquidity. There simply was not much of it on hand because Union control of the Mississippi kept shipments from crossing the river. In fact, the Trans-Mississippi supply of Confederate currency is estimated to have dropped to $17 million in January 1865 from $160 million allocated to the region in February 1864. It remained in short supply in the west through the end of the war, even though it was printed with abandon in the east. People in Texas boycotted Confederate paper money and insisted on being paid in gold. As a professional cattleman who traded for more than twenty years in different currencies as well as in bartered goods on the Texas and Louisiana frontier, Duncan routinely calculated exchange values to avoid losing money. Financially unsophisticated consumers like most folks in Civil War Texas and throughout the South did not understand variable currency and real property valuations and could not calculate exchange rates easily, especially in times of raging inflation. As a result, they often foundered on the wrong and costly side of basic transactions.[6]

The final five days of Duncan's furlough passed quickly. He arrived back in Camp Lubbock at dark after catching the afternoon train into Houston from Liberty. He admitted he was "unusually low spirited today. Got my things on a cart and I went on foot. Road [was] muddy." The sun lifted his mood the next morning, rising in clear skies as he made his way into downtown Houston on personal business. On the way, he stopped at the hospital to visit three of his men: privates Richey, Pruett, and LeBlanc. He judged Pruett as "pretty sick," but said "all [were] doing tolerable." Leaving the hospital, Duncan continued into Houston where he sold six $20 bonds for ninety cents on the dollar in gold. He also met a man from Liberty to discuss starting a new sawmill.

Duncan's mind wandered daily from military matters to civilian business. He was exploring investment options that might be feasible when the war ended. His army duties on some days did not permit him much time to consider the future. He was Officer of the Day when a soldier reported that Private Pruett, one of the soldiers he visited in the hospital, had died. Duncan "sent four men in to see to burying him." Two days later, he met Colonel Spaight in Houston for dinner. Their conversation included opinions of "five men [who] deserted from Co. H" the previous night. The missing quintet would not be the last deserters from Company H.

Since Spaight's Battalion had been stationed at Camp Lubbock, Duncan enjoyed frequent access to Houston. In addition to expenditures for brandy, whiskey, and tobacco for himself, most of his purchases were for Celima and the children back in Liberty. One day he borrowed an old horse—he left his personal animals at home when he was assigned to Camp Lubbock—and rode into town for dinner at Perkins restaurant with future business partner Jim Wrigley. Duncan says Wrigley talked so much he "could not get away from him." When Wrigley finally paused for breath, Duncan excused himself and headed for the market. He bought cotton thread for $6, a yard of blue cloth for $6, some buttons for $2, liquor and tobacco for $3, and a bag of candy for forty cents. The next day, he put his purchases in a basket with twelve pounds of coffee and sent everything home to Celima with one of his men.

He was on his way out of camp again two days later when several shots rang out. Duncan hurried to see what was happening. The ruckus turned out to be a gunfight between two Spaight's Battalion soldiers, neither of whom was much of a shot. They missed each other, but a stray bullet from the shoot-out killed an innocent bystander. The unlucky victim was a cavalryman named McFormont from Captain Marsh's company.[7] Discipline was never a shining virtue of the Confederate army and this was a common example. Although soldiers' conduct is said to have improved gradually over the course of the war, military misbehavior was especially typical in Confederate cavalry units whose lack of order was notorious and whose discipline deteriorated as the war evolved. The Inspector General of the Army of Northern Virginia reported in September 1864, "there is not that spirit of respect for and obedience to general orders which should pervade military organization." Six months after that particular I.G. report was published, General Lee issued an armywide circular in which he said too much dependence had been placed on soldiers' innate merit as individuals and not enough consideration given to forging effective military units. Lee did not gild the lily when he said, "Many opportunities have been lost and hundreds of valuable lives have been uselessly sacrificed for want of a strict observance of discipline." Confederate leadership had ignored discipline far too long to make any difference by 1865. Capt. William Duncan experienced the results of that negligence firsthand at Camp Lubbock, Houston, and later in Galveston when desertions, fistfights, and gunfights increased as the war drew to an end.[8]

Another advantage of being stationed at Camp Lubbock for Duncan was Houston's status as a regional commodity market and the primary financial center of the Trans-Mississippi Region after New Orleans was occupied by the Federals. Duncan's brother-in-law, Simeon DeBlanc, arrived in camp one day at the end of January 1865, and Duncan took him into Houston to collect interest on a $2,600 bond Duncan had bought on Simeon's behalf before the war. While Simeon pocketed his cash, Duncan claimed income from an $1,800 bond he had purchased for Celima. His reputation as an easy touch followed him to the Bayou City. Even when he knew chances for repayment were slim, like the time he loaned "John Watson, a gambler, $5 which I never expect to get," he was inclined to help. People were willing to return his favors as a result. Soldiers moved regularly through Liberty on army business between Galveston, Houston, and Beaumont and several Liberty civilians made regular treks into Houston for supplies and to sell produce. These travelers were happy to oblige when Duncan and his family drafted them as de facto postmen. Daughter Emma frequently asked the local Catholic priest to carry letters to her father. Regular courier Ashley Spaight continued to find the occasional bottle of brandy from Duncan on his desk in gratitude after Duncan returned from errands in town.[9]

Chapter 18 **Resolve**

AS THE WAR CREPT SLOWLY TOWARD ITS END, THE flow of reassigned Texas Confederate officers and men increased at Camp Lubbock. Among them was an old friend of Duncan's, Lt. Col. Edward Bradford Pickett. Pickett was a Liberty man who led a cavalry unit of Texas volunteers in battles through Louisiana, Arkansas, in the siege at Chattanooga, and in John Bell Hood's Tennessee campaign. He was captured in Arkansas and later repatriated to the Confederacy in a prisoner exchange. Pickett was elected to the Texas state senate after the war, served as president of the Texas Constitutional Convention in 1875, and became president of the first board of directors of Texas A&M University when it was founded in 1876. He saw plenty of action in his Civil War and he and his Liberty County neighbor, William Duncan, had notes to compare and memories to share at Camp Lubbock.[1]

The weather in Houston was miserable for nine straight days in late January and early February 1865. Cloudy skies and cold rain mixed with sleet driven by north winds were the rule. When a day finally dawned with brilliant sun shining in clear skies, Duncan was inspired to tackle an early spring-cleaning. He encouraged his bed bugs to find new homes by arranging his mattress and blankets "to sun" outside the tent. Then he packed another goodie bag to send home to Celima. His parcel this day included three pairs of shoes, a dozen fine linen handkerchiefs, and one well-made comb. There was extra room in the basket, so the ever-practical Duncan topped it off with three pairs of old socks that needed darning and a bottle of brandy for future toasts. He sent the surprise home to Liberty with two of his men.

With increasing frequency, Spaight asked Duncan to serve as Camp Lubbock's Officer of the Day. A soldier approached him in that capacity on February 10 and reported, "the men of the regiment intended to go to town and take the commissary." Duncan says, "I knew my company was not in it." Although worried about mutinous mischief, Duncan busied himself building a small hut. He was fed up with sleeping in an insect-infested army tent. As Duncan worked on the new hut one morning, several soldiers walked hurriedly past him toward the sound of a single drumbeat. He put his tools down and followed. The group joined a large crowd already gathered outside another officer's tent, shouting complaints about camp conditions and threatening to desert en masse. Duncan listened for a while, then stepped in front of them to appeal for order. "I thought of what I had heard," he says, "and went to the place and talked to them." Duncan's speech was in vain. All but two of the men in the crowd deserted after the incident. The two who did not run were arrested and detained.[2]

William Duncan showed courage that day at Camp Lubbock. A hostile crowd is a complicated, dangerous organism that can only be explained in terms of its origin, nature, and organization. Individuals in a hostile crowd share a preexisting bond; in this instance, it was probably hunger and disgust with intolerable living conditions in Camp Lubbock, sprinkled with fear of a Federal attack. Individuals in a hostile crowd lose critical discrimination and ordinary self-control, yield to natural inclinations usually forbidden by convention or law, and hide behind anonymity. A man of intuitive common sense, William Duncan sensed the dangers of mob violence yet stood before the mutinous soldiers at Camp Lubbock to appeal for calm and patience. It was a situation of considerable personal danger, yet Duncan proved again his was the courage of a natural leader. On a broader scale, the incident was further evidence discipline was disintegrating quickly in Confederate Texas. Colonel Spaight visited Camp Lubbock the next day and Duncan says he "ordered [a] court of investigation in regard to the mutinous conduct of the men." Duncan adds that two of his soldiers, H. V. Barrow and W. S. Barnes, "were arrested and sent to Houston for being concerned in the mutiny." Duncan rode into town the next day to visit them in the stockade.[3]

Confederate survivors in Houston as well as throughout the South were sick, tired, hungry, and afraid. Camp Lubbock rumbled like a volcano about to erupt, yet Duncan focused on his duty and tried to set an example. Taking advantage of another beautiful day to work on his hut, he was interrupted by Colonel Spaight who dropped by to update him on troop unrest and tell him there would be a campwide inspection the next day. Duncan tossed his tools aside and headed for Colonel Pickett's tent to discuss preparations for the inspection. While Pickett and Duncan talked, John Barrow, a relative of H. V. Barrow, was arrested for participation in the mutinous activity and marched off to join the other two soldiers from Duncan's unit in the stockade.[4] Making things gloomier, the second of the three men whom Duncan visited in hospital in early January died. Stress over imprisoned soldiers, campwide desertions, and threats of mutiny weakened Duncan's immune system even further. He felt so bad he asked a junior officer to lead his company during Spaight's review of troops while Captain Marsh commanded the battalion.[5]

Duncan did not abandon his imprisoned men. He rode into Houston almost daily either to visit the three soldiers locked in the stockade or to testify in their court-martial at General Walker's headquarters in the Fannin Hotel on the corner of Fannin and Franklin in downtown Houston. After the court-martial sessions, he stopped by the hospital to visit sick battalion members, including his unrelated fellow officer, Lt. George Duncan, then ran errands. One day he bought a loaf of bread for twenty cents and picked up his laundry from the washer woman, whom he paid thirty-five cents, before riding back to camp. Colonel Spaight presided over another inspection in which Duncan was pleased that reviewing officers "made a flattering report of the command and gave my company the credit of having the cleanest guns, which was very gratifying to me."

It was Saturday two days later when Duncan rode into Houston again to see Lieutenant Duncan in the hospital. While Duncan chatted with his bedridden friend, President Lincoln stood in the rain in Washington and delivered the 703 words of his second inaugural speech to only a few thousand people, including his soon-to-be assassin, John Wilkes Booth. Lincoln asked his audience to think as one. "Fondly do we hope—and fervently do we pray—that this mighty scourge of war may speedily pass away." The next day in Texas, concerned about morale and order at Camp Lubbock, Duncan ordered his company into formation so he could read them the Confederate States of America's Articles of War. Duncan reminded his men why they volunteered to serve in the C.S.A. army and emphasized their continuing responsibilities. After he finished speaking, he "treated them all to a drink of whiskey."[6]

Six days after Lincoln's second inaugural, William Duncan joined in support of Confederate Pres. Jefferson Davis's ritualistic response to the U.S. president, a day of sacrifice Duncan says was "set apart by the President [Davis] for fast and prayer."[7] President Davis appealed to his Confederate brethren to put their trust in the Almighty because Davis realized the inevitable: the only thing that could save the Confederacy at that point was divine intervention. For many Southerners, including possibly William Duncan, it did not matter what Jefferson Davis said. Many Texans felt they should keep fighting their slice of the Civil War beyond defeat of the rest of the Confederacy so they could make a separate peace with the Union. They dreamed of the rebirth of the Republic of Texas.[8] As a frontier cattleman who grew up in the Republic and served in its army, Duncan would have been attracted by the idea, willing to sacrifice further to win a new independence for Texas like the noble, exciting one of his youth that he clearly remembered. The same day he bowed his head in prayer outside Houston with Jefferson Davis leading the ceremony in absentia, Duncan said, "I believe we will soon have to move towards the Mississippi."[9]

If Spaight's new 21st Texas Infantry regiment was headed to the Big Muddy, Duncan's fellow officer from Liberty, Lt. George Duncan, would not march with them. Captain Duncan stopped at the hospital in Houston a week later to see how the lieutenant was feeling and was "told that no company [was] allowed in [his] room." Duncan walked to headquarters where he met Colonel Spaight to request passes for himself and three other soldiers. The next day, he testified at the mutiny court-martial of his men, then attended a meeting of the Houston Masonic lodge. Duncan had been elected a Master Mason in the Liberty lodge nine years earlier.[10] After giving Colonel Spaight's Fannin Hotel staff two days to process his furlough request, Duncan showed up at headquarters Saturday to find a ten-day leave waiting for him. With the pass in his pocket, he checked schedules at the depot and learned a train to Liberty was scheduled to leave Sunday afternoon at 2:00. Hurrying back to camp after sundown to pack his things, Duncan paused at the hospital where Lieutenant Duncan was "no better." When he woke Sunday morning, Captain Duncan learned Lieutenant Duncan died at 4 A.M. After breakfast, Captain Duncan went back into Houston and asked Colonel Spaight for permission to bury the lieutenant that afternoon with full military honors. Spaight said yes, so Duncan arranged the ceremony for 4:00, then headed for the station to catch the 2:00 train. Captain Duncan knew Lieutenant Duncan would not mind if the captain missed his funeral to catch the only train home.[11]

Duncan enjoyed this particular furlough. He went to a picnic in Liberty on Thursday, "had [a] very good dinner, not many there, stayed till late and returned home." He was up early the next morning to hunt turkey and killed one bird. It was, he says, "the first time since I went into the service. Stayed at home the rest of the day till evening, then went out again to look for turkeys. Found one and killed it. Think the war will end." With plenty of giblets in the pantry, Duncan spent the next day in Liberty. He dropped by the depot to check on schedules back to Houston but found nothing posted. While he was at the station, a "train came in from Beaumont with about sixty furloughed soldiers from the other side of the Mississippi." For many southeast Texas Confederate volunteers, this was how their Civil War ended: no minié balls, no artillery rounds, no white flags. Only a dirty, noisy, crowded ride home on the Beaumont-to-Houston train, worried all the way that invading Federal soldiers might not be far behind.

The weather was springtime beautiful a week later and Duncan went for a ride down memory lane on the last day of his furlough. Throughout his marriages to Eliza and Celima, Duncan lived in the Gillard house on their plantation on the east side of the Trinity. He saddled his horse and rode across the river to the site of the house on his father's plantation where

> *I was raised from a little boy. I scarcely recognize anything. All so changed. The spring and pecan tree by it were the same. But the tree was dead with old age. I have known it forty years. Nothing marks the place where the house stood, except*

the brick bats of the chimney and three walnut trees which I planted. The beauti-
ful old oaks are all gone, not a stump left. The yard and where the house stood has
[sic] all been in cultivation. It makes me feel quite sad while standing on the spot
where I had spent my early childhood, to think on the past.

This is the longest single-topic comment Duncan ever made in his diary. It mourns the loss of his youth, the passage of time and probably also the looming Confederate defeat. He shook off his melancholy, climbed back on his horse and rode back to life. "I went hunting in the evening. Killed nothing."[12]

While Duncan visited the site of his childhood home south of West Liberty, Gen. John Magruder reassumed command of the Confederate District of Texas, New Mexico, and Arizona from General Walker in Houston. Magruder had been serving as the commanding officer of the Arkansas Department since being transferred to Little Rock the preceding August. Gen. Edmund Kirby Smith evidently wanted a healthier, if not entirely sober, general back in Houston. Smith was worried about a Union invasion of Texas in the final hours of the war. He transferred General Walker to command John Austin Wharton's cavalry corps, camped near Hempstead. A month later, Smith moved Walker again, this time to command of Alabama Gen. John Forney's division. It was another round of Confederate general musical chairs, but at this eleventh hour of the war, it was whistling in the wind.[13]

Sunday morning, two days after Duncan's return to Camp Lubbock from leave, a courier from Houston headquarters woke him at 8:00 with "an order placing me in [sic] arrest." Taken by surprise and obviously concerned, Duncan hurried to Colonel Spaight's office downtown before guards showed up to clap him in irons. His talk with Spaight was quick and effective. Duncan was issuing clothing to his soldiers the next day when he says he "received orders 57, releasing me from arrest." Duncan immediately "drew up an application to the Colonel asking for a Board of Investigation into my conduct." He was determined to clear his name and the record. The arrest order could have been a case of mistaken identity, but more likely, it was a specious charge cooked up by an enlisted man in the stockade or by an officer who took offense at the way Duncan performed his Officer-of-the-Day duties at Camp Lubbock. Duncan treated the incident as a serious matter and noted the date for both military and personal reasons: "This day twenty-nine years ago my father died. I never fail to think of it, every 3 [sic] of April. . . . General Magruder takes command today, General Walker relieved. Expect to be ordered away soon."[14]

Chapter 19 **Surrender**

VIOLENCE MOVED UP THE CONFEDERATE CHAIN OF command in Houston the next week. Duncan borrowed a horse at Camp Lubbock and rode into town on routine business where he discovered "Colonel Baylor had killed General [John A.] Wharton. Did not do any of the business I went to attend to. Our regiment was ordered to town to [guard] the Quarter[master's warehouse]. Colonel S. got [the order] countermanded. I was greatly gratified. Our regiment and Gillespie's ordered in at 7 1/2 [*sic*] in the morning as escort for the remains of General Wharton."

The Texas Confederacy lost a well-respected officer when Col. George W. Baylor killed General Wharton. Wharton had served as a Breckenridge, Texas, presidential elector and later voted with the majority representing Brazoria County at the state convention on secession. Wharton was also a lawyer and planter of means; the 1860 Brazoria County tax roll showed he owned $167,004 of taxable property, including 135 slaves. When the war began, Wharton was elected captain of Company B, Eighth Texas Cavalry, known as Terry's Texas Rangers. He rose to command the regiment after the deaths of Col. Benjamin F. Terry and Lt. Col. Thomas S. Lubbock. Wharton was wounded at the battle of Shiloh and later earned promotion to brigadier general in Gen. Braxton Bragg's 1862 Kentucky invasion. His leadership at the battle of Chickamauga in the fall of 1863 earned him promotion to the rank of major general. He was transferred in February 1864 to Richard Taylor's Louisiana command and participated in closing actions of the Red River Campaign. Colonel Baylor shot the unarmed Wharton at General Magruder's headquarters in the Fannin Hotel in Houston during "an unpleasant misunderstanding over military matters." Wharton reportedly called Baylor a liar and slapped him in the face, whereupon Baylor pulled his pistol and shot the general to death. Wharton was buried originally in Hempstead, but his body was moved later to the Texas state cemetery in Austin. Three years later in 1868, a court acquitted Baylor of murder charges.[1]

The Wharton killing speaks volumes on conditions at Confederate facilities in Texas early in April 1865. Senior officers pulled guns in offices to settle arguments, proving discipline was precarious even at the highest ranks. Rather than make plans to counter a Federal invasion, commanders discussed possibilities of their men invading supply warehouses. The general order to post guards at Houston-area depots after the shooting confirms deteriorating discipline in the ranks. Soldiers were hungry, their clothes were in rags, and any hope they might have had was long since replaced by despair. Their officers expected them to break down office and warehouse doors any minute and make off with whatever they could carry. They could feel that fear. William Duncan wanted no part of warehouse guard duty. He would much rather march in General Wharton's funeral procession to the train depot. That duty was far less dangerous and much more honorable than drawing a bead on fellow soldiers invading a camp meat locker.

A slow drumbeat began at 4 A.M. in Camp Lubbock outside Houston on April 7, 1865. It did not announce reveille but rather was a signal that the day was set aside to mourn the death of General Wharton. Capt. William Duncan's company was part of two regiments that marched slowly out of Camp Lubbock at 5:30, heading for the "house where the remains of General Wharton was [*sic*] and stayed an hour or two waiting. Finally the order came to forward march and we were then formed in Main Street opposite Mr. Lynch's dwelling, where another delay occurred," explains Duncan. "Finally all was ready and the corpse put into the hearse and the procession started." Duncan reports, "There were a great number of persons of all classes [that] march[ed] [with the] military officers. We marched to the central depot and then back through Main Street to camp, tired down." When the funeral detail arrived back at Camp Lubbock, the men were soaked from a hard rain that began to fall during the funeral procession. The storm continued through the night. Duncan says it turned "Camp Lubbock [into] a mud hole."[2]

Texas soldiers in Houston and Camp Lubbock did not realize the drum they heard that morning reverberated all the way to Virginia. While General Wharton's funeral cortege wound its way through Houston streets to the train station, Union Lt. Gen. Ulysses S. Grant sent Confederate Gen. Robert E. Lee a note saying he hoped the Confederate general understood "the hopelessness of further resistance" and would choose to prevent "any further effusion of blood" by surrendering. Lee considered a last escape, but realized it was futile after his sentries and scouts reported he was almost completely surrounded by the Union army. Lee sent Grant a response Sunday morning saying he was ready. That afternoon, 1,400 miles east of Houston in central Virginia, General Lee, meticulously dressed in full uniform with decorations, and General Grant, scruffy in a faded blue shirt with dirty trousers tucked into mud-splattered boots, sat down at two small, adjacent desks in the parlor of Wilmer and Virginia McLean's house in the central Virginia town of Appomattox Court House. Lee listened respectfully as Grant explained lenient terms President Lincoln had suggested in case of a Confederate surrender. Grant said the Union would parole Lee's entire army and allow them to take their horses or mules home "to put in a crop." Lee responded, "This will have the best possible effect upon the men. It will be very gratifying and will do much toward conciliating our people."

After an hour and a half, the two men signed the surrender document, stood, and shook hands. General Lee bowed to staff officers in Grant's entourage and walked out of the room. He paused just inside the open door to the McLean's porch. A Federal officer who had not been in the parlor with the two generals watched Lee from across the hall. He said later he saw Lee's neck turn red, "a deep crimson flush, that rising from his neck overspread his face and even tinged his broad forehead. . . . Booted and spurred, still vigorous and erect, he stood bareheaded, looking out of the open doorway, sad-faced and weary." Lee walked onto the porch, down the steps, and climbed slowly onto the magnificent gray stallion he called Traveler. Grant followed him onto the porch and removed his hat in respect; the Federal officers present followed his example. Lee raised his hat in response and turned Traveler through the gate onto the road.[3] Grant watched the Confederate general ride slowly out of sight, feeling "sad and depressed" at "the downfall of a foe who had fought so long and valiantly and had suffered so much for a cause, though that cause was, I believe, one of the worst for which a people ever fought."[4]

William Duncan learned of General Lee's surrender twelve days later. It was a cool day made fresher by strong northerly winds. Duncan again served as Officer of the Day, but this time it was at downtown Houston headquarters. "This day completes my three years service as a soldier," says Duncan. "Little did I think, three years ago on this day that I would be in the service at the end of three years. But so it is and God only knows how much longer I will have to stay in the service of my country." That afternoon, a dispatch arrived at the Fannin Hotel announcing, "that Lee and his Army had surrendered to Grant." Duncan says, "I felt more dispondent [sic] than I ever did before since the beginning of the war. Spent the night at the guard house. Slept about an hour. The night was quite cool."[5]

It was Good Friday, seven days before Capt. William Duncan heard about Lee's surrender, when John Wilkes Booth, an actor from Maryland, entered President Lincoln's box at Ford's Theater in Washington, raised a pistol, and fired one shot into the back of Lincoln's head. Lincoln was carried unconscious from the box to a room in the Petersen boardinghouse across the street where he was pronounced dead at 7:22 A.M. the next morning, April 15, 1865. Duncan worked late at Confederate headquarters in Houston the night Lincoln was shot. He slept at the Fannin Hotel downtown rather than return to Camp Lubbock and rose shortly after Lincoln died in Washington, feeling "very badly for want of rest." Duncan walked to the market for a fifty-cent whiskey and coffee, bought newspapers for twenty cents, a gallon of rum for $2.50, and paid fifty cents for fifteen yards of domestic material. He carried his purchases back to the hotel, left them in Colonel Spaight's office, and walked back to Camp Lubbock.[6]

After an uneventful week Duncan attended a large meeting in Houston the next Saturday where several officers spoke. "Many citizens and soldiers present," Duncan says. At that point, only rumors of Lincoln's assassination had made it to Houston. When he returned to camp that night, Duncan "found men good deal out of spirits." He spent the following Sunday at Camp Lubbock. After morning inspection, he sent a letter and bundle home to Celima containing five yards of calico, three-quarters of a yard of linen, one large spool of thread, several pins and needles, and three skeins of silk thread. When he asked a soldier to carry it to Liberty, he heard "news that Lincoln and Seward are assassinated. Colonel S. came out. He and Colonel Gillespie made speeches." Late that afternoon, Duncan received a letter from his eldest daughter Emma, "brought over by the priest." He received official confirmation of Lincoln's death the next day.[7]

General Magruder was certain Lee's surrender and Lincoln's assassination would bring legions of Union soldiers to Texas, so he ordered his troops to relocate as soon as possible to Galveston where he expected the dominant thrust of the invasion. Duncan received his orders on April 27 and reported to headquarters in Houston as Officer of the Day first thing the next morning where he learned "twelve [more] men of Co. H deserted last night." Two days later, after Captain Marsh called the regiment to formation and Duncan inspected his company, he learned seven more men from Company H had deserted the previous night. Duncan sneered to himself, "That company deserves shooting, men and officers." Magruder's Galveston mobilization called for Duncan's company to take the train from Houston to Galveston four days later. As part of his preparations, Duncan made sure the hard work on his Camp Lubbock hut was not wasted. "P. K. Smith came over to my shanty and I made him a present of my shanty and cook house." Colonel Spaight, concerned more than ever that his battalion would evaporate by desertion, attended a dress parade, and Duncan says he "made a few remarks to regiment in regard to the desertion of Co. H." Soldiers loaded artillery, light weapons, and whatever ammunition they had left onto a wagon train that left Camp Lubbock just after noon the next day. The men followed, marching in formation to Houston's train depot where they slept by the tracks that night.[8]

Shortly after dawn the next morning, Duncan carried his stove and four joints of chimney pipe to Houston headquarters where he paid "Handy, Sydner's boy" twenty-five cents to see to its shipment to Liberty with a box of personal belongings. Duncan made it back to the depot in time to board the 9:00 cars for Galveston. He ate dinner on the train with Colonel and Mrs. Spaight and arrived in Galveston around 4 P.M. "Got quarters on the Gulf side," he writes. "Very pleasant place. Ran round great deal. Very tired and half sick. Slept on gallery on pallet."

The next day, Duncan rented a house from a Galveston friend that offered more comfortable accommodations than a bedroll on a porch. Afterward he says he "put on sword and sash and went down in time to see dress parade."[9] While Duncan stood in formal uniform at the parade in Galveston, Gen. Richard Taylor signed a surrender document with Union Maj. Gen. Edward R. S. Canby in Citronelle, Alabama, forty miles north of Mobile. It contained terms almost identical to those Grant gave Lee at Appomattox Court House. Taylor's Department of Alabama, Mississippi, and east Louisiana was the last Confederate army *east* of the Mississippi to surrender.[10]

The next day, six hundred pounds of coffee arrived for the soldiers in Galveston from "the Ladies of Houston." After Duncan gave orders for its distribution, he moved into his newly rented quarters. "I am very pleasantly situated in the second story with galery [*sic*] facing the south," indicating Duncan enjoyed an unobstructed view of the Gulf of Mexico from his porch. He and another officer walked downtown that night for a whiskey and supper that cost $1.75. He "went to preaching" on Sunday, then back into town. "Great many persons, both officers and men, have completely given up all hope," he says. "It provokes me beyond measure." Two officer colleagues, Captain Evans and Lieutenant Douglas, walked home with Duncan the next evening and the three talked late into the night. Duncan says "both of them [are] badly demoralized." When he wrote to Celima the next day, he says he had enjoyed a "nice fish for dinner," then confesses, "I am in the lowest spirits possible at the state of feeling exhibited by the men. They seem determined to give up the cause." He mailed the letter the following morning, harvesting more opinion on his walk to the postbox. "Feeling among the troops no better," he says. "I think Galveston [must be] the most demoralized place in the Confederacy."

There was at least one person in the Confederacy that day more heartsick than William Duncan. Confederate Pres. Jefferson Davis, fleeing toward Texas with two Texans, former Governor Lubbock and former U.S. congressman John H. Reagan, was captured by Union soldiers 175 miles south of Atlanta near Irwinville, Georgia.[11] After surrenders by generals Lee and Taylor and with the C.S.A. president in Union custody, the insignificant Trans-Mississippi Department was the only Confederate region still officially at war.[12]

Unseasonably cool temperatures with strong north winds swept across Galveston's parade ground the next day during a review and inspection by General Magruder. "He spoke," recounts Duncan "and said General Smith had been called on to surrender, but had refused. He [Magruder] begged the troops to be true and all might be well yet. It revived my drooping spirits but seemed to have no effect upon the men." Duncan was Officer of the Day in Galveston the next two days. After visiting several officers on his rounds the first afternoon, Duncan laments, "My hopes all died away again. I believe that all the Patriotic and brave are gone . . . " The next day, accompanied by an enlisted man acting as his bodyguard, Duncan rode to all the Confederate forts and redoubts on Galveston Island. "State of feeling among the troops no better," he says. "I believe the officers more to blame than the men." The following Sunday, William Duncan attended Mass at St. Mary Cathedral, dedicated in 1848 as the cathedral church for the diocese of Galveston that covered the entire state of Texas. Later that day he participated in an afternoon dress parade and heard reports that Confederate troops on Galveston Island would desert en masse that night. The mood on the island was dark and Duncan confesses, "I have the blues."[13]

Weakened by hunger, driven stir-crazy by boredom, and irrational with fear, Confederate soldiers stationed in Galveston spun out of control at the end of May 1865. When William Duncan woke Monday morning, he heard "that about 300 men went as far as the bridge last night and Colonel [Ashbell] Smith[14] met them there and persuaded them to return. I wish they had gone to the devil," Duncan says. The crowd aimed to ransack and escape with whatever supplies it could find on its way home. Duncan was scandalized but did not let the incident obstruct his performance of duty. The Galveston provost marshal ordered him to supervise eighty-four Confederate soldier-prisoners on work details to strengthen Galveston's artillery positions and forts. He and a squad of his men marched the prisoners to a redoubt four miles down the beach where they arrived hot and sweaty. "No water there to drink," he explains. "Very hot. All wanting water. So I marched back and turned over the prisoners." He dropped by Galveston headquarters after dinner and learned "General Kirby Smith had surrendered this department."[15] Once again unconfirmed rumor preceded hard fact in Confederate Texas. It would be seventeen days later, June 2, 1865, that General Smith would sign surrender documents on board a U.S. warship anchored at Galveston. Within days after Smith's surrender, he and Magruder, along with Texas governors Clark and Murrah, fled to Mexico.[16]

Duncan grew increasingly uncomfortable with his assignment to guard imprisoned Confederate soldiers on Galveston Island work details. He knew many were in chains because of trumped-up charges leveled by incompetent officers, and many others had already served inordinately severe sentences and should be freed. Duncan marched his squad back to the guardhouse the following day to take prisoners out to work, but was excused. After he sent his men back to their tents, he lingered at the stockade "to examine papers [of the] prisoners and try to get released all that were entitled to it." He combed through the records into the night, choosing to sleep at the guardhouse. The next morning he received a tip that more trouble was brewing in Galveston. He headed for the headquarters armory where he "drew Enfield and 100 rounds of amunition [*sic*] for myself." With loaded rifle in hand, Duncan stopped in to see Col. Ashbell Smith, the Galveston garrison commander and "got Colonel Smith to examine papers of prisoners. Reported favorable on some [and] told me to bring them up in the morning." Duncan then heard "Spaight's regiment was going off," indicating the rumor du jour had the 21st Infantry deserting en masse. The officers held a meeting that night to consider options. Captain Duncan says he "talked to some of my company. They were all right."[17]

Duncan made progress the next two days on his prisoner release project. "Dugan and me [*sic*] got out thirty-four," he says. "I took fourteen to my company and Dugan took the rest." Another meeting was called for all officers "on account of the determination of the men to go home." Duncan did not attend because he was busy settling the newly freed soldiers into his company's campground. He walked back to Galveston headquarters on Sunday "to help prisoners out [but] could not do anything." Duncan was sitting in Colonel Smith's office that afternoon "when he [Smith] rec'd. [*sic*] telegram to evacuate the Island and send the troops home."[18] The news flashed across the island like a tropical storm, leaving order in tatters and the situation chaotic.[19] The Civil War for these Texans in Galveston was over.

Duncan was as excited as anyone about the war ending and finally being able to go home for good, but he did not intend to abandon those soldiers still in chains. He stayed at headquarters "to attend to business for [the] prisoners, to get some out and get others off to their commands." While he worked, one of his Company F cavalrymen burst into the office and "told me our command were robbing the blockade runner that [came] in last night. I went there." Duncan's description of what he saw at the Galveston dock is depressing. "Never saw such a sight," he says. "Hundreds of crazy men, pulling and hauling and running in every direction with goods of every description. None of my company there. Guards sent to stop them. [They] would [either] join or be over-powered. Our command was ordered off [the island] at once."

After a year of boredom, gunfights, and near riots at Camp Lubbock, in Houston, and on Galveston Island, southeast Texas Confederate army bureaucracy moved quickly to churn out official demobilization and discharge orders for the Galveston-based Confederates. Four companies of Spaight's (original) Battalion with soldiers from Jefferson, Tyler, and Newton counties were told to take the train up to Houston and connect to the eastbound Beaumont train that ran through Liberty. The Liberty County men were ordered to catch a steamboat at the Galveston docks that would take them across the bay and up the Trinity River to West Liberty. "Packed up and hauled to boat in greatest haste," Duncan says. "Started about 2:00 P.M. Never started towards home before since the war began [*sic*] so gloomy and unhappy."

Duncan's steamboat reached Anahuac at the top of Trinity Bay on the northeast coast of Galveston Bay before nightfall and a handful of men disembarked. After the brief stop, the boat made steam northwestward for Wallisville where it docked again, this time for the night. Ever the shopper, Duncan bought a one-dollar pair of pants for Sabine during the voyage. The steamboat left Wallisville at dawn and chugged up the Trinity to Moss Bluff, Colonel Spaight's hometown that had given its name to his original unit. Several men jumped ashore, after which the boat motored up to West Liberty, arriving around 1 P.M. Duncan says he "put all my things in [Charley] Lund's [warehouse] and I started home" on foot. He met his father-in-law, Dr. Gillard, on the way and Gillard loaned Duncan his horse. It is safe to say the forty-seven-year-old Duncan rode the horse home at least in a brisk canter if not a gallop. When he walked into the house, he smiled and "found all well."[20]

The Duncan-Gillard residence on the east bank of the Trinity River south of Liberty will have been one of the few places in Texas in late May 1865 where all was said to be well. The day after Duncan's Civil War ended, General Magruder signed his final order in Houston as commanding officer of the Confederate district of Texas. Addressed to Col. Ashbell Smith and Galveston attorney William Pitt Ballinger, Magruder directed the two "to proceed to New Orleans or such other place as may be necessary to negotiate with the commanding general of the Federal troops at or near that place or with the proper authorities of the United States for the cessation of hostilities between the United States and the District of Texas on the terms and conditions which have been conveyed to you."[21] Smith and Ballinger arrived in New Orleans on May 29 to present their credentials to Union Gen. Edward R. S. Canby, but there would be no negotiations. Canby told his Texas callers he had no authority to discuss surrender terms. In fact, at that moment, another Union general was preparing several hundred troops to leave New Orleans by boat with a course set for Galveston. His orders did not involve negotiations either. On the contrary, his mission was to announce and enforce indisputable Union conditions for the surrender of Confederate Texas.[22]

Chapter 20 Home

DUNCAN WAS UP EARLY THE NEXT MORNING. HE hitched a team to a wagon and headed for West Liberty to pick up his stored baggage. At the ferry dock on the Trinity River he "heard Lund's had been broken [into] and everything taken, mine with the rest." After crossing the Trinity, he drove to Lund's warehouse and "found my trunk and all my boxes broken open—everything gone. Some of my papers [were] scattered over the floor.[1] My clothes all taken and my blankets, pots and miscellaneous tricts [*sic*]. Tryed [*sic*] to find some thing. Just before the cars started in the evening, [I] found a vest, bottle [of] brandy and towel in possession of Marsh's negro. [I] know that Marsh was [an] accessory to the robbery [*sic*]." Duncan does not clarify whether the Marsh to whom he refers is the same Captain Marsh from Sabine Pass who commanded cavalry Company A of Spaight's Battalion, but it is reasonable to assume he was.[2] Marsh would not have forgiven Duncan for stopping his effort to transfer his and Duncan's companies out of Spaight's Battalion to General Taylor's Louisiana forces in 1863.

Recalling his two terms as Liberty County's sheriff, Duncan knew evidence trails go cold almost immediately as thieves quickly liquidate stolen items that could prove their guilt. Duncan was the victim this time and he knew he must find his possessions soon if he was to find them at all, so he spent the next thirty hours searching West Liberty and Liberty for his stolen property. His local search fruitless, Duncan caught the Houston train and arrived there Saturday around 8 P.M. He walked the city's streets that night, looking for his possessions and inquiring whether anyone knew where stolen items might be for sale. "No news," he says. "Houston quiet." Wandering through the market the next day, Duncan was somewhat encouraged when he says he "got some of my stolen things. Haversack, flannel over-shirt and old hat from negro and heard of others." Duncan spent one more night in Houston before giving up and borrowing the fare for the 9 A.M. train back to Liberty "from Palmer's negro." The cars arrived at the Liberty depot around 1 P.M. Duncan grabbed something to eat then "found Sabine in town with my horse" and rode home.[3]

Fear of Union vengeance smothered the South for months after the Civil War. Reliable news was at a premium and Duncan rode into town almost daily to read papers brought by the train. While there, he perked up his ears to the Liberty grapevine, always more prolific than those in most Texas towns because of the steady flow of travelers across the Atascosito Trail. After reading several Northern papers on the second of June, Duncan shook his head, "News from Yankee papers indicate that we have very little to hope for." He was back in Liberty three days later and the news was worse. "Got papers," he says, "news that we are all prisoners of war and have nothing to hope for from Yankee clemency. [They say] we deserve the worse [*sic*] that can be inflicted. We are the meanest and lowest, most degraded people on earth." Weighed down with the gloom of a defeated Confederate survivor, Duncan tried to brighten his day by walking into a shop on the Liberty square to buy his eldest daughter Emma a new dress and bonnet for $5.50.[4]

Federal government reprisals against former Confederate soldiers were not Duncan's only worry. With dissolution of the C.S.A. army and disappearance of its near worthless payroll, hundreds of Texas families fell deeper into poverty. Many formerly law-abiding people became thieves, robbers, and even murderers in their panic to survive. Without formal law enforcement, individuals were left to defend themselves. Duncan stayed home the day after he bought Emma her new dress and "shot off and reloaded my pistol." He realized he might need it at any moment and was making sure the gun was in smooth working order. To make matters worse, southeast Texas was in the middle of a long, dusty drought. The hot sun shriveled the few crops that had been planted and prospects for harvests of even the smallest size were next to nil. Famine and despair were on the march and Duncan did not escape their stress. It exacerbated his internal organ erosion from decades of excessive alcohol consumption, near-fatal food poisoning on Galveston Bay, and a lifetime of poor nourishment on the cattle trail. On top of pain from physical ailments and concern about civil disorder, Duncan worried about money and his prospects for earning any. The unhealthful combination began to exact painful tolls on him in mid-June. He took to his bed for three days, "not able to do anything . . . with pain in the region of kidneys and liver. Took calamel [*sic*], two grains at a time, every two hours, then a dose [of] oil."

His mind would not settle and after two days of self-medication for kidney and liver complaints he climbed onto his horse and rode into town to get the news. On the way home, he stopped by Colonel Pickett's house to see if he knew anything worth knowing. The next afternoon, Celima's uncle Jerome DeBlanc came over, and Duncan says, "he and I took a drink of some gin of a lot that we had and used on our bear hunts in 1859 and 1860." The aged gin probably dulled Duncan's anxiety but undoubtedly made his stomach pain worse.[5] It was with him the next day when Duncan read in the paper that "General Hood and [the] balance of Texas prisoners [were] in Galveston on their way home." The young man who would soon ask for Emma's hand in marriage, Jerome De-Blanc's son Oscar, was one of them. Duncan stayed home that weekend, missing church services and blaming it on the rain. It let up after dinner Sunday so he and daughters Emma and Kate went for an afternoon horseback ride along the Trinity.[6]

The next morning U.S. Maj. Gen. Gordon Granger arrived by boat in Galveston with 1,800 Federal soldiers. Granger was there to assume responsibilities as the Union commander of the Department of Texas. He was appointed to the post by General Philip Sheridan, U.S. commander of the Military Division of the Southwest. In his formal remarks, Granger proclaimed the emancipation of Texas slaves. The event is memorialized in Texas as the annual Juneteenth holiday, on which black citizens celebrate the anniversary of slavery's end and their ancestors' freedom in food, music, song, dance, and church services. General Granger spoke directly to the former slaves, advising them against congregating around towns or military posts, and encouraging them to find work. In fact, Granger told them they should remain in the rooms, huts, and shacks on their former owners' farms and plantations and sign labor agreements with them until they might receive assistance from the U.S. Freedman's Bureau, at that time yet to be established in Texas.[7]

The general also declared void all laws of the Confederate government, directed persons in possession of public property to turn it in to the U.S. Army, and ordered all privately owned cotton delivered to the army for which individuals would be compensated. Acting under the Amnesty Proclamation issued by President Johnson on May 29, 1865, Granger paroled Texas men who served in the Confederate army and ordered them to travel to Houston to swear an oath of allegiance to the United States.[8] The proclamation promised "amnesty and pardon, with restoration of all rights of property, except to slaves," to "all persons who have directly or indirectly, participated in the existing rebellion."[9] Ineligible for the blanket renewal of civil rights were high-ranking ex-Confederates and those owning property valued at more than $20,000.[10] Although Duncan owned more than 4,000 acres of Texas land, its value did not approach $20,000 in 1865. Duncan read Granger's message in the newspaper. "Papers contained Gen. Grangers [sic] orders declaring negroes [sic] free," he says "and ordering every one connected with the army to come forward and be paroled." To preserve order and prepare for the procession of former Confederate soldiers seeking amnesty, the U.S. Army marched into Houston the day after Granger stepped foot in Galveston. Their assignment in the Bayou City would be brief; they would withdraw by November.[11]

The next day was Sunday and Duncan left his two youngest children, Chessie and Julia, at home with Celima, who soon would give birth to another baby. Duncan took older daughters Emma and Kate, along with Mrs. Jerome DeBlanc and several members of her family, to Colonel and Mrs. Spaight's house in Moss Bluff. "When we got to the Colonel's, he and all, except Mrs. S, were ready to go to preaching," Duncan says. "We all went, a mile below the Colonel's. Saw a number of persons, male and female. Returned to [the] Colonel's to dinner [and] stayed till late and came home." While Duncan and his family enjoyed Spaight's hospitality, the U.S. Amnesty Office opened in Houston, calling all Texas Confederates to come forward to swear allegiance to the United States. Although William Duncan was not required to file formal documents seeking pardon, he made plans to head for Houston because he was bubbling with ideas to reinvent his business life.[12]

The first step he realized he had to take to avoid possible commercial restrictions that a bank, customer, or supplier might impose on a former Confederate officer was to apply for amnesty. Without a pardon, it might be difficult to borrow money, enter into contracts, form legally constituted businesses like joint ventures, or even trade assets with certain buyers and sellers, especially with the government itself. Duncan certainly could not vote without a pardon. That is why he and four friends climbed onto the noon train on June 27, arriving in downtown Houston around 3:30. The quartet walked straight to the provost marshal's office and Duncan "took [the] Amnesty oath."[13] Here is what he pledged: "I, William Berry Duncan, do solemnly swear, in presence of Almighty God, that I will henceforth faithfully support, protect, and defend the Constitution of the United States, and the union of the States thereunder; and that I will, in like manner, abide by, and faithfully support all laws and proclamations which have been made during the existing rebellion with reference to the emancipation of slaves. So help me God."[14]

From there Duncan headed to the Houston street market where he bought ten yards of gingham cloth for thirty-five cents a yard, five mouse traps for fifty cents, a padlock for seventy-five cents, three combs, a pair of gloves, and some candy. Then he collected a $20 debt from a Houston man for Colonel Spaight and says he "went to [a] Yankee dress parade. Their drill is perfect." Even though he was a newly sworn U.S. civilian, Duncan still appreciated precision in military drill after spending many hours as a Confederate officer over the last three years trying to get it right himself.[15]

While a welcomed rain sprinkled the parched fields of Liberty County two days later, Duncan gave Sabine $20 and sent him to buy ten yards of linen. Then Duncan dispatched a wagon to haul twenty bushels of corn back from a neighbor's farm. As it rolled through the gate, three local women arrived at the house. Things were bustling at the Duncan-Gillard homestead with everyone's attention centered on Celima; she was about to deliver that new baby. Around bedtime, she complained of contractions whose frequency increased steadily as the night progressed. Duncan says "she called me at 12 and told me [she] was going to be sick. [I] called up [the] negroes and sent for Fanny. She arrived at 2:00 A.M." With Fanny helping Celima, Duncan tried to sleep through the rain as it pelted onto the roof. He got up at 6 A.M. and found Celima's labor progressing satisfactorily but probably not fast enough to suit her. An hour later, she "delivered of a fine boy, weight ten pounds." Celima and William Duncan named their new son, Emery Lee. Fanny helped Celima get organized with the newborn, then left the house after William slipped $6 into her hands. He followed Fanny out the door, climbed onto his horse, and rode into Liberty, allegedly to pick up mail but in reality to announce the birth of his new son. He bought a newspaper with "no news" and returned home to find "wife and boy doing well."[16]

With pardon in hand, healthy infant son in cradle, and wife and daughters in good health, William Duncan began to reestablish himself as a Texas citizen and Liberty County neighbor. The day after celebrating Emma's sixteenth birthday, Duncan heard that "Mrs. Robinson's little girl was dying. I ate dinner and went. Found child still alive. [She] died at sunset." Duncan sat up with Mrs. Robinson nearly all night. He returned home for breakfast and a short nap, then "went to the burying" with Emma and Kate. Another mourner at the funeral told Duncan a mutual friend had "died this morning with [a] hemorage [*sic*] of the stomach."

Life was still fragile in postwar Texas; it was after all still the American western frontier. But frontier circumstances did not prevent General Granger and his staff from establishing a Federal presence. The day after the Robinson's child's funeral, a U.S. officer outlined the first conditions for Reconstruction to Liberty County residents. Duncan says he "went to Liberty to hear the speech. . . . Good many whites and negroes [*sic*] present. [The] speech did not amount to much," Duncan adds. More important to him was arrival the next week of "a company of Federal troops and a Provost Marshal for Liberty." Showing his down-to-earth practicality and commonsense intention to adjust to the new day, Duncan paid a courtesy call that afternoon on U.S. Army Maj. A. H. Mayer, Liberty's newly appointed provost marshal and the de facto Federal law in town.[17] Mayer served also as the Liberty-area agent for the Freedman's Bureau until he resigned in March 1868. Whether an issue involved community order or emancipated slaves, former Liberty County sheriff William Duncan wanted a good relationship with Provost Marshal Mayer from the get-go. There was no telling when Duncan might need Mayer's help or whether he might be able to offer Mayer his own.[18]

William Duncan's prewar drover pals from south-central and southeast Texas began to move herds onto the Atascosito Trail toward New Orleans with increasing frequency in mid-July 1865. Despite the Civil War's disruption,

New Orleans reemerged quickly as a major cattle market, providing gulf coast cattlemen, farmers, and traders access to many customers through its river access and Gulf of Mexico port. Reports arrived at the Duncan house one morning that three droves of south-central Texas cattle were approaching Liberty on the Atascosito Trail. He rode out to meet them and "found three, one of Foster's, very fine, from San Patricio County," 230 miles southwest of Liberty along the coast near Corpus Christi, "one of Lee and Robinson from Colorado County, 250 [cattle]," 115 miles west of Liberty on the Atascosito Trail whose county seat is Columbus, "and one from Sanders from Guadalupe County,"[19] 205 miles west of Liberty whose county seat is Seguin. Another herd arrived from McMullen County, whose county seat is Tilden, seventy-five miles south of San Antonio and three hundred miles west of Liberty. "They are very fine indeed, 400 in number," Duncan said.[20] Two other cattlemen—drovers Roach and Wheaton—arrived during the month with herds from the area around Washington-on-the-Brazos in Washington County, seventy miles northwest of Houston where Texas declared its independence from Mexico in 1836.

Chatting with his old friends again, then watching cowboys move cattle through dust clouds toward Louisiana, reminded Duncan how lucrative the cattle business could be. But the Wheaton herd helped Duncan recall cattle driving's downside—long hours in the saddle herding essentially wild animals occasionally for nothing. Duncan is curt in his report: "Wheaton's drove broke [the] pen last night and all got away."[21] Duncan had paid his dues on the cattle trail and he did not cotton to the idea of doing it again, especially in the even more unpredictable postwar market that was complicated by carpetbaggers,[22] scalawags,[23] rustlers, and other outlaws. His warm bed in Liberty was less risky, much safer, and more appealing than a bedroll on hard ground or in the mud of the coastal plains.

Despite his decision to avoid the cattle trail, Duncan remained a trader at heart, always looking for deals where he could buy low, sell high, and pocket a margin. He tried to buy Jerome DeBlanc's cotton crop for fifteen cents a pound, "as I was satisfied I could sell it in Houston at eighteen cents, thereby make a handsome speculation. But he had sold it a few minutes before I got there at fifteen cents." Duncan could have used the money to settle his account at the convent school that had reopened in Liberty. Kate had joined Emma in its classroom and Duncan owed tuition to the nuns even though the Mother Superior was into him for a few cows and some corn. "Her account [her bill to Duncan totaled] $108.75, my account [owed Duncan by] her [was] $44.35, leaving me in her debt $63.90." Duncan paid the good sister and afterward went shopping and bought eight yards of calico for $3.60, soap for twenty-five cents, newspapers for another quarter, and candy for ten cents, then rode home for dinner.

At the end of the week, Duncan renewed his contract with Sabine. It is the first of several mentions in Duncan's diary of contracts he made with former slaves. Freedmen saw Duncan as a desirable employer and Duncan hired several. Like many slaves and masters across the South, Sabine and Duncan had a close relationship. Sabine had been a member of Duncan's extended family since he arrived in Liberty as an infant with the Gillards shortly after his birth in 1845 and remained at Duncan's side throughout much of the war. Duncan's quick execution of contracts with Sabine and other former slaves indicate he probably would have been one of many Southern slave owners who would have accepted President's Lincoln's contemplated late-war offer to buy Southern slaves and then immediately hire them back as employees.[24]

As Duncan eased his way back into civilian life, he hit occasional snags. He went riding with Emma and Kate, fixed the water well, made a swing for the children, mended a harness, and attended a "negro wedding at night" in late August. But the last day of the month was a bitter one. "Today I lost my favorite bear dog," he writes. "Died of distemper. I regret the loss very much. Makes me quite sad." He tried to put memories of his hunting dog out of mind the next day when he took all the children to a fish fry at Turkey Creek. There "were few fish but plenty to eat." Four days later, a large herd of more than five hundred cattle arrived outside Liberty. Duncan talked to its drover about the cattle market and the possibility of doing a deal. Although he might have considered a joint financial investment, he was not interested in saddling up for a drive.

Liver and kidney disease had plenty to do with his decision. For the rest of September, he suffered "great pain . . . from my head to my knees . . . between my shoulders, all down my back." Dr. Breshear arrived around 9 A.M. to examine Duncan after a particularly difficult night. The doctor prescribed two-every-four-hour pills and all-day poultices for high fever and severe pain. "Thought I would pass a good night," Duncan says, "but instead, I suffered all night. Did not get two hours' sleep" as rain fell outside his window. The fever finally broke a week later, permitting him to feel just "tolerable." He climbed onto his horse, rode into Liberty, and learned that "Colin Lacour and Minter had shot at each other two or three times yesterday evening." Duncan gives no injury report. Taking a dangerous step back onto a slippery slope, he pulled a chair up on the last Friday night in September to his first card game in Liberty since the war ended and promptly lost $63. He returned to the table the next night and recouped $19. Unfazed by the $44 net loss, he enjoyed a day at home on Sunday. "This has been a beautiful day, a real fall day, cool and clear."[25]

After Duncan attended church services two weeks later, he rode over to visit Ed White, his fellow former Liberty County sheriff, for Sunday dinner. When he walked through White's front door, he found Celima in the parlor with the baby. Celima might have skipped Mass that Sunday to care for Emery Lee or she and her husband could have decided to attend different church services. Duncan and his parents were baptized Catholics in 1831 to meet the Mexican government's requirement that anyone to whom they gave a land grant must be a Catholic, but Duncan frequently alternated attendance at Catholic Mass with participation in Protestant services. After the war, Celima and the children continued to practice Catholicism while Duncan often joined services at local Protestant churches. William Duncan was not a zealot, not to Catholicism, not to Protestantism, not even to the Confederacy. However, he was a community-minded person. Spreading his church attendance between Catholics and Protestants offered him fellowship and opportunities to help needy people in the county. With other public-spirited citizens in town, he regularly helped handle arrangements and attended funerals regardless of denomination for destitute former soldiers, widows, and orphans after the war.[26]

Chapter 21 Struggle

DESPITE MISSING SUNDAY MASS OCCASIONALLY TO attend Protestant services, Duncan continued to supply food to the Ursuline convent in Liberty after the war, sending eighty-nine pounds of beef to the Mother Superior in October. On the first Sunday in November, he drove Celima, Emma, Kate, and baby Emery to Liberty's Catholic church where Emery was baptized. Duncan tipped the priest a dollar. He treated Sabine-the-freedman with the same thoughtfulness he showed to Sabine-the-slave, buying him a pair of shoes one Sunday and paying him $2.50 in gold two days later. Duncan financed his expenses at this time by redeeming investments made before the war and gambling. He rode into Liberty one Friday and exchanged a $30 Louisiana bank note into $20 worth of gold coin, then sat in on a card game and won $99.[1]

Duncan's return to marathon poker games in Liberty's saloons frightened Celima. When he arrived home at dawn after one particularly long night of shots and straights, he found her roaming the house angrily. "She told me it was time for us to get to some other place." Her reasons will have ranged from fear at being left alone with the children in their house south of town at a time of increased postwar lawlessness, to anxiety that Duncan was losing too much money, to concern her husband was becoming a drunk. She may also have felt isolated in the Reconstruction-era economic crisis that saw the demise of Creoles as a wealthy, landowning class. After the war, the racial connotation of Creole became predominant over its ethnic heritage. For most light-skinned Creoles like the Gillards and their niece, Celima LeBlanc Duncan, Creole had come to mean Caucasian purity, while for blacks it meant miscegenation. Delusional Creoles of all skin tones often denied their ancestors' sexual relations but warmly claimed their cultural identity, pointing to their shared French language. It is possible Celima, more light-skinned than dark, felt isolated by racist treatment from some of her Anglo-Protestant neighbors in Liberty County. Describing the Creole social position in the twentieth century, a Creole woman said, "Whites think we're black and blacks think we're stuck up."[2] Whatever her motivation, Celima Duncan was exceedingly unhappy with her husband and frightened by her situation on the Gillard plantation in October 1865.[3]

Mired in conflict between his bad habits and Celima's plea, Duncan sank further into the snares of gambling and alcohol. After his wife's scolding that morning, he took an hour's nap, then rode back to Liberty and bought ten yards of calico, five-and-a-half yards of flannel, ten pounds of coffee, two pounds of crackers, and six yards of "domestic" cloth to use as diapers. Perhaps thinking his purchases might atone for his destructive behavior, Duncan nevertheless yielded again to intemperance on his way out of town. He found another card game, sat down, played all night, and lost $115. Celima was mad as a hornet when she found out, but her anger dissolved into panic three days later. William dealt himself into yet *another* card game in Liberty, this one organized by Simeon DeBlanc, Celima's brother. Duncan admits they "played all day and half the night. Lost $214." The next morning, he paid for it with more than cash. "I was awoke before day with most excutiating [*sic*] pain [in] the region of kidney," says Duncan. "Called up Celima and she [summoned] the negroes [*sic*]. They made fire and prepared bath. And [a] great many remedies. Was not able to go to town today. Took medicine and remained quiet all day."[4]

Celima's sense of doom darkened when her husband, in considerable pain, struggled out of bed the next day and rode to her Uncle Jerome's house and borrowed $100. Climbing awkwardly back onto his horse, Duncan headed into Liberty to pay debts from the card games. While making his rounds, Duncan did a questionable deal with a New Orleans–bound man. In exchange for a $10 gold piece, Duncan gave the fellow two Louisiana bank notes, one of $43 and another of $5, surrendering eighty cents of each dollar of face value. Louisiana's Bank Act of 1842 was the first law passed in the United States requiring banks to keep a gold or silver reserve against notes and deposits,[5] and the two notes Duncan exchanged would have been worth much more than twenty cents on the dollar. Duncan's trade on the Liberty town square that day illustrates the weakness of the postwar economy, the sad state of his personal finances, and exceptionally poor judgment on his part. The once-prosperous Texas cattle drover was stretching himself thin with gambling losses made more dangerous by the poor Texas economy. With no steady income, he was liquidating valuable financial assets at a loss. Duncan's lengthening string of bad luck reveals he abandoned table-stakes discipline at the card table and washed down his poor judgment with too much whiskey. His behavior put his family and himself in harm's way. Like many ex-Confederate soldiers across the South, Duncan's civilian reconstruction was not going well.[6]

Not to excuse his conduct but rather attempt to understand it, Duncan's business as a Texas cattleman and farmer involved gambling by definition.

Rustlers, stampedes, bad weather, and weak markets could cause large losses in the blink of an eye. Poker and drinking cemented his status as one of the boys. Poker is traditionally considered a "man's game" where learning to play cards is identified with adulthood and part of growing up. Taking a chance—a gamble—is an escape from routine and thus intrinsically pleasurable.[7] William Duncan's gambling, drinking, and borrowing to cover losses amid Celima's pleas to reform in October 1865 suggest the former Confederate officer had slipped into posttraumatic stress disorder (PTSD). Unnamed in the nineteenth century, the condition is frequently signaled by compulsive gambling and substance abuse. Like all persons with addictive tendencies, former soldiers suffering PTSD often deny it while they struggle to complete transitions back to civilian life. If Duncan suffered from the Civil War version of PTSD, it could have stemmed from guilt that he *did not see* violent action in the war. Contemporary clinicians who treat posttraumatic stress disorder call this the survivor theory, explained by patterns of denial, repression, and emotional avoidance after a traumatic event. In Duncan's case, it is possible his decadent postwar behavior stemmed from guilt over being a Confederate survivor.[8]

Gambling losses, hangovers, more frequent, longer-lasting bouts of pain, and deterioration of the relationship between him and his wife seem to have coalesced, albeit gradually, into a wake-up call for William Duncan. He realized he needed to clean up his act and get back to making honest money. When he rode out to meet two more herds arriving in the Liberty area from the west, one of the drovers mentioned he needed a new horse. Spotting an immediate opportunity to monetize an asset, Duncan invited the man to his farm where he sold him a horse for $60 in Federal greenbacks.[9]

The quickest way for a Reconstruction-era Liberty County, Texas, householder to put food on the table was by hunting, so Duncan drafted a former slave to accompany him to a bayou near his house to hunt wild cows—Duncan describes the outing simply "to hunt beef." The pair did not bag any game on their first hunt in November but two days later, Duncan's luck improved and he "killed a beef and three ducks." There are always chores to be done on a farm and Duncan turned his attention to them as well. He put Sabine and another former slave named Swain to work cutting hay, for which he paid Swain $2.50 and Sabine fifty cents. A few days later, he paid a friend $2 for one hundred bundles of fodder for his horses and sent Sabine with a wagon to haul the hay back to the plantation. When Sabine returned with the hay and finished stacking it in the barn, Duncan slipped him another fifty cents.

Ten days later, he put together his first joint-venture business deal since the war ended. His talkative friend James Wrigley engaged him to "go up country" to buy cotton. Investor Wrigley gave trader Duncan $1,500 in cash and Duncan prepared to ride north into the area around Livingston to make the purchases. Their plan appeared simple at first glance: offer less valuable paper money to strapped, small inland farmers for their cotton, then haul it down to Galveston and sell it for gold. Its twofold profit proposition was more complex; they aimed to make money on the purchase-sale margin *and* on the currency spread. Before leaving on his buying trip, Duncan stopped by Ed White's house and "got him to promise to count the rails I have the negroes [*sic*] splitting." Trading cotton, cutting hay, buying fodder, building and repairing fences, all point to Duncan's decisions to rebuild his life in farming and ranching, reduce participation in lubricated card games, and leave healthier, younger men to make money driving cattle to Louisiana on the Atascosito Trail.[10]

Duncan spent the first two weeks of December 1865 sixty miles north of Liberty in Trinity and Polk counties, searching for cotton. It was cold, dark and rainy and cotton pickings were slim. One farmer had eight bales of cotton for sale and wanted twenty-five cents a bale; Duncan said no. Another offered eight bales, also at twenty-five cents. Duncan offered him half that—eight bales for a dollar, or twelve-and-half-cents each—and the farmer took his counter. Another man tendered six bales, but Duncan turned them down because the cotton was not ginned. Another farmer had six or eight bales—he did not know which—but told Duncan he planned to keep it until spring. Another said he had five bales in the barn but aimed to take it to Galveston himself. By that time, Duncan knew his cotton scheme was doomed. The harvest had been paltry, those inland farmers were more financially sophisticated than Duncan and Wrigley expected, and in the end it would take months just to find, let alone buy, $1,500 worth. He turned his horse south and rode home over freezing mud and ice along the Trinity. When he caught up with Wrigley five days later, Duncan "returned him his money, after deducting my wages and expenses—$113.60—paying him $1,386.40."[11]

Most of his former slaves along with several freedmen from other Liberty County plantations approached Duncan for work after the war. The applicants were usually unskilled farm workers. Occasionally, a craftsman, most often a carpenter, presented himself for employment. Duncan says he "was bothered a good deal with negroes wanting to make bargains to stay with me." Louis, one of Duncan's former slaves, decided to test the job market by applying for employment to Duncan's friend, Pryor Bryan. Louis returned from Bryan's without a job, so Duncan came up with a plan to offer him one. He worked out a deal with his father-in-law, Edward Gillard, for Duncan to lease a portion of Gillard's fields, then drafted a sharecropping agreement with Louis, his two sons, Reuben and Texas, and another freedman, Benjamin Moseley. Duncan explains, "I furnished tea, tools and feed and provisions for himself, Reuben and Texas and give him one third of all the crop."[12]

The agreement stipulated the freedmen would "conduct themselves faithfully, honestly, civilly and diligently to perform all labor on said plantation that may be required by said Duncan or his agent, proper and necessary in order to produce a crop of cotton, corn and potatoes and preparing the same for market." The contract provided for lost labor penalties, including fifty cents a day if the worker refused or neglected his daily assignment, $2 a day if he was absent without leave, and dismissal and forfeiture of his share of the crop if absent more than one day without prior clearance. The freedmen agreed to "take good care of all utensils, tools and implements" and to be "gentle to all work animals under their charge." Duncan promised "to treat his hirelings with justice and kindness, to furnish them and their families with quarters on his plantation and land for gardens and the privilege of cutting fire wood from some portion of the premises." He also agreed to provide rations to the freedmen free of charge and "to furnish the usual meat and bread rations to the families of said freemen to be accounted for at the market price out of their shares of the crop." The fact Duncan agreed to furnish provisions for Louis and his group of freedmen suggests Duncan felt something more than a fiduciary responsibility to help them succeed. The deal with Louis was one of several new investments Duncan made in his return to the civilian business world after the war.[13]

Duncan's work pace quickened over the next three weeks. He bought a yoke of oxen on a year's credit for $25.50 in U.S. greenbacks and paid a former slave youth to drive them home for fifty cents. Three days later, he bought three used plows for $6, again on credit. He spent several hours helping former slaves, now his employees, build a cabin, then took a Sunday break to attend church with Colonel Spaight and "after church went home with [widow] Mrs. Lt. Duncan" for dinner. Back to work the next day, Duncan purchased thirty-three bushels of corn from a neighboring farmer and six bushels of potatoes for fifty cents from another, aiming to plant them as seed for his first crops. He delivered three used plows to the blacksmith's shop in Liberty for repair, paid $140 and $120 for two mules, $6 for another plow, and spent all day Saturday building a fence. He skipped church on Sunday to buy a two-horse plow for $15, paying the seller in Liberty the next day when he was in town for his lodge meeting. Aside from welcoming a new son to his family, swearing renewed allegiance to the United States, and wandering unproductively north of Liberty for two weeks on a fruitless cotton-buying venture, Duncan had essentially squandered the last seven months of 1865 in a haze of gambling and alcohol. His wife's frightened intervention made him realize the mess he was making of his life. At the end of the year he started to mend his ways, but good intentions do not always add up to a virtuous rebirth. Before the lodge meeting that night in Liberty, he bought himself a gallon of whiskey for $3.[14]

Duncan rode into town on the first of February with freedmen Louis, Reuben, Texas, and Ben "to enter into written contract with them" that a local lawyer helped him draft. After the signing, Duncan ate dinner with the attorney and bought a horse from him for $75. He did not indicate whether he paid cash or bought the horse on credit, but Duncan was using credit extensively to finance his new farming ventures. His friend, W. J. Swilley, the man who sold Duncan a horse during the war, then took it back and helped him find another before Duncan's posting to Louisiana, provided Duncan seed corn, potatoes, and selected equipment in exchange for a promissory note for $352.40 due in four months. No chore was too small for Duncan, proving he was making progress in his personal reinvention. He spent an entire Saturday planting Irish potatoes in a new garden near the house. Sabine and other employees joined Duncan in cultivation of what he called "the patch," and it soon yielded food not only for his family but also for his new freedmen employees, plus enough surplus to fill regular wagon loads to sell at Liberty's weekly farmer's market in the town square. Duncan expanded his crop slate over the next few weeks, adding oats, sugar cane, black-eyed peas, butterbeans, black beans, sweet peas, tomatoes, and watermelons to his original corn and potato plantings.[15]

Duncan's busy workload, undoubtedly made lighter with occasional nips of whiskey out of Celima's sight, caught up with him in mid-February 1866. After settling a bill for horse collars with a man in Liberty, Duncan dropped by the convent to visit daughter Chessie. "I am unwell today, with kidney infection," he says. His kidney discomfort was compounded when the [Mother] "Superior talked an hour." A pattern of pain unfolded the next week that would repeat itself with growing intensity over the next eighteen months. The day after his convent visit, Duncan reports he was "quite unwell with pain in kidney and bladder." Gritting his teeth, he worked all day cleaning, salting, and hanging beef from a slaughtered cow in the family meat locker, "suffering all the while." In the afternoon, he rode to his leased land on the Gillard plantation to settle a dispute with his and Dr. Gillard's freedmen over its boundaries. The ride and his role as mediator took their toll; Duncan was "unwell with pain at night." The next day about noon, he says he "got so bad off that I was obliged to quit work. Took laudanum and other things. Applied hot poultices and everything that could be thought of. Bath also. Nothing gave any relief."[16]

He felt somewhat better the next day as northern gale-force winds blew over Liberty County. The winter temperatures arrived in time for Duncan to escort daughter Emma to Amanda Day's wedding at her house outside West Liberty. They took the train across the Trinity with a festive crowd. "From West Liberty, some rode in ox carts, some in hacks and some walked. I was one of the latter." There was plenty to eat and drink at the wedding and Duncan partied all night. As he walked with several others to the West Liberty depot the next morning, he realized he had forgotten his pistol. Returning to the wedding site, he found his weapon and hurried to the depot in time for the train back across the river. When it pulled into Liberty, one of Duncan's men was there with a carriage to take Emma to her Uncle Simeon's place in town while Duncan rode home with a friend. Standing water from overnight rains made him late the next morning to a funeral of a widow whom Duncan's lodge was burying because she died alone and indigent.[17]

From sickbed to wedding to widow's funeral, Duncan returned to his heavy schedule on the farm. He paid $4.75 for a tree iron and pair of trace chains to speed his entry into the lumber business. He planned to cut Trinity River basin timber into fence posts, railroad ties, and building materials for the local and Houston markets. Many days he worked inside the barn, making or repairing plows, horse collars, bridles, wagon tongues, wheel rims known as "felloes," an occasional pair of shoes, and a toy wagon for the children. Duncan's forty-eighth birthday fell on a Friday, and he says "the children made a nice cake in honor of the event." Three days later, Jerome DeBlanc's son, Oscar, the Confederate veteran from John Bell Hood's command, called on Emma and mentioned to Duncan that, "Jerome was going bear hunting tomorrow and wanted me to go. I had to decline." Duncan had not lost passion for hunting, but perhaps he had lost his taste for bear. He could be found in the swamp many afternoons, looking to get a shot at a wild turkey whose meat was tastier and its bite less sharp.[18]

Duncan's postwar heartbeat was adjusting to a more civilian rhythm, but Reconstruction issues were never far from his mind. One Saturday night in late March 1866, he rode into Liberty to attend a meeting where Colonel Spaight was the featured speaker. Spaight was elected by Liberty voters on January 8 as their delegate to a convention ordered held in all Confederate states by Pres. Andrew Johnson.[19] The Texas convention convened in Austin on February 7 and declared the state's act of secession null and void, accepted slavery's abolition, repudiated the state's war debt, and granted freedmen basic rights.[20] The most contentious issue at the convention involved the former slaves. Delegates lined up in three camps. One supported laws to protect basic civil rights for freedmen. The other two opposed granting any rights to blacks beyond emancipation and in fact favored new laws to restrict rights of black Americans. Such laws became known across the South after the war as black codes. Led by conservative Unionist James W. Throckmorton, the convention drafted a constitution to submit to Texas citizens that gave freedmen the right to purchase and sell property, to sue and be sued, to enter legally binding contracts, and to testify in court cases involving other blacks. But it deprived blacks of the vote, access to public office and public schools, and denied them the right to jury participation. The convention set June 25 for a statewide vote to ratify the draft constitution and elect new state representatives. Spaight's speech that night in Liberty was probably a briefing to county citizens on what transpired at the Austin meeting and a presentation of the draft constitution.[21]

After the meeting, Duncan says, "Jelks was shot and killed by Gibson about 11 at night." Raw nerves and irrational fear filled Texas in 1866, and denial of the franchise to freedmen was seen by some as an effort to reestablish an antebellum political paradigm in the state. The gunfight after Spaight's presentation could have been between two men on different sides of the freedmen's rights debate. One would rather be damned than support a former slave's right to vote, the other, a Texan who saw no harm in it. False bravado probably emboldened by whiskey caused the argument to spill into the street. Guns were drawn, shots fired, and one man lay dead in the dirt in a fight over black Texans' civil rights. Beyond question are two facts: state voters approved the new constitution in June and reconstruction-era Texas remained a frontier land where bullets frequently settled arguments.[22]

Celima woke the heavy-sleeping Duncan late on a Friday night two weeks later to warn him a wild storm was battering the roof. When he got up the next morning, he found deep drifts of hailstones around the house and devastation in the garden. "Corn, Irish potatoes and everything also was cut to pieces. I never saw such distruction [*sic*] by hail," says Duncan. He rode over his land that afternoon and "found heaps of hail still unmelted" and much of his corn, cotton, and potato crops destroyed. He organized his workers, oxen, and horses two days later to move into the fields with plows to open ditches so the standing water could escape. Then Duncan began the disheartening, tedious, and costly process of plowing under the battered crops.

While his employees replanted the fields, Duncan restocked the family's meat locker. Range cattle continued to run wild across the coastal plains and free steaks were on offer to the best shot. Duncan took one of his new employees with him onto the prairie to hunt wild steers, but found only a "fresh beef head with ears cut off." Another hunter had beaten him to that prize. Two days later, they returned to the plains outside Liberty and bagged a deer as well as a branded west Texas cow that had obviously escaped from a passing herd. Duncan skinned and dressed the meat the next day, sending a 125-pound quarter to his friend Pryor Bryan and two quarters weighing 208 pounds to in-laws Gillard.[23]

Two days later, Duncan welcomed a financial windfall delivered by William Dugat, his sister Sidney Duncan Dugat's brother-in-law. Dugat handed Duncan $592 from the sale of nineteen cattle from his Refugio County herd. They must have been well-fed cows sold into a strong south-central Texas market to fetch $31.15 per head, a value that reminded Duncan of prewar New Orleans prices. He rode west the following Sunday afternoon to meet another herd approaching Liberty from Nueces County, describing the six-hundred-head drove as "first rate." Looking over the grazing cows headed for New Orleans and thinking of the dwindling pile of cash in his home safe, Duncan was tempted once again to return to the trail. But he knew cattle driving was a former life and for him, there was no going back. He had loans coming due and work to be done on the farm, so he turned his horse around and headed home, stopping briefly for a chat at Pryor Bryan's house.

He was back at Pryor's place a week later, getting organized he says "to kill a beef in the morning." After coffee, the two friends rode onto the prairie, killed a wild cow, and by 10 A.M. had hauled it back to the house. They agreed each man would take half the meat. While they dressed the carcass, "Old Jim Williams came out with [a] note from [the Mother] Superior dunning me for the balance of her account for tuition and board. I sent to her by Jim, $39.60 so I am out of her debt, once more." Duncan was grateful to the Ursuline nuns for educating his daughters but had learned to pay them what he owed when they asked to avoid another speech by the Mother Superior in the convent parlor.[24]

Duncan declared a holiday two days later, giving his freedmen the day off so everyone could go mayhaw hunting.[25] The mayhaw is a small, applelike fruit of small trees of the Hawthorn family that flourish in wet, swampy floodplain soils along creeks and rivers in the South. The mayhaws ripen during late April and early May in east and southeast Texas and harvesters often use boats as tools for collection in the bayous. Mayhaws make delicious jams and jellies and some folks press them into wine. Collecting mayhaws was a celebrated annual cultural event along the Trinity River, enjoyed by many people including William Duncan and his freedmen employees in Reconstruction-era Liberty County.[26]

After Duncan joined Ashley Spaight's unit and swore allegiance to the Confederate States of America in 1862, he never reneged on his vow to serve, even though he felt doubt and regret on many occasions. After giving his word to Louis and other former slaves he hired that he would provide food and other provisions to them as part of their sharecropping agreement, Duncan aimed to keep that pledge too. A week after the mayhaw hunt, he took Texas with him on a hunting trip with Pryor Bryan. Duncan and Bryan were on horseback while Texas drove a wagon across the prairie when they shot a wild cow. They loaded it into the wagon and hauled it back to Pryor's barn. The meat dressed out to 140 pounds per quarter and they agreed to split it. Pryor kept two quarters and Duncan says he "divided mine among negroes."[27]

Duncan took his family, including Celima and baby Emery, into Liberty on regular Saturday outings. On one such morning, he handed Celima and Emma $10 each with which to shop and had portrait photographs taken of everyone but the two youngest children. "Julie and the baby would not sit," he shrugged. While the family enjoyed its day in town, Duncan watched the sky. Farmers owe their livelihoods to Mother Nature who is known to wreck harvests occasionally. It began to rain and blow Sunday evening just as dark fell over Liberty County, and Duncan was concerned. "It was hardly dry enough to work before this," he thought. His anxiety was well founded. So much rain poured onto Liberty County overnight that every spot on the farm was under water the next morning. Duncan's crop forecast after the deluge was dire, reporting, "Looking like [more] rain. Don't know what I shall do if it continues to rain. Prospects of crop declined about twenty-five pr. ct. [*sic*]."[28]

The more it rained, the more his debt obligations preyed on Duncan's mind. Should he pay them in full, pay them in part, pay them in gold, greenbacks, or barter, or refinance? He decided to repay Jerome DeBlanc in gold for the $160 Duncan borrowed several months earlier. Then his friend Swilley dropped by "to ask me to pay him before the note was due." Duncan wondered whether he might find an answer for his debt management dilemma from his sister Sidney's husband, Joseph Dugat. He climbed on his horse and rode to the Trinity River ferry, paid fifty cents to cross, then continued in heavy rain to the Dugat place near West Liberty. He arrived soaking wet just before dark but was glad he made the trip. Joseph agreed to loan him $200.

The next morning, Duncan let water drain off the trail before heading home around 11:00. Once again, he forgot his pistol and rode back to the Dugat house to fetch it. When he got to the river, the ferry was on the other side, so he talked a man with a small boat into rowing him across and paid a boy ten cents to swim his horse to the other side. He rode into Liberty and learned a surprise party was planned that night at Bryan's place. He trotted home, ate a bite of supper, and took daughter Kate with him to the party. "Had [a] nice dance till 1 1/2 o'clck. A.M. [and] came home." Even though Duncan was not in the best of health and had plenty on his mind, he was not inclined to miss a night of music and dancing at his friend's house.[29]

Chapter 22 Progress

DUNCAN AND PRYOR BRYAN WERE HUNTING THE next afternoon when his friend gave Duncan an earful of disturbing information. "While we were out," Duncan explains, "Bryan told me that Buckfield told him that Henry Barrow intended to shoot me when I least expected it. Very unexpected news to me."[1] Henry Barrow was a Liberty native who farmed in Jefferson County when he joined Duncan's unit in 1864. His brother, John, a rancher from Refugio County, had earlier transferred into Duncan's command from Company K of the 21st Texas cavalry.[2] They were two of the men arrested in February 1865 at Camp Lubbock and later court-martialed for mutiny. Henry Barrow apparently nursed a vendetta against Duncan for what Barrow thought was unfair treatment or allegedly false testimony by Duncan. Bryan's warning to Duncan was evidence of how military grudges could fester among civilians in post–Civil War Texas. Duncan does not tell of an attempt on his life, so the threat might only have been testosterone talk. Yet it obviously concerned him.

In an effort to reestablish a relationship with Henry Barrow, Duncan drafted an agreement between the Barrow brothers and himself whereby Duncan offered to hire them to look after his cattle in Refugio County. Duncan took the agreement into Liberty on July 23, two months after Pryor Bryan warned him that Henry was gunning for him. Duncan reports he "saw Ben [Barrow] and gave him the papers, but H. V. slipped through without my seeing him. Followed [him] to the river and gave it up." Duncan wrote the Barrows on August 13, intending to ask his sister's father-in-law, William Dugat, to carry the letter to them in Refugio County, but Duncan never sent the letter.[3] Instead he had a cordial business discussion with Ben Barrow and made a deal with him to look after some of his cattle out west. In January 1867, Ben wrote to Duncan with a report on how things were going. "You never seen snow treat cattle so bad in all your life as it did in this county," said Ben. "Of all the shivering of horses and cattle the like was never seen in this county. No grass to be seen, beeves is in very bad shape. We want a little rain in this county, the beeves ain't so very fine. Will send you a list of your calves branded in 1866. So I told you of all the news worth any importance, Duncan."[4]

Duncan will have agreed with Benjamin Franklin that "in this world nothing is certain but death and taxes" when he "started to Liberty to see about paying National Tax," but met a man on the way who told him "he [had] gotten Baldwin to attend to it." Duncan obviously owed Baldwin some money. Duncan continued on to Liberty where he paid another man $24 in Federal greenbacks to pay his state and county taxes, proving the former Liberty County sheriff and tax assessor paid taxes as responsibly as he settled gambling debts. Duncan's friend W. J. Swilley asked him in mid-May to repay another loan before its due date and Duncan spotted a chance to save some money. He owed Swilley $352.50, so he offered him $300 in gold to settle. Swilley took the deal.[5]

Pleased to be able to clear one of his larger debts at a discount, Duncan redoubled his efforts on the farm, hoeing in the garden patch as well as occasionally plowing in the large cotton fields while his freedmen worked alongside. The more he worked, the more he complained of severe pain in his back and stomach. The pain came and went, granting him enough relief some days to permit him to work or hunt, but on other days, driving him to bed. His pain was tolerable enough at the end of June to permit him to take Emma to Pryor Bryan's son's wedding. At the ceremony, Duncan heard his former colleague from infantry Company E of Spaight's Battalion, Captain O'Brien from Beaumont, had died. It was another example of false frontier gossip; George O'Brien lived until 1909. Nevertheless, the news did not stop Duncan from dancing with the wedding party until dawn.[6]

Eldest daughter Emma's seventeenth birthday fell on a Tuesday in 1866. She invited several girlfriends to the house for a sleepover. Their all-night chatting, dancing, and watching the sun rise took a toll on Emma. Duncan reports she had a "hard chill and high fever" when her friends left the next day. They were the first symptoms of what would be Emma's ten-day battle with high fever that frightened Duncan. He took charge of her care, keeping careful track of changes in her condition as the hours passed. He demanded not one but two doctors make daily house calls and insisted one of them spend the night on four consecutive days. Duncan was clearly worried when he writes, "Emma suffered greatly all night and was very sick this morning. I thought the symptoms very bad indeed. [I] let [Dr. James P.] Cooke have my horse to go to Liberty, as he had to go. I begged him to get [Dr. C. D.] Breshear to come out. I wrote by him to Breshear to come without fail."

The same day that Duncan recorded these thoughts, four ladies from Liberty along with the entire Jerome DeBlanc family came to the house to help care for Emma. It was the first night the exhausted Duncan had slept since Emma became ill. But he did not rest well. "I was awoke [*sic*] at light by Mrs. Gillard who was frightened out of her senses, saying Emma was very bad off and wanted the priest," says Duncan. "I was astounded as [I] was not expecting [her] to get so bad in so short a time. Hurried to her and was satisfied it [was] a false alarm, told them so and told Emma there [was] nothing the matter with her. It was hard to convince her. But she finally, and a dozen fools who were around her, became convinced she was not dying." Duncan grew short-tempered with Emma when he felt she was getting better but showing signs of hypochondria, milking her symptoms for sympathy. Nonetheless he watched over her all day as Dr. Cooke confirmed Duncan's suspicions that evening that Emma was on the mend. "She was doing very well at night," says Duncan, "and I went to bed."[7]

As Emma's strength continued to build, Duncan went back to farming, hunting, and searching for investments, but nothing came easily. Duncan had begun to sell rough-cut timber that he and his freedmen harvested to sawmill owner and Duncan's erstwhile cotton co-venturer, Jim Wrigley. It may have been during one of their tree-cutting sessions that Duncan reports he "cut my hand badly." It would not be long before the gravity of his injury became clear. For the time being, he wrapped the hand in rags and went back to work. His first cotton crop began to mature in early August and Duncan hired additional workers for the harvest. He personally made several sacks and one of his hired hands filled one with forty-two pounds of cotton the first day in the field.[8]

While his employees picked cotton, Duncan took the train into Houston, met Jim Wrigley at the depot, and the two men drove to Wrigley's Harrisburg lumberyard in eastern Harris County. Harrisburg was a port town established in 1825 on Buffalo Bayou east of today's downtown Houston. It enjoyed continuous growth until Mexican General Santa Anna burned it to the ground on April 16, 1836, five days before Gen. Sam Houston and his Texas soldiers defeated that same 1,500-man Mexican army a few miles north at the Battle of San Jacinto.[9] As the Republic of Texas prospered in its early days, the Harrisburg port community was rebuilt into the first railroad terminal in the region, complete with switching yards and workshops. In addition to Jim Wrigley's lumberyard, it was the home of a steam saw- and gristmill, three hotels, and several shops.[10] In Harrisburg that day in 1866, William Duncan picked out a pair of mules and a wagon for which he paid Wrigley $300, indicating he and Wrigley were building a formal commercial relationship in the lumber business.[11]

Duncan spent the following Sunday scouting harvestable timber stands on his land along the Trinity. It was the middle of summer on the upper Texas gulf coast and mosquito and tick populations were exploding. Duncan spent two days in late August rounding up his horses that he let graze wild on the plains to "doctor them for ticks."[12] Ticks spread diseases like anemia, sleeping sickness, Lyme disease, and piroplasmosis, making horses at least irritable and at worst, dead. Equine piroplasmosis causes fever, anemia, jaundiced mucous membranes, swollen abdomens, constipation, colic, and labored breathing. Ticks often invade horses' ears, making them droopy and causing the horse to be head shy—irritating for the horse and dangerous for its rider. Because ticks breathe through holes in their abdomens called spiracles, they can be suffocated with alcohol or chloroform at sites on the horse where they feed. It is a far more effective treatment than pinching them one-by-one off a horse's hide.

Duncan never heard of piroplasmosis but he knew alcohol helped control ticks on horses. In the meantime, rather than drive his new wagon and two new mules home from Harrisburg, Duncan arranged for a steamboat to haul them across Trinity Bay and up the river to Liberty, arriving at the dock on August 29. The freight bill was $12.60 in gold, but Duncan paid it with $18 in U.S. currency. Driving his new wagon and mule team home through Liberty, he stopped to buy candles, starch, a bolt of gingham cloth, five pounds of white sugar, and a pair of shoes for Texas for $2.50. After he picked up a repaired coffee pot—the bill was twenty cents—he knocked back two one-dollar whiskies at the bar.[13]

The next day Duncan planted several rows of Irish potatoes and entered the hog business by cutting and installing fence posts for a pigsty.[14] On Sunday, he took Texas and Reuben "down to Spaight's to catch a wild horse of Emma's." They found the horse "and gave him chase, but could not drive him," says Duncan. It was too hot to keep trying, so Duncan and his men gave up and rode home. The following Friday, one of Duncan's young freedmen employees, Jacob, came down with what Duncan diagnosed as "cholera morbus," an acute gastroenteritis also called summer diarrhea. Its symptoms in addition to loose bowels are vomiting and cramps, caused by improperly prepared food. It occurs in summer and autumn, especially in children, and today it is commonly called food poisoning or intestinal flu. It has no relationship to the virulent, deadly Asiatic cholera.[15] Duncan sent one of his men into Liberty to fetch Jacob's mother while Duncan "attended him all day till in the night." His overnight care of the sick young man is another insight into Duncan's character. It made no difference to Duncan that Jacob was black. The boy was better the next morning.[16]

After butchering another wild cow shot on the prairie Wednesday by his friend Ed White, Duncan inspected his cotton fields to see how the harvest was coming. He was crushed when he "found cotton ruined with rain and worms. Won't make a quarter [of the] crop." Duncan was sorely disappointed as most farmers are when crops fail to reach forecasts. He and his men worked long and hard to take one step forward, but Murphy's Law forced them to retreat another five. Troubled by irreparable damage to his cotton crop, Duncan nevertheless shouldered civic duty again the next week. Summoned to serve on a grand jury in Liberty, his fellow jurors promptly elected him foreman. The grand jury worked from early morning until late afternoon, Monday through Saturday, with Duncan complaining about being locked in the jury room all day. The grand jury finished its work Saturday afternoon and Duncan stayed home Sunday in what he admits was a "very bad humor about private matters." His relationship with Celima might have been deteriorating further, although a problem on the farm was certainly part of his foul mood. While he had been in town at the courthouse, grazing cattle invaded his fields. He says he "tryed [*sic*] to get negroes to repair [the] fence" but it was Sunday and he "could not get them at it." His men went to work Monday morning on the fences and spent the next five days repairing them.[17]

Duncan felt most freedmen he hired were good workers. He is occasionally sarcastic—"negroes picking or pretending to pick cotton and cut hay"—but rarely fired anyone except when he "paid Jim $3.25 and let him go." When Duncan sacked Jim, he took up the slack himself. While the men pulled and hauled corn, Duncan "worked at [the] crib. [I] hauled one load for me and one for [the] negroes. Tyre came off [the] wagon, I put it on. Sowed turnips." When weekends arrived, his freedmen enjoyed their new independence, often attending political events in Liberty. Duncan says, "all [the] negroes gone to town" on Saturday, October 13, 1866 "to hear Freedman speech." The next Saturday, Duncan reports "negroes all going to town to Sam's trial." No word on what charges had been filed against Sam or his trial's outcome, but he must have appreciated plenty of support in the gallery. The following Monday, Duncan rode into Liberty and "got negro contract approved," by Provost Marshal Mayer, illustrating how Duncan cooperated with the Federal government in its monitoring of former slave owners' treatment of their emancipated employees.[18]

The weather remained wet but turned much cooler the third week of October, and Duncan's health suffered mightily. Typical of his daily condition reports, he writes he was "very unwell . . . got so sick that I had to go to bed. Had chill and high fever all day. Began to take medicine at 4 P.M. and continued until 12." He felt worse with each new day. "Felt very badly this morning and continued getting worse. Had chill and high fever with pain in head and back. Sent for Dr. Breshear." When the fever eased, he struggled out of bed and headed to work. Asked to appraise the property of a deceased fellow Mason in early November, Duncan rode to the departed's home after breakfast. "Worked till 11 and took a hard chill. Had fire made and sat by about an hour till chill went off. Fever came on and then I came home, [so] sick I could scarcely sit on my horse. Went to bed and burned up with fever till midnight. Pd [*sic*] little negro to wait on me."[19]

Duncan felt somewhat better in mid-December after being painfully ill for more than five weeks. Routine chores kept him busy until Christmas Day. "This is the first Christmas I have spent at home since 1860," he reflected. "Today I was alone with my own family, as Mr. and Mrs. Gillard were at the Mill. Emma was not home, but in town." Duncan went into Liberty the next day, as did the freedmen who lived on his place, to attend a speech by Provost

Marshal Mayer. Besides providing updates on issues for the freed slaves, the event was a chance for Mayer to collect feedback on how things were going from their points of view. The next day, Duncan "could not get [the] negroes to work, as Texas was to marry today." Duncan had planned to haul cotton to the gin, but understood how his black employees wanted to celebrate the wedding. While the freedmen partied, Duncan organized his mules, oxen, and wagons to begin loading cotton the next morning.[20]

It dawned cold and rainy and Duncan found the "negroes of course not fit to work on account of their frolicing [sic], so [I] put off the hauling cotton till Monday." Duncan did not begrudge the lost workday. The weather was nasty and he understood how folks can be worse for wear after attending a rousing wedding reception because he enjoyed a party too. It was still very cold Sunday morning so Duncan made fires in the hearths and brewed coffee two hours before dawn, his normal rising time. On an exceptionally cold morning, the first thoughts of farmers and ranchers go to their crops and livestock, and Duncan was no exception. He worked until mid-afternoon "feeding animals, horses, mules, oxen and cows." Then he climbed on his horse and rode to the public cotton gin to get the key for the next day's ginning. From there he traveled to Wrigley's for a deal-making supper, saying he "stayed till late. We agreed to go into the wood business in co-partnership." After a bitterly cold ride, Duncan arrived home at midnight. The former Confederate cavalry officer was in ill health but nonetheless gaining traction in his return to business in postwar Texas. As he extinguished his lantern moments into the new year, snow began to fall on Liberty County. It was New Year's Day, 1867, the second full year of Reconstruction in post–Civil War America and the first day of what would be a fateful one for William Duncan.[21]

He went into Liberty the next morning to pick up medicine and a pair of saddle blankets for $2.50. He dropped by Major Mayer's office for a short visit and afterward rode to Wrigley's warehouse on the river. When he dismounted, Duncan's horse reared onto its hind legs, ripping the reins out of his hands, and galloped away. His business with Wrigley finished, Duncan borrowed another horse and rode home to find his breakaway mount standing patiently at the gate, casting a wary eye at its owner. His new horse blankets were nowhere in sight. Duncan stabled the two horses, made a fire, and went to bed.[22]

The next Sunday, he struck a father-in-law deal to expand his farming business. Duncan negotiated an agreement with Dr. Gillard to rent a piece of his land for the next year in exchange for three bales of cotton and one hundred bushels of corn. Duncan's plan included another sharecropping contract, this one with freedmen Zeno and Mart. Dr. Gillard agreed to give Duncan full control of the field, permission to move fences as he pleased, use of two mules, one yoke of oxen, and all the farming implements he could spare. After shaking hands on the deal, Duncan climbed on his horse and rode through the designated field, planning what he would plant as soon as weather permitted. In the meantime, it was time to renew the first sharecropping contract Duncan had made with Louis and his co-workers the previous year. Duncan "told negroes to gear up wagon and mules to go to Liberty to make contract. Louis said he wanted to settle first. [I] talked short to him and left him." Louis and his workmates headed for town and Duncan followed, "but did not enter into contract. Told negroes they had better go home."

While Duncan let emotions cool between him and Louis, he renewed his contract with Sabine, agreeing to pay him $12.50 per month plus rations, and promised to pay any medical bills. Duncan then worked out a new one-year deal with Jacob in which Duncan explains, "I am to feed and clothe him and give him medical attention and one dollar pr [sic] month." The difference in these two contracts shows how highly Duncan valued Sabine's service and friendship. Duncan held another meeting with Louis and his co-workers a week later in Liberty. Duncan reports he "settled with negroes [and] they came out in debt. [They] were greatly dissatisfied but entered into [a] contract for another year."[23]

The former slaves naturally expected to earn money under their sharecropping agreement but probably did not fully understand the terms of the contract. Contracts and their financial ramifications were second nature to Duncan. He knew earnings come only from revenues after deducting operating costs, debt service, and taxes. The freedmen probably thought gross revenues were profits in which they should share. Floods and insect infestation had reduced the corn and cotton yields significantly and costs would have climbed if Duncan had replanted any of the fields. Gross revenues from the harvest might have been lower than expected because of lower commodity prices in a too-much-supply, not-enough-demand soft market. The freedmen likely did not understand these financial concepts.

Economics is called the dismal science. Business issues can be complicated for educated folks and downright mysterious for illiterate souls. For people like William Duncan, capital and operating costs, soft markets, financial terms, and real property losses were facts of life. When income expectations were not met for newly emancipated former slaves—many of whom were in business with unscrupulous landowners who took advantage of their lack of sophistication—they were bitterly disappointed. Strained agri-business relationships like the one freedman Louis and farmer Duncan found themselves in 1867 Liberty County, Texas were common throughout the South during Reconstruction.

Duncan moved from tense sharecropping contracts to the timber business two days later. He rode out to the Trinity River "with freedman Lund to show lines of my land to establish [a] wood yard." Freedman Lund was probably one of Charley Lund's former slaves who took Lund's surname like many former slaves across the South took their owner's names after gaining their freedom. Another stop to chat in Major Mayer's office in Liberty highlighted Duncan's ride into Liberty the next day. Duncan and the U.S. Army provost marshal had become good friends. Six days later, after Duncan assigned new hire Boudreau and old hand Sabine to mend fences while other workers split rails for posts, he went hunting and killed a Brant goose and a duck. Duncan hired new employees more frequently in 1867, usually as day laborers for specific jobs. Boudreau worked five days building fences with Sabine at seventy-five cents a day, Sam hauled rails out to the fence line for Boudreau and Sabine for the same pay, and Tucker hired on at a dollar a day to help Duncan on a two-day project to repair the barn. Duncan paid more for skilled carpentry than he did for unskilled manual labor because of their intrinsic values, not because he favored one freedman over another.[24]

After breakfast two days later, Duncan and Sabine drove a wagon into the woods "and got two sticks and took them to the mill and had them sawed for cart tongues." When he needed something, the nineteenth-century farmer—just like his twenty-first-century counterpart today—tried to do it himself. While he rested at the house the following Sunday, a man dropped by to tell Duncan "he had a hog for me." The man was not bearing gifts; he sold livestock door to door. Duncan "sent for it; when it came, cut up and salted it. Wt—163 lbs at five cents = $8.40." Either Duncan's math was off or he tipped the pig peddler thirty-five cents for delivering the hog. In either case, Duncan did not pay the man for a week and then only $5 of what he owed. Cash buyers in Reconstruction Texas had strong purchasing power and could drive a seller crazy with low offers and demands for extended payment terms. If vendors agreed to sell, they were forced to swallow buyers' demands and endure slow pay, regardless of how much it stuck in their craws.[25]

When Duncan returned to the house for midday dinner on February 21, he found an unexpected guest from Refugio County. Gus Burk had arrived "on Mrs. Winfree's business." Duncan explains that he "entered into an agreement with him as agt. [sic] for Mrs. Winfree to give him [Burk] all the beeves in my western stock after March 1st until the notes which she holds against me are paid." The Barrow brothers had initially ignored Duncan's offer to look after his Refugio County herd, and here was a chance to care for it while using the cattle to clear a debt to Mrs. Winfree without selling them. She and Burk had cooked up a scheme in which Duncan would lease the herd to Mrs. Winfree and she would contract with Burk to manage it. The plan called for Burk to add a certain number of Duncan's yearlings to Burk's New Orleans–bound droves and split their sales revenue with Mrs. Winfree until she recouped what Duncan owed her. At that point, the lease would expire and Duncan would get his herd back.

It was a good deal in which all three parties shared an economic benefit rather than a bad deal that favored one at the expense of the other. Mrs. Winfree got her money back, Gus Burk made some incremental cash, and William

Duncan retired a debt to Mrs. Winfree without having to liquidate assets. While Reconstruction-era politicians in Washington, Austin, and other Southern state capitals bickered about ending the Civil War well after its last shot was fired, this Duncan-Winfree-Burk cattle deal showed how ordinary folks in postwar Texas rebuilt their lives. It was also an example of frontier Texas hospitality. After they agreed terms, Duncan invited Burk to stay the night.[26]

The next morning around 3:00, while Burk slept soundly in the Duncans' guest room, Celima woke Duncan "who told me she was sick and that it was necessary to send for the midwife. I started Sabine after old Fanny who arrived about light and at 6 o'clock, a boy was born."[27] The baby was Duncan's eighth child, his fourth son and the fifth offspring born to him and Celima. Two of the boys died as infants, but Emery Lee, eighteen months old at this time, was doing well. Duncan and Celima named their new son William after Duncan's father, the new baby's deceased oldest brother who died in August 1854, and of course, after Duncan himself.[28] Wishing Gus Burk a safe journey back to Refugio County, Duncan climbed on his horse and headed into Liberty. He left mother, infant, siblings, and their attendants to buy a new wagon, yoke, and ox, paying $25 cash for the ox and yoke and writing a $60 note due next January for the wagon. In eight days, Duncan would celebrate his forty-ninth birthday. In ominous diary omissions, Duncan does not mention anticipating or observing the special day.[29]

Chapter 23 **Rest**

DUNCAN WAS TROUBLED FIVE DAYS LATER. AFTER a day planting sugarcane with Sabine behind the plow, Duncan loaded his pistol and took it into the field. It was the first time he had fired it since he left the army in May 1865. He does not mention what prompted him to test the weapon but it could have been a report that Henry Barrow was back in Liberty, causing Duncan to prepare to defend himself. Whether or not Barrow was on the prowl, a hard freeze turned heavy rain into sleet over Liberty, putting a temporary halt to corn planting and most other work except timber hauling. Wind and rain pummeled Liberty County so hard that much of Duncan's fencing was destroyed. The Trinity rose in its banks and Duncan feared the rough-cut logs he kept stacked by the river were in danger. But the spring equinox brought back the sun and things gradually returned to normal in the Duncan fields and at his lumberyard. Unfortunately for Duncan at this point in his life, "normal" also meant recurrence of high fever and severe pain. His symptoms ebbed and flowed in their virulence, so he was able to function in the respites. When he felt better, he was more interested in hunting turkeys than in work.[1]

The rains returned and Duncan says "everything in [the] field looks like it was washed away. Never saw harder rain fall than fell on me yesterday evening as I came out from Liberty." The normally healthy Sabine got sick and Duncan missed having his help for almost a week, even though Sabine climbed out of bed for a few hours on three days to help cultivate a corn field and potato patch. Provost Marshal Mayer invited Duncan and five other Liberty men to his house for supper and poker at midweek. "We had [a] fine red fish supper and ice cream," Duncan says. "I stayed all night and slept. [The] others played cards." It was the only time William Duncan ever recorded that he slept through a card game, proof-positive of how awful he felt.[2]

Duncan gave his men the day off on Good Friday and everyone except Sabine, George, and Duncan himself took advantage of it. While Duncan planted new cotton and corn beds, Sabine and George plowed ditches along the edges of the field so standing water from the next heavy rain would drain before damaging the crops. Duncan, Emma, and Kate were late to Mass on Easter Sunday and Duncan reports, "After it was over [we] all went to [the] Methodist Church." He reports, "I did not do much" on Easter Monday. The following day, he did less. "I am very unwell this morning; tryed [sic] to work in gardin [sic]. Could not. Came to the house and lay down a while. Could not eat breakfast. Had considerable fever and severe pains all over." Duncan's health was deteriorating at an increasingly rapid rate. In addition to chronic high fever and pain he blamed on kidney and liver disease, the laceration he suffered on his hand the previous July was badly infected. He was miserable: "have fever every day . . . suffering very much with hand . . . suffered greatly with thumb . . . doctored my hand with hot lie [sic] and egg and salt and turpentine." Duncan took every remedy he could find, trying to win relief. Nothing worked. His panic grew more intense with the pain.[3]

William Duncan was dying. Not from an old war wound or a bullet fired by Henry Barrow, but from a septic infection of the cut on his hand. He did not admit it to himself and it is doubtful he said much about it to others until the end. Yet he knew his time was short and so probably did those around him. His immune system was shot, unable to fight the infection and permitting his unhealthy lifestyle to catch up with him. Thousands of mosquitoes, ticks, and horseflies had injected their venom in him while he worked cattle for years on the plains, bayous, and rivers along the Atascosito Trail. Riding his horse through oppressive heat, numbing cold, and torrential rain on thousands of days had robbed his stamina. A frontier diet of unsanitary water, often-spoiled salted meat, and bug-infested biscuits had eaten away at his digestive tract. The toxic episode of food poisoning during the war had almost finished him off and his body had not forgotten it. Through it all, his habitual answer to pain had been self-medication with whiskey-by-the-gallon, the most harmful folk medicine on the nineteenth-century Texas frontier. No wonder William Duncan slipped toward death when the cut on his hand became infected; his body could not stand the abuse any longer.

Duncan became obsessed with his pain. He admitted it almost daily beginning Easter week in 1867 but worked through it whenever he could. "Feel very badly," he writes one rainy morning. "Negroes went to planting Lewis and Ben's corn. I went out with Geo. [sic] and Sabine and planted some of the C. Stone corn, 18 rows. Got so unwell that I had to quit. Came home and lay down." Duncan was not out of commission for long. The following Sunday, after heavy rain fell all night, he awakened to find "my fence down in several places. I hired a negro and made him take a mule and big plough and run furrows till 12 o'clock to let off water. Paid him fifty cents. I was very unwell all day." Late the next afternoon, he climbed on his horse and rode into Liberty for his lodge meeting. "Very unwell," he moans to himself. "Did not stay." Duncan tried to overcome his pain with hard work on the farm and brief diversions with friends, but the effort became increasingly difficult as the days passed.[4]

During life on the frontier and his Confederate service in the Civil War, William Duncan learned anger was wasted energy. Survival depended on being aware of your surroundings, alert to the near occasion of threat and ever sensitive to the people around you. People need energy for such awareness. Duncan conserved his and rarely lost his cool to outlaw cowboys, drunken officers, mutinous soldiers, or impatient freedmen. Not even to the weather. When heavy spring rains fell onto Liberty County one Sunday in early May, Duncan took advantage of the downpour and "stayed in bed all day," commenting that he "never saw so much rain fall in same length of time." The fields were too muddy to work the next morning, so he hitched a pony to the buggy and took daughter Kate to school while "Sabine and George shelled a little corn [and] other negroes pretended to their corn. In the evening," he continues, "[I] rode in [the] prairie with Sab. and Geo. [sic] and got up some calves and yearlings." When Duncan entered his dying process, he did not give up. He simply played the cards he was dealt as best he could.[5]

No one enjoyed a bargain more than Duncan. He was a practical cattleman and farmer and as such, an inveterate trader. If he saw a chance to improve his lot, he jumped at it. Despite almost constant, usually horrible pain, Duncan remained true to his commercial genes and did two final business deals at the end of his life. The joint venture in the lumber business with Jim Wrigley was not going well. In two meetings at the end of May and the first week of June 1867, the two unwound their agreement. Duncan explains, I "saw Wrigley [and] he said I had better have wood measured and discharge [the] hands." A week later after supper at Wrigley's house near the Trinity, Duncan says, "he and I went to [the] River to settle wood yd. [sic] matters. I sold out my interest in the yard to him. He allowed me $1 per cord and takes the wood. The amt. pd. [sic] all that I owed him and a little over which he is to pay me in cash. I got home at 2 o'clk [sic]."[6]

Duncan negotiated one other agreement in his last days and it was personal. Jerome DeBlanc's son, Oscar, the former soldier in John Bell Hood's command, had proposed marriage to Emma, Duncan's oldest daughter. Oscar pursued Emma since he returned from the war and Duncan kept an accounting of their courtship, revealing he was never keen on the relationship. In mid-June, he reports, "I went to Jerome's to see Oscar. Did not see him." Six weeks later, Duncan says he "met Oscar by appt. [sic] Settled our trouble amicably." That same night, he felt excruciating pain "in the palm of my hand." Four days later, Jerome "came over and rode with me to the bridge. We concluded it were [sic] best [to] break off the engagement existing between Oscar and Emma." After "suffering very much in the night with my hand" and "too sick to do any thing [*sic*] till after dinner . . . I passed by Jeromes [*sic*] on my way to town and he rode with me. [I] gave him the ring which Oscar gave Emma." Duncan does not mention how Emma felt about her father's intervention in her romance. He is typically brief when he writes he "went and saw Emma. Told her I would come for her tomorrow. My hand very bad."[7]

When he was homesick during his military service and things happened he considered dishonorable, irresponsible, or unlawful, William Duncan admitted to being depressed. His emotions during his final weeks were linked to the intensity of physical pain with which he struggled. On a cool morning in early May, he reports, "I feel much better." The next day, he was "very unwell this morning, was all night." In midmonth he felt "better satisfied than usual with days [*sic*] work" and a week later, he "got up this morning feeling very well, as I had slept out on the river bank. First time I believe I have slept out since the war ended." Six days later, rain and pain sent Duncan's emotions tumbling. "It seems that I will be unable to make any thing with all my work and exertion," he writes. "River rising and likely to take off my wood and George who was to haul it returned this morning saying he was sick, leaving my oxen in the swamp. Quite unwell."[8]

Duncan's last days took shape the way he always lived: he worked, cut deals, settled debts, and generally did what he could to provide for his family after he was gone. There were no card games in town or hunting trips along the Trinity. He called on Provost Marshal Mayer in Liberty, asked Sabine to deliver a letter to Colonel Spaight in Moss Bluff, and mailed another to McQuoid, Mehle & Co. of New Orleans.[9] The letter to the colonel does not survive, but it probably asked lawyer Spaight to help Celima with his estate. The other letter was similar. McQuoid, Mehle was Duncan's Louisiana cattle broker who maintained offices on Front Street near Louisiana Avenue in Jefferson City, now part of New Orleans. They called themselves "commission merchants" who represented clients in several businesses including the cattle market.[10] They earned their fees from a percentage of the sales price of an asset they bought or sold on behalf of a client. Duncan asked McQuoid, Mehle about prices in the New Orleans cattle market, indicating he wanted to sell some cattle to raise cash to pay off several debts totaling more than $4,000.[11] Noting a tone of urgency in Duncan's letter, McQuoid, Mehle assured him of their prompt attention to his request. They responded to Duncan's inquiry within the week: "We could not advise you to ship anything here at present as our market is entirely overstocked with all kinds of stock just now. Such cattle as would come from your country are bringing from $14 to $25 per head and some of the poor classes, less. . . . The market for small stock [calves and yearlings] is flat and they are selling from $4 to $6 per head. We will write to you every week or two . . . and should there be an opportunity

FIG. 10.
William B. Duncan's 1867
grave and late-twentieth-
century commemorative
headstone in the Liberty,
Texas city cemetery.

for you to make anything, we will let you know at once."[12] Duncan tried everything he could to make it easier for Celima and the children after he died, but
the New Orleans cattle market was not cooperating.[13]

Less than a month before his final breath, Duncan rode slowly into his
fields and "found thousands of cotton worms. [I] told negroes to quit the cotton and begin to save fodder." He knew Louis and his mates would be sorely
disappointed but there was nothing he or anyone could do. On the last day of
July, Duncan says he "suffered last night worse than I ever have and can get no
peace today." The next day, his pain intensified and Celima wilted from the
stress. "Suffering martyrdom with my hand," he writes. "Stayed all day at home.
Celima had chill and fever. Simeon sent in great haste for Mr. Gillard . . . after
dinner [the] pain of hand was unbearable." For the next two weeks, Duncan's
dying consumed him all the time. "Suffered awfully all night and no better,"
he says. "No rest except obtained by taking laudanum," he reports the next day.
"Suffered intensely last night. Up all night poulticing. . . . Suffered awfully.
"Pain became perfectly unbearable."[14]

When he was conscious during his last week, Duncan dictated his thoughts
to Emma who transcribed them into the diary. When he was incoherent, she

composed entries on his behalf. A steady stream of visitors called, but few stayed long. After Jim Wrigley dropped by near sundown on Saturday, August 16, and promised to call again, Duncan pronounced himself "Much better today, clear of fever." It was wishful thinking. He scrawled, "got worse, suffering very much" the following day. Emma wrote the next entry in her own words. "Suffered very much during the night. Was delirious, got worse toward morning, sent for the doctor."[15] A twentieth-century psychiatrist and recognized authority on caring for people near death says "there is a time in a [dying] patient's life when the pain ceases to be, when the mind slips off into a dreamless state, when the need for food becomes minimal and the awareness of the environment all but disappears in darkness. . . . It is the hardest time for the next of kin as he either wishes to take off, to get it over with; or he desperately clings to something that he is in the process of losing forever. It is the time for the therapy of silence."[16]

William Berry Duncan was forty-nine years old when he died on Tuesday, August 19, 1867.[17] He rests today in the shade of four big trees in the old City Cemetery in Liberty, Texas, less than fifty feet from a murky bayou of the Trinity River (see figure 10). Except for Friday nights in the fall as cheers reach the cemetery when the Liberty Panthers host a visiting opponent at the high school football stadium across the road, Duncan's gravesite is a quiet place where purple martins, yellow warblers, and orange-and-black Monarch butterflies stop to rest on their semiannual migrations along the North American Central flyway. Darlene Mott works in Liberty, knows something of William Duncan's life, and drops by the old cemetery to see him every year on March 2, Texas Independence Day and his birthday. She pours a bottle of water on his grave to quench the thirst he developed from decades of driving cattle on the Atascosito Trail, riding across Louisiana and Texas in the Civil War, and farming in Liberty County. Miss Mott tidies Duncan's gravesite and remembers the pioneer Texas cattleman, Liberty County sheriff, and Confederate cavalry officer and what his life must have been like on the Texas frontier in the nineteenth century. "William Duncan was a good and decent man," she says, "an ordinary yet special person, far-from-perfect but nevertheless, a good man. He helped build the Republic of Texas and helped rebuild the United States after the war between the states. I am grateful for his legacy of courage, integrity and sacrifice."[18]

Epilogue

THE CIVIL WAR ROBBED MILLIONS OF NINETEENTH-century Americans their last rations of Time, Talent, and Treasure. It was the end of Time for more than 620,000 from both North and South. For millions of survivors, especially Southerners like William Duncan, the war ignored their Talent and squandered their Treasure. Justifiably obscured in much of history by the terrible total of dead, financial devastation of the South was overwhelming. Southern banks reported aggregated capital in 1860 of $61 million. Ten years later, their capital had dropped to $17 million leaving them feeble and their limited available credit usuriously expensive. Currency in circulation fell from $51 million in 1860 to $15 million ten years later. Reconstruction politics placed a backbreaking additional economic burden on the former Confederate states. Individual shares of Northern war debt and pensions assigned them by the Federal government totaled at least $1 billion. Without state, federal, foreign, or divine assistance, individuals in the South struggled to create productive capital. Shortages of skilled labor, raw material, and finished goods—largely irrelevant in the end because the war destroyed Southern markets—made it a next-to-impossible task. A Mobile furniture dealer explained in 1866, "Everybody wanted to buy and nobody had any money." If a merchant refused his customers credit, he infuriated them. If he granted them financing, he arranged his own bankruptcy. The Alabama retailer threw his losing cards onto the table and closed the store.

Total property valuation in the former Confederate States of America in 1860 was assessed at $4,363,030,367. Ten years later the 1870 census valued property in those same states at $2,141,834,788, 49 percent of the prewar value. Actual property depreciation was much greater since the 1870 census did not account for the war's reduction in currency values, estimated to have been at least 20 percent. The value of farms in the mostly agrarian Confederate states dropped 39 percent during the 1860s, from $1.427 billion in 1860 to $866 million in 1870. Total farm livestock, that is, all domesticated animals, decreased 20 percent in Texas alone from 1860 to 1866. Texas land at the end of the war was valued from one-tenth to one-fourth its 1860 price. This meant the 4,197 acres William Duncan owned in 1860, along with his other miscellaneous personal property, dropped in value from $184,944 to between $18,494 and $51,784 in twenty-first-century inflation-adjusted dollars.[1]

These depressed financial data presume a relatively balanced, functional economy that the former Confederacy did not enjoy. The actual worth of an asset is undetermined until a buyer actually acquires it. Absent a closed transaction, valuations are estimates, and in the postwar South, often not worth the paper on which they were written. People with cash or marketable assets were especially rare in Reconstruction Texas, so even if Duncan wanted to sell land, chances are he could not find buyers. If someone stepped up with an offer, they were likely opportunistic Northern carpetbaggers offering ridiculously low bids. Duncan did not sell any land after the war, suggesting at that particular time that his land was worthless. Texas banks like others across the South had little capital to lend, regardless of available collateral, leaving Duncan unable to borrow much—if anything—against his land. An active trader and consumer who helped build the Texas antebellum economy, the Civil War transformed William Duncan and thousands like him across the South into emasculated investors fighting for economic traction. It was no fun for Duncan, no good for Texas and crushing for the South.

When Duncan returned home in May 1865 after three-plus years' service as a Confederate cavalry officer, he found the social fabric of Texas in tatters. Crime raged across the state and desperate poverty reinforced natural frontier stresses like assimilation, miscegenation and prejudice. Racial, ethnic, cultural, class, gender, and regional bigotry frequently sparked fistfights that often escalated into gunfights. Bad weather made things worse with drought, pelting rain, floods, and insects devastating crops. Thousands of destitute whites and black former slaves contributed to fragile postwar Texas society. The black population had risen dramatically when many former Louisiana slaves were sent to Texas during the war to escape Union emancipation. Illiterate, aimless, and unconnected to a social support unit, many of them turned to crime just to eat. Poverty and famine were their common denominators. The robbery of Lund's warehouse in West Liberty and theft of his possessions on his first night home was personal proof for Duncan of postwar Texas anarchy.

Like thousands of public-spirited men and women who built the American frontier and continue to develop grassroots America, William Duncan's political service before the war helped tame Texas as much as his economic activity helped strengthen it. But significantly shrunken postwar assets robbed his risk-taking spirit, and poor health discouraged him from participating in elective or appointive political activity. The state could have used his commonsense moderation in its public arena after the war to counter fractious partisanship that was rule rather than exception in Reconstruction Texas. When Gov. J. W. Throckmorton submitted the Thirteenth and Fourteenth Amendments of the U.S. Constitution to the Texas legislature for ratification as required by the Federal government, Throckmorton told legislators it was unnecessary for them to accept the Thirteenth Amendment that freed the slaves because it had already been ratified by 75 percent of the states. As for the Fourteenth Amendment that granted U.S. citizenship to former slaves, Throckmorton recommended its rejection. Following his lead, the Texas legislature returned the Thirteenth Amendment to the secretary of state without action and voted sixty-seven to five to reject the Fourteenth. While William Duncan battled to rebuild his civilian life in Liberty County, Texas politicians found ways to keep fighting the war long after shooting ended on the battlefield.

When former Texas secessionists won their state legislative majority in 1866, they appointed O. M. Roberts, former president of the Texas Secession Convention, and David G. Burnett, ex-president of the Republic of Texas and another secessionist, to the U.S. Senate. They also elected several former Texas Confederates to seats in the U.S. House of Representatives. Northerners in Congress considered the Texas senate appointments and house elections evidence of continued rebellion and blocked Texas delegates from taking seats in Congress. In the process, the Northern-controlled Congress proclaimed new state governments in Texas and other Southern states unconstitutional because they were created without congressional approval. National anger against Texas came to full boil in early 1867. Radical Republicans and Unionists passed the Congressional Reconstruction Act on March 2, 1867—William Duncan's forty-ninth birthday—that withdrew Texas statehood from the Union and declared the state a "conquered province" governed by Federal military rule. This law finally and unequivocally confirmed Duncan's fear of a "foreign" Union invasion of Texas and other former Confederate states that sent him and thousands of other Southerners to war in the first place.[2]

The way of life Duncan aimed to defend as a Texas Confederate officer depended to some extent on slavery. He leaves no evidence he rationalized owning slaves by quoting Genesis or Leviticus like many slave owners were wont to do.[3] His reasons were more temporal and certainly more commercial. Slaves were cheap labor that Duncan used to round up and drive more cattle to market, harvest greater yields from his crops, and fundamentally, earn more money. Yet Duncan does not appear to have employed Anthony Parent's *Foul Means* to manage his slaves.[4] His almost paternal relationship with young Sabine who accompanied, assisted, and even nursed him through most of his Civil War travels, his unqualified trust in midwife Fanny to help wife Celima give birth to his children, his quick hiring of Sabine, Texas, Louis, Reuben, Swain, and other freedmen after the war, his care of young Jacob, and his prompt compliance with Federal regulations over the employment of former slaves all suggest Duncan was more benevolent than he was draconian as a slave owner.

This is not to sanction William Duncan's ownership of slaves or suggest his particular practice of slavery was more acceptable than another. It does however support Ira Berlin, author of *Many Thousands Gone: The First Two Centuries of Slavery in North America*, when he cautions against a doctrinaire, simplistic view on any aspect of slavery because its history is convoluted, uneven, and outright messy. In the midst of slavery's reprehensible racism, black and white people met often in America as equals aligned against those they considered a common enemy. William Duncan and Sabine riding with the Texas Volunteers of the Confederate States of America are two examples. Yes, Sabine was Duncan's slave. He also was a skilled horseman, trained in frontier survival, comfortable interacting with blacks, whites, Creoles, Cajuns, and Indians, and familiar with the Texas and Louisiana gulf coast. He was also part of Duncan's family. Sabine remained with William Duncan until the end of Duncan's life—proof this particular pioneer Texas slave owner created at least a tolerable world for his slaves.[5]

What became of twenty-two-year-old Sabine after Duncan died? He did not leave a diary or letters—at least none have been found. After Duncan's death, Sabine might have remained in Liberty County as a sharecropper or moved to Galveston or maybe New Orleans where either port's shipping, rail, and associated support economy would have given him access to a wide range of jobs. He might have signed on as a cowboy for one of Duncan's fellow drovers and driven herds east to New Orleans or north to Kansas railheads. As a skilled horseman, Sabine could even have ridden west to join the buffalo soldiers of the U.S. 10th Cavalry regiment, one of four all-black regiments of the regular U.S. Army formed after the Civil War who fought Native Americans in frontier America's Indian Wars. If he avoided Comanche warriors, racist cattle rustlers, and murderous outlaws and his luck held—Duncan taught him when it comes to luck, a person usually makes his own—it is likely Sabine succeeded because Duncan had shown him how to ride, wrangle, and find his way. That was how Duncan lived: riding, wrangling, and finding his way with kindness, integrity, respect for tradition, and resilience to life's challenges on the Texas frontier. To know pioneer William Berry Duncan and the people in his life is to understand why Texas is unique among states, why the United States is unique among countries, and why William Shakespeare was right when he wrote, "There is a history in all men's lives."[6]

Notes

CHAPTER I

1. William B. Duncan, Original Diary, March 1, 2, 29, 1862, Julia Duncan Welder Collection, Sam Houston Regional Library and Research Center (hereafter SHRL), Liberty, Texas.

2. James M. McPherson, *For Cause and Comrades: Why Men Fought in the Civil War* (New York: Oxford University Press, 1997), 17, 21, 23.

3. Diana J. Kleiner, *Handbook of Texas Online,* s.v. "Liberty County," http://www .tsha.utexas.edu/handbook/online/articles/LL/hc18.html (accessed October 21, 2006).

4. Miriam Partlow, *Liberty, Liberty County, and the Atascosito District* (Austin: Pemberton Press, 1974), 81, 211.

5. Ashley Spaight served from 1881 to 1883 as the commissioner of the Department of Insurance, Statistics, and History, the predecessor agency of the Texas State Library whose Sam Houston Regional Library and Research Center houses the Julia Duncan Welder Collection in which the William B. Duncan files are preserved. Spaight died in Galveston in 1911. Robert Wooster, *Handbook of Texas Online,* s.v. "Ashley W. Spaight," http://www.tsha.utexas.edu/handbook/online/articles/SS/fsp1.html (accessed December 6, 2006).

6. Charles R. Walker, M.D., "Spaight's Battalion, C.S.A.," *Texas Gulf Historical and Biographical Record* 8, no. 1 (Beaumont, Tex.: Texas Gulf Historical Society, November 1972): 22.

7. W. T. Block, "Confederacy's Col. Spaight Well-Respected," *Beaumont Enterprise,* January 25, 2003.

8. Walker, "Spaight's Battalion, C.S.A.," 23.

9. Descriptive Roll of Commissioned Officers, Company (F) Spaight's Battalion of Texas Mounted Volunteers, C.S. Army. In SHRL, Liberty, Texas.

10. Murray N. Rothbard, "The Panic of 1819: Contemporary Opinion and Policy," *Journal of Finance* 15, no. 3 (1960): 421.

11. Eugene C. Barker, "Stephen F. Austin," *Mississippi Valley Historical Review* 5, no. 1 (1918): 22.

12. Marvin Fischbaum, review of *Trails to Texas: Southern Roots of Western Cattle Ranching*, by Terry G. Jordan, *Journal of Economic History* 41, no. 4 (1981): 933.

13. Frank L. Owsley, "Plain Folk of the Old South" (Baton Rouge, 1949), in *Cows, Ticks, and Disease: A Medical Interpretation of the Southern Cattle Industry* by Tamara Miner Haygood, in *Journal of Southern History* 52, no. 4 (1986): 554.

14. Descriptive Roll of Commissioned Officers, Company F, Spaight's Battalion of Texas Mounted Volunteers C.S. Army. In SHRL, Liberty, Texas.

15. Fred Kniffen, "The Western Cattle Complex: Notes on Differentiation and Diffusion," *Western Folklore* 12, no. 3, Oregon Number (1953): 182–83.

16. Eugene C. Barker, ed., *The Austin Papers* (Washington, D.C.: Historical Manuscripts Commission, 1924).

17. Partlow, *Liberty, Liberty County, and the Atascosito District*, 66.

18. The Atascosito District Census of 1826 spells Duncan's stepmother's maiden name as "Oden," while a will (No. 272) for the estate of Michael Odom filed June 1822, in the Probate Court of St. Landry Parish, Louisiana, lists Jane as one of Michael's children, indicating the transcriber of the Mexican census misspelled her maiden name. Probate filing copy in possession of Mrs. Mary Welder Urban, Dayton, Texas, a great-granddaughter of William B. Duncan.

19. Mary McMillan Osburn, ed., *The Atascosito Census of 1826*, in *Texans* 1, no. 4 (1963): 4–5.

20. Jo Ann Carrigan, "Privilege, Prejudice, and the Strangers' Disease in Nineteenth-Century New Orleans," *Journal of Southern History* 36, no. 4 (1970): 573–74.

21. Partlow, *Liberty, Liberty County, and the Atascosito District*, 75.

22. W. Duncan, Auborne, Trinity River, Texas, to Henry Moss, November 22, 1835. In Julia Duncan Welder Collection, SHRL Liberty, Texas.

23. Photostats of baptismal certificates of William Duncan, Jane Oden Duncan, and William B. Duncan, signed by Revered Michael Muldoon, December 13, 1831. William B. Duncan Papers, SHRL, Liberty, Texas.

24. Partlow, *Liberty, Liberty County, and the Atascosito District*, 83–84.

25. Margaret Swett Henson, *Handbook of Texas Online*, s.v. "John Davis Bradburn," http://www.tsha.utexas.edu/handbook/online/articles/BB/fbr9.html (accessed October 18, 2006).

26. Partlow, *Liberty, Liberty County, and the Atascosito District*, 86.

27. The Gillard home, built with lumber cut in Dr. Gillard's sawmill on his Trinity River plantation south of Liberty, is preserved at the Sam Houston Regional Library and Research Center in Liberty, Texas.

28. William B. Duncan grew up on his father's plantation along the *west* side of the Trinity south of West Liberty, today's town of Dayton. As a married man, he lived in the Gillard house on their plantation on the *east* side of the Trinity. Mrs. Mary Urban, Dayton, Texas, great-granddaughter of William B. Duncan, telephone interview with author, December 2, 2006.

29. Wm. Bollaert, "Notes on the Coast Region of the Texan Territory: Taken during a Visit in 1842," *Journal of the Royal Geographical Society of London* 13 (1843): 235–36.

30. Partlow, *Liberty, Liberty County, and the Atascosito District*, 128, 193.

31. William B. Duncan, Original Diary, April 3, 1865.

32. William B. Duncan was drafted into the Republic of Texas army June 28, 1836, ordered to report for duty July 7, 1836, and discharged October 7, 1836. *Draft* and *Discharge Notices,* William B. Duncan papers, SHRL, Liberty, Texas.

33. Herbert Gambrell, *Handbook of Texas Online,* s.v. "Mirabeau Buonaparte Lamar," http://www.tsha.utexas.edu/handbook/online/articles/LL/fla15.html (accessed October 16, 2006).

34. Partlow, *Liberty, Liberty County, and the Atascosito District,* 350–51.

35. Sam Houston to William Duncan, December 6, 1847, Julia Duncan Welder Collection, SHRL, Liberty, Texas.

36. Wayne Gard, *The Chisholm Trail* (Norman: University of Oklahoma Press, 1954), 25; also, *Galveston Weekly News,* December 2, 1856. In W. T. Block, *A History of Jefferson County, Texas, from Wilderness to Reconstruction* (Nederland, Tex.: Nederland Publishing, 1976), chapter 11. Also, Partlow, *Liberty, Liberty County, and the Atascosito District,* 19–20.

37. Walter J. Matherly, "The Emergence of the Metropolitan Community in the South," *Social Forces* 14, no. 3 (1936): 316.

38. William B. Duncan, Original Diary, October 9, 1861.

39. Kevin R. Young, *To the Tyrants Never Yield: A Texas Civil War Sampler* (Plano, Tex.: Wordware Publishing, 1992), 17–18; also, *Goliad, Birthplace of Texas Ranching,* http://www.goliad.org/goliad.html (accessed May 7, 2006).

40. William B. Duncan, Original Diary, October 22, 31, 1861.

41. William B. Duncan, Personal Bible, July 25, 1845, SHRL, Liberty, Texas. Duncan's daughter, Chessie, died on July 18, 1878 at age seventeen.

42. William B. Duncan, Original Diary, November 2, 1861.

43. Ibid., November 3, 5, 10, 11, 13 and 15, 1861.

44. The herd totaled 946 head, of which Duncan owned 375 (40 percent), his codrovers owned 240 (25 percent), and Duncan's investor, Gilbert, owned 331 (35 percent). Gross revenues from the sale totaled $26,015, with Duncan's share at $10,406. If his costs were 25 percent of revenues, the gain on his own cattle would have exceeded $7,804. Friend Gilbert's gross margin would have been $5,094. Duncan's fee for handling Gilbert's investment was probably a commission on his gross revenue; for example, 15 percent or $764.

45. Samuel H. Williamson, "Five Ways to Compute the Relative Value of a U.S. Dollar Amount, 1790–2007," www.MeasuringWorth.com, 2008. Using an inflation calculation known as the GDP deflator, a ratio of nominal Gross Domestic Product (GDP) to real GDP, Duncan's estimated $8,568 net income from his 1861 cattle drive equates to approximately $165,042 in 2007 relative value.

CHAPTER 2

1. Bollaert, "Notes on the Coast Region of the Texan Territory: Taken during a Visit in 1842," 241.

2. James P. Baughman, "The Evolution of Rail-Water Systems of Transportation in the Gulf Southwest, 1836–1890," *Journal of Southern History* 34, no. 3 (1968): 358.

3. William Duncan's largest land holding was a 1,476-acre inheritance from his father's 4,400-acre head-right along the Trinity River granted to Duncan the elder in 1831 by the Mexican government. His next largest holding, 1,107 acres, lay west of

Liberty in Montgomery County. He owned 946 acres to the northeast in Hardin County, 403 acres to the south in Chambers County, and 265 acres west of Liberty along the San Jacinto River.

4. William B. Duncan, 1861 Property Tax Assessment, William B. Duncan papers, June 1861 bills, SHRL, Liberty, Texas. The amount in 1861 dollars was $11,559; its 2005 estimated value, $184,944, is calculated with a 16x multiplier.

5. William B. Duncan, Receipt from Assessor and Collector's Office, Refugio County, Texas, March 1, 1861, William B. Duncan papers, June 1861 bills, SHRL, Liberty, Texas. The amount paid was $17.92 for 1,128 head of cattle reported owned in Refugio County.

6. Shannon Tomkins, "Trinity River Wildlife Refuge Sees a Growth Spurt," *Houston Chronicle*, May 19, 2006, C14.

7. William Ransom Hogan, "Amusements in the Republic of Texas," *Journal of Southern History* 3, no. 4 (1937): 412.

8. William B. Duncan, Original Diary, April–December 1861.

9. Gillard papers, SHRL, Liberty, Texas.

10. "Tontas" means clown or foolish in French. "Mon tont," or "my foolish little clown" is a term of endearment. The Duncans called daughter Celima Catherine, "Tont" as well as Kate. William B. Duncan, Personal Bible, July 25, 1845.

11. William B. Duncan, Personal Bible, July 25, 1845, SHRL, Liberty, Texas.

12. Julia Duncan Welder is responsible for the preservation of her father's diaries and papers that are part of the Julia Duncan Welder Collection in the Sam Houston Regional Library and Research Center, Liberty, Texas.

13. Liberty County, Texas, Census of 1850, page 287, entry H287, SHRL, Liberty, Texas.

14. Partlow, *Liberty, Liberty County, and the Atascosito District*, 189.

15. Mary Welder Urban, great-granddaughter of William B. Duncan, interview by author, January 5, 2007, Dayton, Texas.

16. Jacques M. Henry and Carl L. Bankston, III, "Propositions for a Structuralist Analysis of Creolism," *Current Anthropology* 39, no. 4 (1998): 562, 564.

17. City of St. Martinville, s.v. "Our History," http://www.cityofsaintmartinville .com/english/index.htm (accessed October 24, 2006).

18. "Atchafalaya National Wildlife Refuge," Southeast Louisiana National Wildlife Refuges, U.S. Fish and Wildlife Service, www.fws.gov/ (accessed October 24, 2006).

19. Lauren C. Post, "The Rice Country of Southwestern Louisiana," *Geographical Review* 30, no. 4 (1940): 579.

20. Edward Joseph Duncan was born to Celima and William on March 26, 1859. William B. Duncan, Personal Bible, July 25, 1845.

21. William B. Duncan, Original Diary, January 3, 9, 10, 1861.

22. Eliza delivered two daughters and one son before she died; Emma was born July 10, 1849; William, born October 14, 1853, and died August 29, 1854, and Celima Catherine Duncan, named after Eliza's cousin and Duncan's future second wife, was born June 26, 1855. William B. Duncan, Personal Bible, July 25, 1845.

23. Liberty County Convention Election Returns, February 23, 1861, SHRL, Liberty, Texas.

24. Edward P. White served as Liberty County sheriff from 1862 to 1865. Partlow, *Liberty, Liberty County, and the Atascosito District,* Appendix, Exhibit E, County Officials of Liberty County, 350–52.

25. William B. Duncan, Original Diary, February 23, 25, 1861.

26. Ludwell H. Johnson, "Fort Sumter and Confederate Diplomacy," *Journal of Southern History* 26, no. 4 (1960): 441–77.

27. Alwyn Barr, "Texas Coastal Defense 1861–1865," *Southwestern Historical Quarterly Online* 065, no. 1 (1961): 4; http://www.tsha.utexas.edu/shqonline/apager .php?vol=065&pag=004 (Accessed December 22, 2007).

28. William B. Duncan, Original Diary, July 11–12, August 4, 29, 31, September 2, 1861.

29. Celima Duncan, Liberty, Texas, to William B. Duncan, September 12, 1861, Julia Duncan Welder Collection, SHRL, Liberty, Texas.

30. Celima Duncan, Liberty, Texas, to William B. Duncan, October 1, 1861, Julia Duncan Welder Collection, SHRL, Liberty, Texas.

31. Ralph Ramos, "Big Man on Texas Frontier," *Beaumont Enterprise-Journal,* February 23, 1975, Section C.

32. G. H. Willis, "Confession of G. H. Willis, One of the Three Who Attempted to Rob and Murder J. M. Dark and Family in Batson Prairie on the Night of the 16th of September, 1861," SHRL, Liberty, Texas, typewritten, photocopied.

33. John W. Crozier, "Statement of the Chief Justice of Hardin County, 17 Sept. 1861," SHRL, Liberty, Texas, typewritten, photocopied.

34. Celima Duncan, Liberty, Texas, to William B. Duncan, October 1, 1861, SHRL, Liberty, Texas.

CHAPTER 3

1. William B. Duncan, Original Diary, December 3, 10, 18, 1861.

2. Block, *A History of Jefferson County, Texas from Wilderness to Reconstruction,* chapter 11.

3. Emma Duncan was born July 10, 1849, to William and his first wife, Eliza Gillard Duncan. William B. Duncan, Personal Bible, July 25, 1845.

4. Partlow, *Liberty, Liberty County, and the Atascosito District,* 256.

5. William B. Duncan, Original Diary, January 18, 22; February 6, 11, 12; March 1, 2, 8, 10; April 3, 1862.

6. Ralph A. Wooster, *Texas and Texans in the Civil War* (Austin: Eakin Press, 1995), 95.

7. John C. L. Scribner, "Civil War," Texas Military Forces Museum (Austin: Camp Mabry), www.texasmilitaryforcesmuseum.org/ (accessed April 7, 2006).

8. William B. Duncan, Original Diary, March 15, 18, 19; April 4–10, 1862.

9. Russell K. Brown, "Fallen Stars," *Military Affairs* 45, no. 1 (1981): 10.

10. "The Rebel General Killed. General Albert Sidney Johnston," *New York Times,* April 10, 1862.

11. William B. Duncan, Original Diary, April 17, 23, 27, 30, 1862.

12. Ibid., May 6–10, 12, 17, 19, 1862.

13. Ibid., May 24, 1862.

14. Charles W. Ramsdell, "General Robert E. Lee's Horse Supply, 1862–1865," *American Historical Review* 35, no. 4 (1930): 758–60.

15. William B. Duncan, Original Diary, May 26, 28, 31, 1862.

16. Thomas W. Cutrer, *Handbook of Texas Online*, s.v. "John George Walker," http://www.tsha.utexas.edu/handbook/online/articles/WW/fwa20.html (accessed September 12, 2006).

17. W. T. Block, *Sapphire City of The Neches: A Brief History of Port Neches, Texas from Wilderness to Industrialization* (Austin: Nortex Press, 1987), 19.

18. William B. Duncan, Original Diary, June 6, 1862.

19. William Duncan, Sabine Pass, Texas, to Celima Duncan, Liberty, Texas, May 26, 1862, SHRL, Liberty, Texas.

20. William B. Duncan, Original Diary, June 7, 8, 1862.

21. Duncan often uses the term, *the cars,* to mean the train.

22. William B. Duncan, Original Diary, June 9–15, 1862.

23. William T. Windham, "The Problem of Supply in the Trans-Mississippi Confederacy," *Journal of Southern History* 27, no. 2 (1961): 150.

24. Paul O. Hébert to Secretary of War Judah Benjamin, September 27, 1861, Official Records, Ser. I, IV, 112. In Windham, "The Problem of Supply in the Trans-Mississippi Confederacy," 51.

25. Francis R. Lubbock to Judah P. Benjamin, March 7, 1862, Official Records, Ser. IV, I, 980. In ibid., 151.

CHAPTER 4

1. William B. Duncan, Original Diary, June 30; July 3–4, 7, 11–12, 15–31; August 2, 4, 1862.

2. Descriptive Roll of Commissioned Officers, Company F, Spaight's of Texas Mounted Volunteers C.S. Army. SHRL, Liberty, Texas.

3. William B. Duncan, Original Diary, August 6, 7, 10, 1862.

4. Willard A. and Porter W. Heaps, *The Singing Sixties: The Spirit of Civil War Days from the Music of the Times* (Norman: University of Oklahoma Press, 1960), 132.

5. William B. Duncan, Original Diary, August 8 and 9, 1862.

6. Barr, "Texas Coastal Defense, 1861–1865," 12.

7. Murphy Givens, "Town Bitterly Divided during the Civil War," *Corpus Christi Caller-Times,* January 11, 2006.

8. William B. Duncan, Original Diary, August 18, 1862.

9. Many people in the American South eat dinner at midday and supper in the evening. These terms are used here because they were part of William Duncan's vernacular.

10. William B. Duncan, Original Diary, August 19–26, 1862.

11. Frank Fenner and David O. White, *Medical Virology* (New York: Academic Press, 1976), 363.

12. William B. Duncan, Original Diary, September 4, 6–8, 10–12, 1862.

13. Walker, *Spaight's Battalion,* 23.

14. X. B. Debray, Col. and C. M. Mason, Capt., Commanding Officer and Acting Assistant Adjutant-General, respectively, Sub-Military District of Houston, Texas, "Engagement at Sabine Pass, Tex., Sept. 24–25, 1862."

15. William B. Duncan, Original Diary, September 25–30, 1862.

16. A. W. Spaight, Lieut. Col. and R. M. Franklin, Commanding Officer and Acting Assistant Adjutant-General, respectively, Spaight's Texas Battalion, "Engagement at Sabine Pass, Tex., Sept. 24–25, 1862."

17. Walker, *Spaight's Battalion,* 22.

18. Barr, "Texas Coastal Defense, 1861–1865," 12–13

19. William B. Duncan, Original Diary, October 1, 1862.

20. Partlow, *Liberty, Liberty County, and the Atascosito District,* 75.

21. William B. Duncan, Original Diary, October 15, 1862.

22. Ibid., October 25; November 5, 30; December 1–5, 8–26, 28–31, 1862.

23. William J. Cooper, *Jefferson Davis, American* (New York: Vintage Books, 2001), 441–43.

24. Robin E. Baker and Dale Baum, "The Texas Voter and the Crisis of the Union, 1859–1861," *Journal of Southern History* 53, no. 3 (1987): 395.

25. Michael A. Morrison, review of *The Shattering of Texas Unionism: Politics in the Lone Star State during the Civil War Era,* by Dale Baum, in *Journal of Southern History* 66, no. 3 (2000): 638–39.

26. Stanley E. Siegel, review of *Texas Divided: Loyalty and Dissent in the Lone Star State, 1856–1874,* by James Marten, in *American Historical Review* 96, no. 3 (1991): 964.

27. Partlow, *Liberty, Liberty County, and the Atascosito District,* 209.

28. Walker, *Spaight's Battalion,* 23.

29. Paul D. Casdorph, review of *Battle on the Bay: The Civil War Struggle for Galveston,* by Edward T. Cotham Jr., in *Journal of Southern History,* 65, no. 4 (1999): 880.

CHAPTER 5

1. Bern Anderson, "The Naval Strategy of the Civil War," *Military Affairs* 26, no. 1 (1962): 13.

2. Gerald M. Capers Jr., "Confederates and Yankees in Occupied New Orleans, 1862–1865, *Journal of Southern History* 30, no. 4 (1964): 406.

3. Jim Dan Hill, review of *David Glasgow Farragut: Admiral in the Making,* by Charles Lee Lewis, in *American Historical Review* 47, no. 3 (1942): 638.

4. Stephen W. Sears, *Landscape Turned Red: The Battle of Antietam* (New York: Houghton Mifflin, 1983), 33.

5. Frank E. Vandiver, review of Prince John Magruder: His Life and Campaigns, by Paul D. Casdorph, in *Journal of American History* 85, no. 1 (1998): 248.

6. Mary Chestnut, *Original Diary, May 29, 1862,* in *Mary Chestnut's Civil War,* ed. C. Vann Woodward (New Haven, Conn.: Yale University Press, 1981), 352.

7. Celima Duncan, Liberty, Texas, to William B. Duncan, January 2, 1863, 1861. Julia Duncan Welder Collection, SHRL, Liberty, Texas.

8. Edward T. Cotham Jr., *Battle on the Bay: The Civil War Struggle for Galveston* (Austin: University of Texas Press, 1998), 124–34. Also Barr, "Texas Coastal Defense, 1861–1865," 14–16.

9. Casdorph, review of *Battle on the Bay,* 880.

10. Barr, "Texas Coastal Defense, 1861–1865," 18.

11. William B. Duncan, Original Diary, January 1–3, 10, 20, 1863.

12. Block, "Civil War Comes to Jefferson County, Texas: The Road to Gettysburg, 1861–1863," 10–18.

13. Walker, *Spaight's Battalion,* 23.

14. William B. Duncan, Original Diary, January 21, 1863.

15. Spaight's Battalion jacket (Confederate Records, National Archives, Washington, D.C.), in Cooper K. Ragan, ed. "Notes and Documents: The Diary of Captain George W. O'Bryan [*sic*], 1863," *Southwestern Historical Quarterly* 67, nos. 1, 2, 3 (1963–64): 9.

16. Walker, *Spaight's Battalion,* 23.

17. Block, *Civil War Comes to Jefferson County,* 10–18.

18. William B. Duncan, Original Diary, January 22, 23, 25, 27, 1863.

19. Bell Irvin Wiley, "A Time of Greatness," *Journal of Southern History* 22, no. 1 (1956): 4, 5.

20. Walker, *Spaight's Battalion,* 24.

21. William Duncan, Sabine Pass, Texas, to Celima Duncan, Liberty, Texas, January 9, 1863. Julia Duncan Welder Collection, SHRL, Liberty, Texas.

22. William B. Duncan, Original Diary, January 30, 31, 1863.

CHAPTER 6

1. William B. Duncan, Original Diary, February 1, 1863.

2. The correct title is "Yes, We Think of Thee at Home" (words by John H. Hewitt, music by E. Clarke Ilsley), in Heaps and Heaps, *The Singing Sixties,* 234.

3. William Duncan, Sabine Pass, Texas, to Celima Duncan, Liberty, Texas, February 2, 1863, SHRL, Liberty, Texas.

4. W. T. Block, "Scrappy Kate Dorman Left Her Mark," *Beaumont Enterprise,* August 18, 1974.

5. W. T. Block, "Catherine Magill Dorman: Confederate Heroine of Sabine Pass," www.wtblock.com (accessed April 28, 2006).

6. William Duncan, Sabine Pass, Texas, to Celima Duncan, Liberty, Texas, January 29, 1863. Julia Duncan Welder Collection, SHRL, Liberty, Texas.

7. William B. Duncan, Original Diary, February 2, 3, 7, 9, 10, 23, 25, 1863.

8. William Duncan, Sabine Pass, Texas, to Celima Duncan, Liberty, Texas, February 1, 1863, SHRL, Liberty, Texas.

9. William B. Duncan, Original Diary, February 3, 17, 1863.

10. William Duncan, Sabine Pass, Texas, to Celima Duncan, Liberty, Texas, January 16, 1863, SHRL, Liberty, Texas.

11. William B. Duncan, Original Diary, February 11–17, 21, 1863.

12. Charles W. Ramsdell, "The Problem of Public Morale in the Southern Confederacy," in J. Cutler Andrews, "The Confederate Press and Public Morale," *Journal of Southern History* 32, no. 4 (1966): 445–46.

13. Andrews, "The Confederate Press and Public Morale," 446.

14. Gary W. Gallagher, *The Confederate War* (Cambridge, Mass.: Harvard University Press, 1997), 36–40.

15. William B. Duncan, Original Diary, February 22, 1863.

16. Cooper, *Jefferson Davis, American,* 377.

17. Stanley Lebergott, "Why the South Lost: Commercial Purpose in the Confederacy, 1861–1865," *Journal of American History* 70, no. 1 (1983): 68, 70.

18. Walker, *Spaight's Battalion*, 22.

19. Christopher S. Dwyer, "Raiding Strategy: As Applied by the Western Confederate Cavalry in the American Civil War," *Journal of Military History* 63, no. 2 (1999): 268.

20. William B. Duncan, Original Diary, February 28, 1863.

21. Celima Duncan, Liberty, Texas, to William B. Duncan, February 27, 1863, SHRL, Liberty, Texas.

CHAPTER 7

1. William B. Duncan, Original Diary, March 2, 4, 8, 9, 1863.

2. S. F. Du Pont, et al., "The U.S. Coast Survey and the Blockade, 1861," Official Naval Records, Series I, 16: 654–55, in *The Denbigh Project, Institute of Nautical Archaeology*, Texas A&M University, www.nautarch.tamu.edu (accessed May 2, 2006).

3. William B. Duncan, Original Diary, March 11, 1863.

4. Benjamin N. Schoenfeld, "The Psychological Characteristics of Leadership," *Social Forces* 26, no. 4 (1948): 393.

5. E. L. Munson Jr., "Leadership for American Army Leaders," *Infantry Journal* (Washington, D.C., 1942); Schoenfeld, "The Psychological Characteristics of Leadership," 395.

6. William B. Duncan, Original Diary, March 17, 1863.

7. McPherson, *For Cause and Comrades*, 138.

8. James M. Wright to Louisa F. Wright, November 27, 1864. Wright papers in private possession, in McPherson, *For Cause and Comrades*, 162.

9. McPherson, *For Cause and Comrades*, 137, 138, 169.

10. William B. Duncan, Original Diary, March 19, 1863.

11. Ibid., March 20, 24, 27, 30, 31; April 2, 4, 1863.

12. The Immaculate Conception Catholic Church in Liberty, founded in 1756, is one of the oldest churches operating today in Texas. William B. Duncan, Original Diary, April 5, 1863.

13. Ibid., April 8, 9, 13, 1863.

CHAPTER 8

1. William B. Duncan, Original Diary, April 18, 1863.

2. G. W. Schlesselman, "The Gulf Coast Oyster Industry of the United States," *Geographical Review* 45, no. 4 (1955): 533.

3. William B. Duncan, Original Diary, April 19, 1863.

4. Jane E. Schultz, "The Inhospitable Hospital: Gender and Professionalism in Civil War Medicine," *Signs* 17, no. 2 (1992): 369–71.

5. William B. Duncan, Original Diary, April 19–21, 1863.

6. Several receipts made out to Duncan for subscription payments to *Sartain's Union Magazine, New Orleans Weekly Delta, Galveston Weekly News*, the *Galveston Tri-Weekly News* (1864), and the *Liberty State Gazetta* are preserved in the William Duncan papers, SHRL, Liberty, Texas.

7. Duncan's subscription to *Sartain's Union Magazine of Literature and Art* is another indication of his intellectual capacity. It was a short-lived literary magazine first published in January 1849 that ceased publication in 1852, a critical success but financial failure.

8. Taylor was the son of Pres. Zachary Taylor and the brother-in-law of C.S.A. Pres. Jefferson Davis.

9. Windham, "The Problem of Supply in the Trans-Mississippi Confederacy," 151.

10. Harry T. Williams, *Lincoln and His Generals* (New York: Alfred A. Knopf, 1952; reprint, New York: Gramercy Books, 2000), 189.

11. Joseph T. Glatthaar, "4th Texas Cavalry Regiment," Department of History, University of Houston, www.bauer.uh.edu/parks/tex/ (accessed May 11, 2006).

12. William B. Duncan, Original Diary, April 22, 23, 26–30; May 1–7, 1863.

CHAPTER 9

1. William B. Duncan, Original Diary, May 8–9, 1863.

2. Bell Irvin Wiley, *The Life of Johnny Reb: The Common Soldier of the Confederacy* (2005 printing: Baton Rouge: Louisiana State University Press, 1943), 256, 259–60.

3. William B. Duncan, Original Diary, May 10–14, 1863.

4. William T. Chambers, "The Gulf Port City Region of Texas," *Economic Geography* 7, no. 1 (1931): 76.

5. The Battle of Mansfield (Louisiana) is its Confederate name; the Union knew it as the Battle at Sabine Crossroads, a road junction approximately forty miles south of Shreveport. Waldo W. Moore, "The Defense of Shreveport—The Confederacy's Last Redoubt," *Military Affairs* 17, no. 2 (1953): 77.

6. William B. Duncan, Original Diary, May 15, 1863.

7. Ragan, ed., "Notes and Documents, The Diary of Captain George W. O'Bryan [*sic*], 1863," 6.

8. William B. Duncan, Original Diary, May 16–21, 1863.

CHAPTER 10

1. William B. Duncan, Original Diary, May 23, 1863.

2. Reggie Talley, "Monroe County Champion Trees: Black Gum," *Arkansas Gardener*, January 2002.

3. William B. Duncan, Original Diary, May 24, 1863.

4. Dwyer, "Raiding Strategy," 268.

5. William B. Duncan, Original Diary, May 25–28, 1863.

6. Simeon DeBlanc was four years younger than his sister, Celima; he was born in Louisiana in 1847. See 1850 Liberty County Census, SHRL, Liberty, Texas.

7. William B. Duncan, Original Diary, May 29, 1863.

8. John P. Dawson and Frank E. Cooper, "The Effect of Inflation on Private Contracts: United States, 1861–1879," *Michigan Law Review* 33, no. 5 (1935): 707.

9. Ramsdell, "General Robert E. Lee's Horse Supply, 1862–1865," 771.

10. Dawson and Cooper, "The Effect of Inflation on Private Contracts," 709; also, William B. Duncan, Original Diary, May 30, 1863.

11. W. T. Block, "The Opelousas Trail: Bellowing Cows Marked First Trail to New Orleans," http://www.wtblock.com/wtblockjr/opelousa.htm (accessed May 31, 2006); also, *Beaumont Enterprise*, 1975.

12. William B. Duncan, Original Diary, May 31–June 13, 1863.

13. Washington, Louisiana Historical Society, s.v. "Washington, Gateway to the Southwest," www.townofwashingtonla.org/history (accessed June 28, 2006).

14. William B. Duncan, Original Diary, June 13–23, 1863.

15. Ludwell H. Johnson, III, review of *The South Reports the Civil War*, by J. Cutler Andrews *American Historical Review* 76, no. 2 (1971): 561.

16. James G. Randall, "The Newspaper Problem in Its Bearing upon Military Secrecy during the Civil War," *American Historical Review* 23, no. 2 (1918): 313–14.

17. *CWSAC Battle Summaries*, s.v. "LaFourche Crossing, June 20–21, 1863," The American Battlefield Protection Program, Heritage Preservation Services, National Park Services, U.S. Department of the Interior, www.cr.nps.gov/ (accessed July 15, 2006).

18. Tom Green County in west central Texas was established by the Texas legislature and named for General Green on March 13, 1874. Its county seat is San Angelo.

19. Sherod Hunter, Major, commanding Mosquito Fleet, Baylor's (Texas) Cavalry, Battle of Brashear (Morgan City), 23 June 1863. Official Records: Series 1, XXVI, Part 1, Brashear City, June 26, 1863.

CHAPTER 11

1. William B. Duncan, Original Diary, June 24–July 1, 1863.

2. J. P. Dyer, "Some Aspects of Cavalry Operations in the Army of Tennessee," *Journal of Southern History* 8, no. 2 (1942): 212–13.

3. Colonel Alfred Roman, Assistant Inspector-General, Confederate Army, December 28, 1864, in Beauregard Papers (Division of Manuscripts, Library of Congress). In Dyer, "Some Aspects of Cavalry Operations in the Army of Tennessee," 210–25.

4. William B. Duncan, Original Diary, July 2, 4, 1863.

5. Peter Marshall, "Ambrotype," About Photography, http://photography.about .com/library/glossary/bldef_ambrotype.htm (accessed October 25, 2006); also, "The Ambrotype Art," *Scientific American* 12, no. 18 (New York) (January 10, 1857): 138.

6. William B. Duncan, Original Diary, July 5–6, 9–10, 1863.

7. Ibid., July 14–31; August 1–2, 1863.

8. Spaight's Battalion, Company F, Descriptive Roll Book, SHRL, Liberty, Texas.

9. William B. Duncan, Original Diary, August 1, 2, 1863.

CHAPTER 12

1. William B. Duncan, Original Diary, August 4–6, 1863.

2. Ibid., August 8, 9, 11, 21, 1863.

3. David T. Courtwright, "The Hidden Epidemic: Opiate Addiction and Cocaine Use in the South, 1860–1920," *Journal of Southern History* 49, no. 1 (1983): 64, 72.

4. William B. Duncan, Original Diary, August 12–21, 24, 1863.

5. Cooper, *Jefferson Davis, American*, 487.

6. T. Michael Parrish, review of *The Papers of Jefferson Davis,* vol. 9, January–September 1863, by Jefferson Davis, Lynda Lasswell Crist, Mary Seaton Dix, and Kenneth H. Williams, *Journal of Southern History* 64, no. 2 (1998): 371.

7. Cooper, *Jefferson Davis, American,* 485–86.

8. William B. Duncan, Original Diary, August 28, 1863.

9. Ibid., August 29–31, 1863.

10. Cooper, *Jefferson Davis, American,* 481–82, 530–31.

11. William B. Duncan, Original Diary, September 1–6, 1863.

12. Sabine River Authority of Texas s.v. "Description of Sabine River Basin," www.sra.dst.tx.us/basin/overview (accessed July 11, 2006).

13. William B. Duncan, Original Diary, September 7, 1863.

14. Ibid., September 8, 1863.

CHAPTER 13

1. W. T. Block, "The Battle of Sabine Pass—Its Causes and Effects," wtblock.com (accessed June 3, 2006).

2. Edward T. Cotham Jr., *Sabine Pass: The Confederacy's Thermopylae* (Austin: University of Texas Press, 2004), 47–49.

3. *CWSAC Battle Summaries,* s.v. "Sabine Pass II, Sept. 8, 1863." The American Battlefield Protection Program, Heritage Preservation Services, National Park Services, U.S. Department of the Interior, www.cr.nps.gov/ (accessed June 3, 2006).

4. William B. Duncan, Original Diary, September 9–13, 1863.

5. Peter S. Bearman, "Desertion as Localism: Army Unit Solidarity and Group Norms in the U.S. Civil War," *Social Forces* 70, no. 2 (1991): 322–23.

6. William B. Duncan, Original Diary, September 14, 15, 1863.

7. Notice to absentees of Spaight's Battalion, Liberty, Texas, September 15, 1863, in William B. Duncan papers, SHRL, Liberty, Texas.

8. Walker, *Spaight's Battalion,* 25.

9. *CWSAC Battle Summaries,* s.v. "Stirling's Plantation, September 29, 1863." The American Battlefield Protection Program, Heritage Preservation Services, National Park Services, U.S. Department of the Interior, www.cr.nps.gov/ (accessed October 19, 2006).

10. William B. Duncan, Original Diary, September 26, 30; October 1–25; November 1, 1863.

CHAPTER 14

1. William B. Duncan, Original Diary, November 19, 1863.

2. Ibid., November 2–12, 14–16, 19, 20, 22–26, 1863.

3. Ibid., November 27–30; December 1, 3, 4, 1863.

4. John G. Moore, "Mobility and Strategy in the Civil War," *Military Affairs* 24, no. 2, Civil War issue (1960): 69, 75.

5. Baughman, "The Evolution of Rail-Water Systems of Transportation in the Gulf Southwest, 1836–1890," 362.

6. Moore, "Mobility and Strategy in the Civil War," 74.

7. William B. Duncan, Original Diary, December 5–7, 1863.

8. Ibid., December 9, 10, 12, 13, 1863.

CHAPTER 15

1. William B. Duncan, Original Diary, December 15–23, 1863.

2. Ibid., December 24–28, 30, 31, 1863.

3. William B. Duncan, San Jacinto (River) at Sims, to Celima Duncan, Liberty, Texas, January 5, 1864, SHRL, Liberty, Texas.

4. Governor Pendleton Murrah to the Extra Session of the Tenth Legislature, May 11, 1864. Executive record books, reel 3477, Texas Secretary of State, Archives and Information Services Division, Texas State Library and Archives Commission.

5. "Camps, Forts and Posts in Texas, 1861–1865," Adjutant General RG 401 Civil War Records, 1861–65, Texas State Archives.

6. William B. Duncan, Camp near Houston, to Celima Duncan, Liberty, Texas, January 11, 1864, SHRL, Liberty, Texas.

7. Ibid., 330.

8. Morning Report, February 11, 1864, Company F, Spaight's Battalion, SHRL, Liberty, Texas.

9. Crute, *Units of the Confederate States Army,* 337.

10. William B. Duncan, Beaumont, to Celima Duncan, Liberty, Texas, February 3, 1864, SHRL, Liberty, Texas.

11. William B. Duncan, Beaumont, to Celima Duncan, Liberty, Texas, February 8, 1864, SHRL, Liberty, Texas.

12. William B. Duncan, Beaumont, to Celima Duncan, Liberty, Texas, February 21, 1864, SHRL, Liberty, Texas.

13. William B. Duncan, Beaumont, to Celima Duncan, Liberty, Texas, February 12, 1864, SHRL, Liberty, Texas.

14. William Duncan to Celima Duncan, February 8, 1864, SHRL, Liberty, Texas.

15. William B. Duncan, Beaumont, to Celima Duncan, Liberty, Texas, February 16, 1864, SHRL, Liberty, Texas.

16. William B. Duncan, Beaumont, to Celima Duncan, Liberty, Texas, February 21, 1864, SHRL, Liberty, Texas.

17. Morning Report, February 24, 1864, Company F, Spaight's Battalion, SHRL, Liberty, Texas.

18. William B. Duncan, Camp near Beaumont, to Celima Duncan, Liberty, Texas, February 24, 1864, SHRL, Liberty, Texas.

19. William B. Duncan, Camp near Beaumont, to Celima Duncan, Liberty, Texas, March 7, 1864, SHRL, Liberty, Texas.

20. Morning Report, March 7, 1864, Company F, Spaight's Battalion, SHRL, Liberty, Texas.

21. Morning Report, March 10, 1864, Company F, Spaight's Battalion, SHRL, Liberty, Texas.

22. Morning Reports, March 15, 21, 1864, Company F, Spaight's Battalion, SHRL, Liberty, Texas.

23. William B. Duncan, Old Camp near Beaumont, to Celima Duncan, Liberty, Texas, March 22, 1864, SHRL, Liberty, Texas.

24. Morning Report, April 6–7, 1864, Company F, Spaight's Battalion, SHRL, Liberty, Texas.

25. Robert Wooster, *Handbook of Texas Online,* s.v. "Burr's Ferry," http://www.tsha
.utexas.edu/handbook/online/articles/BB/rtb2.html (accessed November 2, 2006).

26. Morning Report, April 10, 1864, Company F, Spaight's Battalion, SHRL, Liberty, Texas.

27. Morning Reports, April 21–22, 1864, Company F, Spaight's Battalion, SHRL, Liberty, Texas.

28. William B. Duncan to Captain Giraud, Engineering Department, receipt for $1,413.50 in Duncan's handwriting dated April 23, 1864, William Duncan papers, SHRL, Liberty, Texas.

29. Morning Reports, April 27–30, 1864, Company F, Spaight's Battalion, SHRL, Liberty, Texas.

30. William B. Duncan, Niblett's Bluff, to Celima Duncan, Liberty, Texas, May 1, 1864, SHRL, Liberty, Texas.

31. Morning Report, May 2, 1864, Company F, Spaight's Battalion, SHRL, Liberty, Texas.

32. William B. Duncan, Houston, to Celima Duncan, Liberty, Texas, April 26, 1864, SHRL, Liberty, Texas.

33. Walker, *Spaight's Battalion,* 25, 26.

34. Morning Reports, May 5–14, 1864, Company F, Spaight's Battalion, SHRL, Liberty, Texas.

35. James M. McPherson, *Ordeal by Fire,* vol. 2, *The Civil War,* 3rd ed. (New York: McGraw Hill, 2001), 447.

36. Morning Reports, May 5–14, 1864, Company F, Spaight's Battalion, SHRL, Liberty, Texas.

CHAPTER 16

1. William B. Duncan, on board steamer *Sunflower* between Niblett's Bluff and Beaumont, May 2, 1864, to Celima Duncan, Liberty, Texas, SHRL, Liberty, Texas.

2. Charles C. Lund was county treasurer of Liberty County from 1856 to 1861. Partlow, Appendix, Exhibit E, County Officials of Liberty County, 350–52.

3. Miller, E. T., "The State Finances of Texas during the Civil War," *Southwestern Historical Quarterly Online,* pages 1–23, http://www.tsha.utexas.edu/publications/journals/shq/online/vo14/n1/article_2.html (accessed November 2, 2006).

4. William B. Duncan to Celima Duncan, April 26, 1864.

5. Gilbert E. Govan and James W. Livingood, "Chattanooga under Military Occupation, 1863–1865," *Journal of Southern History* 17, no. 1 (1951): 28.

6. McPherson, *Ordeal by Fire,* 445.

7. William B. Duncan to Celima Duncan, May 2, 1864.

8. Morning Report, May 19, 1864, Company F, Spaight's Battalion, SHRL, Liberty, Texas.

9. William B. Duncan, Camp Spindletop, to Celima Duncan, Liberty, Texas, May 20, 1864, SHRL, Liberty, Texas.

10. Walker, *Spaight's Battalion,* 26.

11. William B. Duncan, Beaumont, to Celima Duncan, Liberty, Texas, August 3, 1864, SHRL, Liberty, Texas.

12. "Mobile Bay, Aug. 2–24, 1864," *CWSAC Battle Summaries.* The American Battlefield Protection Program, Heritage Preservation Services, National Park Services, U.S. Department of the Interior, www.cr.nps.gov/ (accessed November 9, 2006).

13. Cutrer, "John George Walker."

14. Morning Report, October 15, 1864, Company F, Spaight's Battalion, SHRL, Liberty, Texas.

15. Walker, *Spaight's Battalion,* 26.

16. William B. Duncan, Camp Lubbock, to Celima Duncan, Liberty, Texas, December 11, 1864, SHRL, Liberty, Texas.

17. Art Leatherwood, *Handbook of Texas Online, s.v.* "Camp Groce," http://www.tsha.utexas.edu/handbook/online/articles/CC/qcc17.html (accessed November 10, 2006).

18. William B. Duncan, Camp Lubbock, to Celima Duncan, Liberty, Texas, December 18, 1864, SHRL, Liberty, Texas.

19. William B. Duncan, Camp Lubbock, to Celima Duncan, Liberty, Texas, December 20, 1864, SHRL, Liberty, Texas.

CHAPTER 17

1. William B. Duncan, Original Diary, January 1, 1865.

2. McPherson, *Ordeal by Fire,* 496–97, 500–501, 503.

3. William B. Duncan, Original Diary, January 2, 4, 1865.

4. Duncan, Camp Lubbock, to Celima Duncan, Liberty, Texas, December 18, 1864, SHRL, Liberty, Texas.

5. William B. Duncan, Original Diary, January 6, 1865.

6. Richard C. K. Burdekin and Marc D. Weidenmier, "Inflation Is Always and Everywhere a Monetary Phenomenon: *Richmond vs. Houston* in 1864," *American Economic Review* 91, no. 5 (2001): 1624.

7. William B. Duncan, Original Diary, January 10–12, 14, 18–19, 21, 1865.

8. Wiley, *The Life of Johnny Reb,* 243.

9. William B. Duncan, Original Diary, January 25, 27, 30; February 2, 1865.

CHAPTER 18

1. Barbara H. Fisher, *Handbook of Texas Online,* s.v. "Edward Bradford Pickett," http://www.tsha.utexas.edu/handbook/online/articles/PP/fpi5.html (accessed September 15, 2006).

2. William B. Duncan, Original Diary, February 4, 6, 7, 10, 11, 1865.

3. Ibid., February 12–14, 1865.

4. Morning Report, Company F, Spaight's Battalion, February 15, 1865, SHRL, Liberty, Texas.

5. William B. Duncan, Original Diary, February 15, 16, 1865.

6. Ibid., February 20, 25, 27; March 1–3, 5, 1865.

7. Ibid., March 10, 1865.

8. Burdekin and Weidenmier, "Inflation Is Always and Everywhere a Monetary Phenomenon: Richmond vs. Houston in 1864," 1627.

9. William B. Duncan, Original Diary, March 10, 1865.

10. Duncan was made a Master Mason on April 4, 1856 in the Grand Lodge, State of Texas of Ancient Free and Accepted Masons, certificate, SHRL, Liberty, Texas.

11. William B. Duncan, Original Diary, March 16–19, 1865.

12. Ibid., March 23–25, 31, 1865.

13. Cutrer, "John George Walker."

14. William B. Duncan, Original Diary, April 2, 3, 1865.

CHAPTER 19

1. William B. Duncan, Original Diary, April 6, 1865; also, Thomas W. Cutrer, *Handbook of Texas Online,* s.v. "George Wythe Baylor," http://www.tsha.utexas.edu/ handbook/online/articles/BB/fbaar.html (accessed October 30, 2006); also, Young, *To the Tyrants Never Yield,* 182–85; Texas State Cemetery, "John Austin Wharton."

2. William B. Duncan, Original Diary, April 7, 8, 1865.

3. Charles Bracelen Flood, *Lee: The Last Years,* 1st Mariner Books ed. (New York: Houghton Mifflin, 1998), 10, 12–13.

4. Ulysses S. Grant, *Personal Memoirs,* 2 vols. (New York, 1885), II, 489, in McPherson, *Ordeal by Fire,* 519.

5. William B. Duncan, Original Diary, April 21, 1865.

6. Ibid., April 14, 15, 1865.

7. Ibid., April 22–24, 1865.

8. Ibid., April 27–28; 30, May 1–2, 1865.

9. Ibid., May 3, 4, 1865.

10. Elizabeth Bethel, "The Freedmen's Bureau in Alabama," *Journal of Southern History* 14, no. 1 (1948): 49.

11. Patrick G. Gerster, review of *A Long Shadow: Jefferson Davis and the Final Days of the Confederacy,* in *Journal of Southern History* 54, no. 1 (1988): 125.

12. William B. Duncan, Original Diary, May 5, 7–9, 1865.

13. Ibid., May 11–14, 1865.

14. Ramsdell, "Texas from the Fall of the Confederacy to the Beginning of Reconstruction."

15. William B. Duncan, Original Diary, May 15, 16, 1865.

16. Ramsdell, "Texas from the Fall of the Confederacy to the Beginning of Reconstruction."

17. William B. Duncan, Original Diary, May 17, 18, 1865.

18. Ibid., May 20, 21, 1865.

19. Ramsdell, "Texas from the Fall of the Confederacy to the Beginning of Reconstruction," *Southwestern Historical Quarterly Online* 11, no. 3 (accessed October 28, 2006).

20. William B. Duncan, Original Diary, May 22, 23, 1865.

21. John Bankhead Magruder, commanding general, Texas and New Mexico District, Confederate States of America, to Col. Ashbell Smith and William Pitt Ballinger, May 24, 1865, Galveston and Texas History Center, Rosenberg Library, Galveston, Texas.

22. C. Richard King, *Handbook of Texas Online,* s.v. "Ballinger, William Pitt," http:// www.tsha.utexas.edu/handbook/online/articles/BB/fba52.html (accessed September 6, 2007).

CHAPTER 20

1. Duncan's 1864 diary was among his missing papers; it was never found. His 1864 military life is reconstructed primarily from Morning Reports, January–December, 1864, Company F, Spaight's Battalion, SHRL, Liberty, Texas.

2. William B. Duncan, Original Diary, May 24, 1865.

3. Ibid., May 25–29, 1865.

4. Ibid., June 2, 5, 1865.

5. Ibid. June 13, 1865.

6. Ibid., June 6, 8, 10–14, 18, 1865.

7. Robert Cochran, review of *Juneteenth Texas: Essays in African-American Folklore* by Francis Abernethy, Patrick Mullen, and Alan Govenar, in *African American Review* 33, no. 4 (1999): 694.

8. James Alex Baggett, *Handbook of Texas Online*, s.v. "Gordon Granger," http://www.tsha.utexas.edu/handbook/online/articles/GG/fgr10.html (accessed September 19, 2006).

9. President Andrew Johnson, Amnesty Proclamation, May 29, 1865, www.sewanee.edu/faculty/Willis/Civil_War/documents (accessed September 19, 2006).

10. Robert A. Calvert, Arnoldo De León, and Gregg Cantrell, *The History of Texas*, 3rd ed. (Wheeling, Ill.: Harlan Davidson, 2002), 150.

11. William B. Duncan, Original Diary, June 21, 1865.

12. Ibid., June 25, 1865.

13. Duncan's official amnesty oath with voter registration was issued October 14, 1865, in SHRL, Liberty, Texas.

14. Johnson, Amnesty Proclamation.

15. William B. Duncan, Original Diary, June 27, 1865.

16. Ibid., June 29, 30, 1865.

17. Ibid., July 10, 11, 13, 17, 1865.

18. *Liberty Gazette*, March 6, 1868, in Partlow, *Liberty, Liberty County, and the Atascosito District*, 216.

19. William B. Duncan, Original Diary, August 1, 1865.

20. Ibid., July 31, 1865.

21. Ibid., July 19, 24, 1865.

22. Peter Kolchin, "Scalawags, Carpetbaggers, and Reconstruction: A Quantitative Look at Southern Congressional Politics, 1868–1872," *Journal of Southern History* 45, no. 1 (1979): 63.

23. Allen W. Trelease, "Who Were the Scalawags?" *Journal of Southern History* 29, no. 4 (1963): 445.

24. William B. Duncan, Original Diary, August 12, 14, 19, 1865.

25. Ibid., August 12, 14, 19, 23, 26, 31; September 1, 5, 18–24, 27, 29–30; October 1, 1865.

26. Ibid., July 11, October 15, 1865; March 9, 10, 1867.

CHAPTER 21

1. William B. Duncan, Original Diary, October 6, 8, 10, 17, 22; November 5, 1865.

2. Ibid., October 20, 1865.

3. The Duncan papers contain an undated, partially completed poem in Celima's hand that reveals her anger over Duncan's all-night drinking and gambling escapades. It reads in part, "One evening as I sat beside Our humble cottage door, Listening for my husband's steps As oft I've done before, Some evil thoughts come in my mind And bitterly I said, 'I never wish to see him more, Oh would that he were dead.'" William Duncan papers, SHRL, Liberty, Texas.

4. William B. Duncan, Original Diary, October 21, 23, 24, 1865.

5. Louisiana State Museum, "Antebellum Louisiana: Urban Life," www.lsm.crt .state.la.us/ (accessed October 17, 2006).

6. William B. Duncan, Original Diary, October 25, 1865.

7. Herbert A. Bloch, "The Sociology of Gambling," *American Journal of Sociology* 57, no. 3 (1951): 217.

8. Joan A. Furey, "For Some, the War Rages on," *American Journal of Nursing* 82, no. 11 (1982): 1695–96, 1698.

9. William B. Duncan, Original Diary, November 14, 1865.

10. Ibid., October 30; November 16, 18, 19, 27, 29, 30, 1865.

11. Ibid., December 1–14, 19, 1865.

12. Ibid., January 3, 4, 1866.

13. Contract between William B. Duncan and freedmen Louis Green, Reuben Green, Texas Green, and Benjamin Moseley, filed February 1, 1866 with the Bureau of Refugees, Freedmen and Abandoned Lands, Liberty, Texas, in SHRL, Liberty, Texas.

14. William B. Duncan, Original Diary, January 11, 16, 19, 21, 22, 24–29, 1866.

15. Ibid., February 1, 9, 10, 28; March 16, 26; April 20, 1866.

16. Ibid., February 11–13, 1866.

17. Ibid.,, February 14–16, 17, 1866.

18. Ibid., February 23, 24, 26, 27; March 2, 5, 18, 20, 22, 24, 28, 1866.

19. Robert Wooster, "Ashley W. Spaight."

20. Carl H. Moneyhon, *Handbook of Texas Online,* s.v. "Reconstruction," http:// www.tsha.utexas.edu/handbook/online/articles/RR/mzr1.html (accessed December 7, 2006).

21. Calvert, De León, and Cantrell, *The History of Texas,* 150–52.

22. William B. Duncan, Original Diary, March 24, 1866.

23. Ibid., April 6, 7, 9, 11–14, 16, 17, 1866.

24. Ibid., April 19, 22, 29, 30, 1866.

25. Ibid., May 2, 1866.

26. Marty Baker and George Ray McEachern, Texas Cooperative Extension, "Texas Mayhaws," January 27, 1997, http://aggie-horticulture.tamu.edu/extension/fruit/ mayhaw/mayhaw.html (accessed October 16, 2006).

27. William B. Duncan, Original Diary, May 12, 1866.

28. Ibid., May 13, 1866.

29. Ibid., May 11, 13–16, 1866.

CHAPTER 22

1. William B. Duncan, Original Diary, May 17, 1866.

2. List of Privates, Descriptive Roll of Commissioned Officers, Company F, Spaight's Battalion of Texas Mounted Volunteers C.S. Army, SHRL, Liberty, Texas.

3. William B. Duncan, Original Diary, July 23; August 13, 1866.

4. Benjamin Willie Barrow, Refugio County, Texas, to William B. Duncan, Liberty, Texas, January 21, 1867, in William B. Duncan papers, SHRL, Liberty, Texas.

5. Benjamin Franklin to M. Leroy, 1789, in John Bartlett, *Familiar Quotations*, 15th ed. (New York: Little, Brown, 1980), 348.

6. William B. Duncan, Original Diary, May 29, 31; June 1, 5–7, 9, 11, 12, 14, 15, 20, 21, 26, 1866.

7. Ibid., July 10, 11–21, 1866.

8. Ibid., July 19; August 14–15, 1866.

9. Calvert, De León, and Cantrell, *The History of Texas*, 83–84.

10. Andrew Forest Muir, *Handbook of Texas Online*, s.v. "Harrisburg, Texas," http://www.tsha.utexas.edu/handbook/online/articles/HH/hvh27.html (accessed September 22, 2006).

11. William B. Duncan, Original Diary, August 16, 1866.

12. Ibid., August 19, 22, 24, 1866.

13. Ibid., August 29, 1866.

14. Ibid., August 30, 1866.

15. M. Fernan-Nunez, "Asiatic Cholera," *American Journal of Nursing* 43, no. 1 (1943): 44.

16. William B. Duncan, Original Diary, September 7, 8, 1866.

17. Ibid., September 7, 8, 12, 17–28, 1866.

18. Ibid., October 10, 13, 19, 20, 22, 1866.

19. Ibid., October 23–November 1, 7, 1866.

20. Ibid., December 25–27, 1866.

21. Ibid., December 28, 30, 1866; January 1, 1867.

22. Ibid., January 2, 1867.

23. Ibid., January 6, 8, 14, 1867.

24. Ibid., January 16, 17, 23, 27, 31; February 4–5, 1867.

25. Ibid., January 25; February 10, 16, 1867.

26. Ibid., February 21, 1867.

27. Ibid., February 22, 1867.

28. William B. Duncan, Personal Bible, July 25, 1845, SHRL, Liberty, Texas.

29. William B. Duncan, Original Diary, February 22; March 2, 1867.

CHAPTER 23

1. William B. Duncan, Original Diary, March 7, 14–17, 20–26; April 1–2, 4–5, 11–12, 1867.

2. Ibid., April 10, 12–19, 1867.

3. Ibid., April 19, 21–23; July 3, 7, 8, 26, 1867.

4. Ibid., April 25, 28, 30, 1867.

5. Ibid., May 5, 6, 1867.

6. Ibid., May 27; June 4, 1867.

7. Ibid., June 13, 25, 29, 30; July 29, 1867.

8. Ibid., May 2, 3, 15, 22, 28, 1867.

9. Ibid., July 1, 8, 9, 11–12, 14, 22, 1867.

10. Kathryn Page, Louisiana State Museum, New Orleans, e-mail to author, October 18, 2006. James McQuoid, Chris. Mehle, James Aycock, James Gitzenger and Hortaire Imbau were listed as members of McQuoid, Mehle & Co. in the 1866 New Orleans City Directory.

11. A note written by Celima in September 1867 itemizes several Duncan debts that total more than $4,000. William B. Duncan papers, SHRL, Liberty, Texas.

12. J. D. Staples, McQuoid & Mehle, New Orleans, to W. B. Duncan, July 18, 1867. William B. Duncan papers, SHRL, Liberty, Texas.

13. Celima DeBlanc Duncan was ninety-one when she died on May 8, 1925. She is buried in Liberty's Catholic cemetery within sight of her husband's grave in the old City Cemetery across the road.

14. William B. Duncan, Original Diary, July 24, 31; August 1, 3, 4–6, 1867.

15. Ibid., August 17, 18, 1867.

16. Elizabeth Kübler-Ross, *On Death and Dying* (New York: Macmillan, 1969), 276.

17. William B. Duncan, Personal Bible, July 25, 1845. Julia Duncan Welder Collection, SHRL, Liberty, Texas.

18. Darlene Mott is an archivist at the Sam Houston Regional Library and Research Center in Liberty, Texas.

EPILOGUE

1. James. L. Sellers, "The Economic Incidence of the Civil War in the South," *Mississippi Valley Historical Review* 14, no. 2 (1927): 183, 187, 188.

2. W. C. Nunn, *Texas under the Carpetbaggers* (Austin: University of Texas Press, 1962), 7, 8, 135, 207, 208.

3. Genesis 9; Leviticus 25, 44–46.

4. Anthony S. Parent Jr., *Foul Means: The Formation of a Slave Society in Virginia, 1660–1740* (Williamsburg, Va.: Omohundro Institute of Early American History and Culture published by the University of North Carolina Press, Chapel Hill, 2003).

5. Ira Berlin, *Many Thousands Gone: The First Two Centuries of Slavery in North America* (Cambridge, Mass.: Harvard University Press, 1998).

6. *King Henry IV*, Part II, Act III, scene i.

Bibliography

PRIMARY SOURCES

Crozier, John W. "Statement of the Chief Justice of Hardin County, 17 Sept. 1861." Duncan papers. Sam Houston Regional Library and Research Center, Liberty, Texas. Typewritten, photocopied.

Debray, X. B., Col., and C. M. Mason, Capt., Commanding Officer and Acting Assistant Adjutant-General, respectively, Sub-Military District of Houston, Texas. "Engagement at Sabine Pass, Texas, Sept. 24–25, 1862." In Official Records, Series 1, Vol. 15, Part 1 (Baton Rouge–Natchez), 143–44.

Descriptive Roll of Commissioned Officers, Company (F) Spaight's Battalion of Texas Mounted Volunteers, C.S. Army. Julia Duncan Wilder Collection. Sam Houston Regional Library and Research Center, Liberty, Texas.

Duncan, W. Auborne, Trinity River, Texas, to Henry Moss, November 22, 1835. Julia Duncan Welder Collection. Sam Houston Regional Library and Research Center, Liberty, Texas.

Duncan, William B. Personal papers. Julia Duncan Welder Collection. Sam Houston Regional Library and Research Center, Liberty, Texas.

————. Master Mason certificate, April 4, 1856. Grand Lodge, State of Texas of Ancient Free and Accepted Masons, Liberty Lodge No. 48.

————. Original Diaries, June 25–September 19, 1843; September 24, 1844–March 1, 1846; October 23–December 14, 1853; May 18, 1854–August 31, 1854; November 4, 1854–February 15, 1855; January 1, 1860–January 17, 1861; February 21, 1858; January 18–September 9, 1861; September 10, 1861–January 12, 1862; January 1, 1862–May 5, 1862; May 6, 1862–December 31, 1862; January 1, 1863–June 1, 1863; June 1, 1863–December 31, 1863; January 1, 1865–December 31, 1865; January 1, 1866–March 4, 1867; March 5, 1867–August 18, 1867. Transcribed by Chessie Duncan Quesenbury. Original documents and transcriptions in the Julia Duncan Welder Collection. Sam Houston Regional Library and Research Center, Liberty, Texas.

————. Personal Bible, July 25, 1845. Julia Duncan Welder Collection. Sam Houston Regional Library and Research Center, Liberty, Texas.

Gillard papers. Julia Duncan Welder Collection. Sam Houston Regional Library and Research Center, Liberty, Texas.

Houston, Sam to William Duncan, December 6, 1847. Julia Duncan Welder Collection. Sam Houston Regional Library and Research Center, Liberty, Texas.

Hunter, Sherod, Maj., commanding Mosquito Fleet, Baylor's (Texas) Cavalry, Battle of Brashear (Morgan City), June 23, 1863. Official Records. Series 1, Vol. 26, Part 1, Brashear City, June 26, 1863.

Johnson, President Andrew. Amnesty Proclamation. May 29, 1865.

Liberty County Convention Election Returns, February 23, 1861. Sam Houston Regional Library and Research Center, Liberty, Texas.

Liberty County, Texas. Census of 1850, p. 287, entry H287. Sam Houston Regional Library and Research Center, Liberty, Texas.

Liberty County, Texas. Index to Deeds, Deed Book F, p. 122. Sam Houston Regional Library and Research Center, Liberty, Texas.

Magruder, John Bankhead, commanding general, Texas and New Mexico District, Confederate States of America, to Col. Ashbell Smith and William Pitt Ballenger, May 24, 1865. Galveston and Texas History Center, Rosenberg Library, Galveston, Texas.

Marshall, Brig. Gen. Humphrey to Gen. A. Sidney Johnston, January 20, 1862. "The War of the Rebellion: A Compilation of the Official Records of the Union and Confederate Armies." Series 1, Vol. 7 (Washington, D.C.: Government Printing Office, 1882).

Morning Reports, January–December 1864, Company F, Spaight's Battalion. Julia Duncan Wilder Collection. Sam Houston Regional Library and Research Center, Liberty, Texas.

Morning Report, Company F, Spaight's Battalion, February 15, 1865. Julia Duncan Wilder Collection. Sam Houston Regional Library and Research Center, Liberty, Texas.

Murrah, Pendleton, Gov. To the Extra Session of the Tenth Legislature, May 11, 1864. Executive record books, reel 3477, Texas Secretary of State, Archives and Information Services Division, Texas State Library and Archives Commission. Sabine Pass, Texas, Engagement at, 24–25 September 1862. Official Records, Series 1, Vol. 15, Part 1 (Baton Rouge–Natchez): 143–44.

Spaight, A. W., Lieut. Col., and R. M. Franklin, Commanding Officer and Acting Assistant Adjutant-General, respectively, Spaight's Texas Battalion. "Engagement at Sabine Pass, Texas, Sept. 24–25, 1862." Official Records, Series 1, Vol. 15, Part 1 (Baton Rouge–Natchez), 144.

Spaight's Battalion, Company F, Descriptive Roll Book, Sam Houston Regional Library and Research Center, Liberty, Texas.

Urban, Mrs. Mary. Dayton, Texas. Great-granddaughter of William B. Duncan. Telephone interview with author, December 2, 2006.

Willis, G. H. "Confession of G. H. Willis, One of the Three Who Attempted to Rob and Murder J. M. Dark and Family in Batson Prairie on the Night of the 16th of September, 1861." Sam Houston Regional Library and Research Center, Liberty, Texas. Typewritten, photocopied.

SECONDARY SOURCES

Adams, George Worthington. "Confederate Medicine." *Journal of Southern History* 6 (May 1940): 151–66.

Alcott, Louisa M. *Hospital Sketches* (1863; Cambridge, Mass.: Harvard University Press, 1960), 36. In Richard H. Shyrock, "A Medical Perspective on the Civil War." *American Quarterly* 14 (Summer 1962): 161–73.

"The Ambrotype Art." *Scientific American* 12 (January 10, 1857): 137–44. Available at http://cdl.library.cornell.edu/cgi-bin/moa/moa-cgi?notisid=ABF2204–0012& byte=164002945 (accessed October 25, 2006).

Anderson, Bern. "The Naval Strategy of the Civil War." *Military Affairs* 26 (Spring 1962): 11–21.

Andrews, J. Cutler. "The Confederate Press and Public Morale." *Journal of Southern History* 32, no. 4 (1966): 445–46.

Ash, Stephen V. *When the Yankees Came: Conflict and Chaos in the Occupied South, 1861–1865.* Chapel Hill: University of North Carolina Press, 1999.

"Atchafalaya National Wildlife Refuge." Southeast Louisiana National Wildlife Refuges, U.S. Fish & Wildlife Service. Available at www.fws.gov (accessed October 24, 2006).

Augustin, George. "History of Yellow Fever (New Orleans, 1909)." *Yellow Fever Deaths in New Orleans, 1817–1905.* New Orleans Public Library Online. Available at http://nutrias.org/facts/feverdeaths.htm (accessed March 22, 2006).

Baggett, James Alex. *Handbook of Texas Online,* s.v. "Gordon Granger." Available at http://www.tsha.utexas.edu/handbook/online/articles/GG/fgr10.html (accessed September 19, 2006).

Baker, Marty, and George Ray McEachern. "Texas Mayhaws" (January 27, 1997). Texas Cooperative Extension, Texas A&M University System, College Station, Texas. Available at http://aggie-horticulture.tamu.edu/extension/fruit/mayhaw/mayhaw .html (accessed October 2, 2006).

Baker, Robin E., and Dale Baum. "The Texas Voter and the Crisis of the Union, 1859–1861." *Journal of Southern History,* 53, no. 3 (1987): 395–420.

Baker, T. Lindsay. *Ghost Towns of Texas.* Norman: University of Oklahoma Press, 1986.

Barker, Eugene C. "Stephen F. Austin." *Mississippi Valley Historical Review* 5, no. 1 (1918): 20–25.

Barker, Eugene C., ed., *The Austin Papers.* 3 vols. (Washington, D.C.: Historical Manuscripts Commission, 1924–28).

Barr, Alwyn. "Confederate Artillery in the Trans-Mississippi." *Military Affairs* 27, no. 2, Civil War Issue (1963): 7–83.

———. "Texas Coastal Defense, 1861–1865." *Southwestern Historical Quarterly* 45, no. 1 (1961): 1–31. Available at http://www.tsha.utexas.edu/shqonline/apager .php?vol=065&pag=009 (Accessed December 22, 2007).

Basler, Roy P. "Abraham Lincoln's Rhetoric." *American Literature* 11, no. 2 (1939): 167–82.

Baughman, J. L., and B. B. Baker Jr., "Oysters in Texas." *Texas Game, Fish and Oyster Commission Bulletin* No. 29 (1951). In Schlesselman 1955, 533.

Baughman, James P. "The Evolution of Rail-Water Systems of Transportation in the Gulf Southwest, 1836–1890." *Journal of Southern History*, 34, no. 3 (1968): 357–81.

Baum, Dale. "Pinpointing Apparent Fraud in the 1861 Texas Secession Referendum." *Journal of Interdisciplinary History* 22, no. 2 (1991): 201–21.

Bearman, Peter S. "Desertion as Localism: Army Unit Solidarity and Group Norms in the U.S. Civil War." *Social Forces* 70, no. 2 (1991): 321–42.

Beazley, Julia. *Handbook of Texas Online*, s.v. "Liendo Plantation." Available at http://www.tsha.utexas.edu/handbook/online/articles/LL/cc11.html (accessed November 10, 2006).

Bergeron, Paul H., ed. *The Papers of Andrew Johnson*, Vol. 8, *May–August 1865.* Knoxville: University of Tennessee Press, 1989.

Beringer, Richard E. "A Profile of the Members of the Confederate Congress." *Journal of Southern History* 33, no. 4 (1967): 518–41.

Berlin, Ira. *Many Thousands Gone: The First Two Centuries of Slavery in North America.* Cambridge, Mass.: Belknap Press of Harvard University Press, 1998.

Bethel, Elizabeth. "The Freedmen's Bureau in Alabama." *Journal of Southern History* 14, no. 1 (1948): 49–92.

Biesele, Megan. *Handbook of Texas Online*, s.v. "Tyler County." Available at http://www.tsha.utexas.edu/handbook/online/articles/TT/hct10.html (accessed October 21, 2006).

Bishop, Curtis. "Lots of Land." *New Handbook of Texas* 4 (Austin: Steck, 1949).

Bloch, Herbert A. "The Sociology of Gambling." *American Journal of Sociology* 57, no. 3 (1951): 215–21.

Block, W. T. "The Battle of Sabine Pass—Its Causes and Effects." Available at wtblock.com (accessed June 3, 2006).

———. "Catherine Magill Dorman: Confederate Heroine of Sabine Pass." Available at www.wtblock.com (accessed April 28, 2006).

———. "Civil War Comes to Jefferson County, Texas: The Road to Gettysburg 1861–1863." *Blue and Gray Magazine* 4, no. 1 (1986): 10–18.

———. "Confederacy's Col. Spaight Well-Respected." *Beaumont Enterprise*, January 25, 2003.

———. *A History of Jefferson County, Texas from Wilderness to Reconstruction.* Nederland, Tex.: Nederland Publishing, 1976. Available at http://www.wtblock.com/wtblockjr/History%20of%20Jefferson%20County (accessed December 24, 2007).

———. "The Opelousas Trail: Bellowing Cows Marked First Trail to New Orleans." Available at http://www.wtblock.com/wtblockjr/opelousa.htm (accessed May 31, 2006). Also, *Beaumont Enterprise*, 1975.

———. *Sapphire City of The Neches: A Brief History of Port Neches, Texas from Wilderness to Industrialization.* Austin: Nortex Press, 1987.

———. "Scrappy Kate Dorman Left Her Mark." *Beaumont Enterprise*, August 18, 1974.

———. "The Swamp Angels: A History of Spaight's 11th Battalion, Texas Volunteers, Confederate States Army." *East Texas Historical Journal* 30, no. 1 (1992): 44–57.

Bollaert, Wm. "Notes on the Coast Region of the Texan Territory: Taken during a Visit in 1842." *Journal of the Royal Geographical Society of London* 13 (1843): 226–44.

Bragg, Jefferson Davis. *Louisiana in the Confederacy*. Baton Rouge: Louisiana State University Press, 1941.

Briggs, Asa. "Cholera and Society in the Nineteenth Century." *Past and Present* 19 (April 1961): 76–96.

Brown, Russell K. "Fallen Stars." *Military Affairs* 45, no. 1 (1981): 9–12.

Brown, William O., Jr., and Richard C. D. Burdekin. "Turning Points in the U.S. Civil War: A British Perspective." *Journal of Economic History* 60, no. 1 (2000): 216–31.

Burdekin, Richard C. K., and Marc D. Weidenmier. "Inflation Is Always and Everywhere a Monetary Phenomenon: Richmond vs. Houston in 1864." *American Economic Review* 91, no. 5 (2001): 1621–30.

Burns, Robert. *To a Mouse*, "The best laid schemes o' mice an' men / Gang aft agley." In *The New Dictionary of Cultural Literacy*, 3rd ed., edited by E. D. Hirsch Jr., Joseph F. Kett, and James Trefil. New York: Houghton Mifflin, 2002.

Calvert, Robert A., Arnoldo De León, and Gregg Cantrell. *The History of Texas*. 3rd ed. Wheeling, Ill.: Harlan Davidson, 2002.

Capers, Gerald M., Jr. "Confederates and Yankees in Occupied New Orleans, 1862–1865." *Journal of Southern History* 30, no. 4 (1964): 405–26.

Carrigan, Jo Ann. "Privilege, Prejudice, and the Strangers' Disease in Nineteenth-Century New Orleans." *Journal of Southern History* 36, no. 4 (1970): 568–78.

Casdorph, Paul D. *Prince John Magruder: His Life and Campaigns*. Print-on-Demand: John Wiley and Sons, 1996.

———. Review of *Battle on the Bay: The Civil War Struggle for Galveston*, by Edward T. Cotham, Jr. *Journal of Southern History*, 65, no. 4 (1999): 880–81.

Chambers, William T. "The Gulf Port City Region of Texas." *Economic Geography* 7, no. 1 (1931): 69–83.

Chestnut, Mary. *Original Diary*. In *Mary Chestnut's Civil War*, edited by C. Vann Woodward. New Haven, Conn.: Yale University Press, 1981.

Christian, Carole E. *Handbook of Texas Online*, s.v. "Washington-on-the-Brazos, Texas." Available at http://www.tsha.utexas.edu/handbook/online/articles/WW/hvw10.html (accessed September 21, 2006).

City of St. Martinville, s.v. "Our History." Available at http://www.cityofsaintmartinville.com/english/index.htm (accessed October 24, 2006).

Cobb, Josephine. "Photographers of the Civil War." *Military Affairs* 26, no. 3, Civil War issue (1962): 127–35.

Cochran, Robert. "Review of *Juneteenth Texas: Essays in African-American Folklore*, by Francis Abernethy, Patrick Mullen, and Alan Govenar." *African American Review* 33, no. 4 (1999): 694–95.

Columbia Law Review. "The Reach of the Thirteenth Amendment" (unidentified author) 47, no. 2 (1947): 299–307.

Cooper, William J. *Jefferson Davis, American*. New York: Vintage Books, 2001.

———. "A Reassessment of Jefferson Davis as War Leader: The Case from Atlanta to Nashville." *Journal of Southern History* 36, no. 2 (1970): 189–204.

Cotham, Edward T., Jr. *Battle on the Bay: The Civil War Struggle for Galveston*. Austin: University of Texas Press, 1998.

———. *Sabine Pass: The Confederacy's Thermopylae*. Austin: University of Texas Press, 2004.

Courtwright, David T. "The Hidden Epidemic: Opiate Addiction and Cocaine Use in the South, 1860–1920." *Journal of Southern History* 49, no. 1 (1983): 57–72.

Crute, Joseph H., Jr. *Units of the Confederate States Army.* Midlothian, Va.: Derwent Books, 1987.

Cunningham, H. H. "Confederate General Hospitals: Establishment and Organization." *Journal of Southern History* 20, no. 3 (1954): 376–94.

Cutrer, Thomas W. *Handbook of Texas Online,* s.v. "George Wythe Baylor." Available at http://www.tsha.utexas.edu/handbook/online/articles/BB/fbaar.html (accessed October 30, 2006).

———. *Handbook of Texas Online,* s.v. "John George Walker." Available at http://www.tsha.utexas.edu/handbook/online/articles/WW/fwa20.html (accessed September 12, 2006).

Davis, Jefferson. *Messages and Papers I,* p. 485. In Stephenson 1915, 89.

———. *Richmond Enquirer,* September 28, 1864. In Stephenson 1915, 89.

———. *Richmond Enquirer,* February 7, 1865. In Stephenson 1915, 89.

Dawson, John P., and Frank E. Cooper. "The Effect of Inflation on Private Contracts: United States, 1861–1879." *Michigan Law Review* 33, no. 5 (1935): 706–57.

Dawson, Joseph G., III. "Review of *This Terrible Sound: The Battle of Chickamauga,* by Peter Cozzens and Keith Rocco." *American Historical Review* 98, no. 5 (1993): 1687–88.

Dehler, Kathleen. "Diaries: Where Women Reveal Themselves." *English Journal* 78, no. 7 (1989): 53–54.

Dorris, J. T. "Pardoning the Leaders of the Confederacy." *Mississippi Valley Historical Review* 15, no. 1 (1928): 3–21.

Doster, James F. Review of *Hood: Cavalier General,* by Richard O'Connor. *Journal of Southern History* 16, no. 1 (1950): 95–96.

Duffy, John. "A Note on Ante-Bellum Southern Nationalism and Medical Practice." *Journal of Southern History* 34, no. 2 (1968): 266–76.

Du Pont, S. F., et al. "The U.S. Coast Survey and the Blockade, 1861." *Official Naval Records,* Series I, 16: 654–55. In *The Denbigh Project,* Institute of Nautical Archaeology, Texas A&M University. Available at www.nautarch.tamu.edu.

Dwyer, Christopher S. "Raiding Strategy: As Applied by the Western Confederate Cavalry in the American Civil War." *Journal of Military History* 63, no. 2 (1999): 263–81.

Dyer, J. P. "Some Aspects of Cavalry Operations in the Army of Tennessee." *Journal of Southern History* 8, no. 2 (1942): 210–25.

Eaton, Clement. Review of *General Edmund Kirby Smith, C.S.A.,* by Joseph Howard Parks. *Journal of Southern History* 21, no. 1 (1955): 122–23.

Etheridge, Elizabeth W. "Review of *Yellow Fever and the South,* by Margaret Humphreys and *Dirt and Disease: Polio before FDR,* by Naomi Rogers." *Reviews in American History* 21, no. 2 (1993): 297–302.

Faust, Drew Gilpin. "Altars of Sacrifice: Confederate Women and the Narratives of War." *Journal of American History* 76, no. 4 (1990): 1200–1228.

———. "Christian Soldiers: The Meaning of Revivalism in the Confederate Army." *Journal of Southern History* 53, no. 1 (1987): 63–90.

Fenner, Frank, and David O. White. *Medical Virology*. New York: Academic Press, 1976.

Fernan-Nunez, M. "Asiatic Cholera," *American Journal of Nursing* 43, no. 1 (1943): 43–44.

Finch, L. Boyd. *Confederate Pathway to the Pacific: Major Sherod Hunter and Arizona Territory, C.S.A.* Tucson: Arizona Historical Society, 1996.

Fischbaum, Marvin. Review of *Trails to Texas: Southern Roots of Western Cattle Ranching,* by Terry G. Jordan. *Journal of Economic History,* 41, no. 4, (1981): 933–34.

Fisher, Barbara H. *Handbook of Texas Online,* s.v. "Edward Bradford Pickett." Available at http://www.tsha.utexas.edu/handbook/online/articles/PP/fpi5.html (accessed September 15, 2006).

Flannery, Tim. *The Eternal Frontier: An Ecological History of North America and Its Peoples.* New York: Atlantic Monthly Press, 2001.

Flood, Charles Bracelen. *Lee: The Last Years.* 1st Mariner Books ed. New York: Houghton Mifflin, 1998.

Forbes, Jack. D. "Frontiers in American History and the Role of the Frontier Historian." *Ethnohistory* 15, no. 2 (1968): 203–35.

Fortier, Alcee. "The Acadians of Louisiana and Their Dialect." *PMLA* 6, no. 1 (1891): 64–94.

Franklin, Benjamin to M. Leroy, 1789. In John Bartlett, *Familiar Quotations,* 15th ed. (New York: Little, Brown, 1980), 348.

Freehling, William W. *The Road to Disunion,* Vol. 1, *Secessionists at Bay, 1776–1854.* New York: Oxford University Press, 1990.

Furey, Joan A. "For Some, the War Rages On." *American Journal of Nursing* 82, no. 11 (1982): 1695–96.

Gallagher, Gary W. *The Confederate War.* Cambridge, Mass.: Harvard University Press, 1997.

Galloway, B. P., ed. *Texas: The Dark Corner of the Confederacy.* Lincoln: University of Nebraska Press, 1994.

Gambrell, Herbert. *Handbook of Texas Online,* s.v. "Mirabeau Buonaparte Lamar." Available at http://www.tsha.utexas.edu/handbook/online/articles/LL/fla15.html (accessed October 16, 2006).

Gard, Wayne. *The Chisholm Trail.* Norman: University of Oklahoma Press, 1954.

Gentry, Judith Fenner. "Review of *The Confederate Governors,* by W. Buck Yearns." *Journal of Southern History* 52, no. 1 (1986): 112–14.

Gerster, Patrick G. Review of *A Long Shadow: Jefferson Davis and the Final Days of the Confederacy. Journal of Southern History* 54, no. 1 (1988): 125–26.

Givens, Murphy. "Town Bitterly Divided during the Civil War." *Corpus Christi Caller-Times,* January 11, 2006.

———. "Union Invasion Force Lands." *Corpus Christi Caller-Times,* January 22, 2004.

Goliad, Birthplace of Texas Ranching. Available at http://www.goliad.org/goliad.html (accessed May 7, 2006).

Gorn, Elliott J., Randy Roberts, and Terry D. Bilhartz. *Constructing the American Past: A Source Book of a People's History.* New York: Pearson Education, 2005.

Govan, Gilbert E., and James W. Livingood. "Chattanooga under Military Occupation, 1863–1865." *Journal of Southern History* 17, no. 1 (1951): 23–47.

Grant, Ulysses S., Lieut. Gen., U.S. Army, Vicksburg, Mississippi, to [Jesse R. Grant], July 6, 1863. In "Letter of Grant to his Father, on the Capture of Vicksburg, 1863." *American Historical Review* 12, no. 1 (1906): 109.

Guthrie, Keith. *Handbook of Texas Online*, s.v. "San Patricio County." Available at http://www.tsha.utexas.edu/handbook/online/articles/SS/hcs4.html (accessed September 20, 2006).

Hall, Courtney Robert Hall. "The Influence of the Medical Department upon Confederate War Operations." *Journal of the American Military History Foundation* 1, no. 2 (1937): 46–54.

Handbook of Texas Online. A joint project of The General Libraries at the University of Texas at Austin (www.lib.utexas.edu) and the Texas State Historical Association (www.tsha.utexas.edu).

Hanna, Kathryn Abbey. "Incidents of the Confederate Blockade." *Journal of Southern History* 11, no. 2 (1945): 214–29.

Hay, Thomas Robson. "Confederate Leadership at Vicksburg." *Mississippi Valley Historical Review* 11, no. 4 (1925): 543–60.

Heaps, Willard A., and Porter W. Heaps. *The Singing Sixties: The Spirit of Civil War Days from the Music of the Times.* Norman: University of Oklahoma Press, 1960.

Hébert, Paul O., Brig. Gen. to C.S.A. Secretary of War Judah Benjamin, September 27, 1861. Official Records, Ser. I, Vol. IV, 112. In William T. Windham, "The Problem of Supply in the Trans-Mississippi Confederacy." *Journal of Southern History* 27, no. 2 (1961): 151.

Heinemann, Edith, and Nada Estes. "Assessing Alcoholic Patients." *American Journal of Nursing* 76, no. 5 (1976): 785–89.

Henry, Jacques M., and Carl L. Bankston, III. "Propositions for a Structuralist Analysis of Creolism." *Current Anthropology* 39, no. 4 (1998): 558–66.

Henson, Margaret Swett. *Handbook of Texas Online*, s.v. "John Davis Bradburn." Available at http://www.tsha.utexas.edu/handbook/online/articles/BB/fbr9.html (accessed October 18, 2006).

Hill, Jim Dan. "Review of *David Glasgow Farragut: Admiral in the Making,* by Charles Lee Lewis." *American Historical Review* 47, no. 3 (1942): 638–40.

Hogan, William Ransom. "Amusements in the Republic of Texas." *Journal of Southern History* 3, no. 4 (1937): 397–421.

Hollandsworth, James G. *The Civil War in Louisiana.* Baton Rouge: Louisiana State University Press, 1991.

Jackson, Jim Bob. *They Pointed Them East.* Liberty, Tex.: By the author, 2004.

Johnson, Arthur M. "The Early Texas Oil Industry: Pipelines and the Birth of an Integrated Oil Industry, 1901–1911." *Journal of Southern History* 32, no. 4 (1966): 516–28.

Johnson, Ludwell H. "Fort Sumter and Confederate Diplomacy." *Journal of Southern History* 26, no. 4 (1960): 441–77.

———. "Review of *The South Reports the Civil War,* by J. Cutler Andrews." *American Historical Review* 76, no. 2 (1971): 561–62.

Johnson, M. D., and Artell Egbert. "Antibiotics." *American Journal of Nursing* 50, no. 11 (1950): 688–90.

Jordan, Terry G. "The Origin of Anglo-American Cattle Ranching in Texas: A Documentation of Diffusion from the Lower South." *Economic Geography* 45, no. 1 (1969): 63–87.

———. *Trails to Texas: Southern Roots of Western Cattle Ranching.* Lincoln: University of Nebraska Press, 1981.

Kennedy, Edwin L., Jr. "Review of *General Stand Watie's Confederate Indians,* by Frank Cunningham." *Military Review* 80, no. 2 (2000): 105–106.

Kleiner, Diana J. *Handbook of Texas Online,* s.v. "Jefferson County." Available at http://www.tsha.utexas.edu/handbook/online/articles/JJ/hcj5.html (accessed October 21, 2006).

———. *Handbook of Texas Online,* s.v. "Liberty County." Available at http://www.tsha.utexas.edu/handbook/online/articles/LL/hc18.html (accessed October 21, 2006).

Klingberg, Frank L. "Predicting the Termination of War: Battle Casualties and Population Losses." *Journal of Conflict Resolution* 10, no. 2 (1966): 129–71.

Kniffen, Fred. "The Western Cattle Complex: Notes on Differentiation and Diffusion." *Western Folklore* 12, no. 3, Oregon Number (1953): 179–85.

Kolchin, Peter. "Scalawags, Carpetbaggers, and Reconstruction: A Quantitative Look at Southern Congressional Politics, 1868–1872." *Journal of Southern History* 45, no. 1 (1979): 63–76.

Kübler-Ross, Elizabeth. *On Death and Dying.* New York: Macmillan, 1969.

"LaFourche Crossing, June 20–21, 1863." *CWSAC Battle Summaries.* The American Battlefield Protection Program, Heritage Preservation Services, National Park Services, U.S. Department of the Interior. Available at www.cr.nps.gov/ (accessed July 15, 2006).

Lambert, Alexander, M.D. "Medicine, a Determining Factor in War." *Science* 50, no. 1279 (1919): 8–11.

Lang, Robert E., Deborah Epstein Popper, and Frank J. Popper. "'Progress of the Nation': The Settlement History of the Enduring American Frontier." *Western Historical Quarterly* 26, no. 3 (1995): 289–307.

Leatherwood, Art. *Handbook of Texas Online,* s.v. "Brazos Santiago, Texas." Available at http://www.tsha.utexas.edu/handbook/online/articles/BB/rrb12.html (accessed September 17, 2006).

———. *Handbook of Texas Online,* s.v. "Camp Groce." Available at http://www.tsha.utexas.edu/handbook/online/articles/CC/qcc17.html (accessed November 10, 2006).

Lebergott, Stanley. "Through the Blockade: The Profitability and Extent of Cotton Smuggling, 1861–1865." *Journal of Economic History* 41, no. 4 (1981): 867–88.

———. "Why the South Lost: Commercial Purpose in the Confederacy, 1861–1865." *Journal of American History* 70, no. 1 (1983): 58–74.

Leffler, John. *Handbook of Texas Online,* s.v. "McMullen County." Available at http://www.tsha.utexas.edu/handbook/online/articles/MM/hcm9.html (accessed September 20, 2006).

Lincoln, Abraham, The White House, to [General George Meade], July 1863, unsent. In McPherson, *Ordeal by Fire,* 359.

Louisiana Civil War Map of Battles. U.S. National Park Service, U.S. Library of Congress. Available at www.americancivilwar.com (accessed frequently, June–December 2006).

Louisiana State Museum. "Antebellum Louisiana: Urban Life." Available at www.lsm .crt.state.la.us (accessed October 6, 2006.)

Lubbock, Francis R. to Judah P. Benjamin, March 7, 1862, Official Records, Ser. IV, Vol. I, 980. In William T. Windham, "The Problem of Supply in the Trans-Mississippi Confederacy." *Journal of Southern History* 27, no. 2 (1961): 151.

Lytle, William M. "Merchant Steam Vessels of the United States, 1807–1868," edited by Forrest R. Holdcamper (Mystic, Conn.: 1952). In William N. Still Jr., "Facilities for the Construction of War Vessels in the Confederacy." *Journal of Southern History* 31, no. 3 (1965): 285–304.

McMurry, Richard M. "Review of *Five Tragic Hours: The Battle of Franklin,* by James Lee McDonough and Thomas L. Connelly." *Journal of Southern History* 50, no. 4 (1984): 653–54.

McPherson, James M. *For Cause and Comrades: Why Men Fought in the Civil War.* New York: Oxford University Press, 1997.

———. *Ordeal by Fire,* Vol. 2, *The Civil War.* 3rd ed. New York: McGraw Hill, 2001.

Mahon, John K. "Civil War Infantry Assault Tactics." *Military Affairs* 25, no. 2 (1961): 57–68.

"Mansfield/Sabine Cross Roads," April 8, 1864. *CWSAC Battle Summaries.* The American Battlefield Protection Program, Heritage Preservation Services, National Park Services, U.S. Department of the Interior. Available at www.cr.nps.gov/ (accessed October 31, 2006).

Marshall, Peter. "Ambrotype." *About Photography.* Available at http://photography. about.com/library/glossary/bldef_ambrotype.htm (accessed October 25, 2006).

Marten, James. "Fatherhood in the Confederacy: Southern Soldiers and Their Children." *Journal of Southern History* 63, no. 2 (1997): 269–92.

Matherly, Walter J. "The Emergence of the Metropolitan Community in the South." *Social Forces* 14, no. 3 (1936): 311–25.

Meredith, Mamie. "Picturesque Town Names in America." *American Speech* 6, no. 6 (1931): 429–32.

Miller, E. T. "The State Finances of Texas during the Civil War." *Southwestern Historical Quarterly Online,* page 1–23. Available at http://www.tsha.utexas.edu/publications/ journals/shq/online/vo14/n1/article_2.html (accessed November 2, 2006).

"Mobile Bay, Aug. 2–24, 1864." *CWSAC Battle Summaries.* The American Battlefield Protection Program, Heritage Preservation Services, National Park Services, U.S. Department of the Interior. Available at www.cr.nps.gov (accessed November 9, 2006).

Moneyhon, Carl H. *Handbook of Texas Online,* s.v. "Reconstruction." Available at http:// www.tsha.utexas.edu/handbook/online/articles/RR/mzr1.html (accessed December 7, 2006).

Moore, John G. "Mobility and Strategy in the Civil War." Military Affairs 24, no. 2, Civil War issue (1960): 68–77.

Moore, Waldo W. "The Defense of Shreveport—The Confederacy's Last Redoubt." *Military Affairs* 17, no. 2 (1953): 72–82.

Morrison, Michael A. Review of *The Shattering of Texas Unionism: Politics in the Lone Star State during the Civil War Era*, by Dale Baum. *Journal of Southern History* 66, no. 3 (2000): 638–39.

Motz, Marilyn Ferris. "Folk Expression of Time and Place: 19th-Century Midwestern Rural Diaries." *Journal of American Folklore* 100, no. 396 (1987): 131–47.

Muir, Andrew Forest. *Handbook of Texas Online*, s.v. "Harrisburg, Texas." Available at http://www.tsha.utexas.edu/handbook/online/articles/HH/hvh27.html (accessed September 22, 2006).

Munson, E. L., Jr. "Leadership for American Army Leaders." *Infantry Journal* (Washington, D.C., 1942) In Benjamin N. Schoenfeld, "The Psychological Characteristics of Leadership," *Social Forces* 26, no. 4 (1948): 395.

Nevins, Allan. *War for the Union: The Organized War, 1863–64*. New York: Scribner's, 1971.

Nichols, James D., Fred A. Johnson, and Byron K. Williams. "Managing North American Waterfowl in the Face of Uncertainty." *Annual Review of Ecology and Systematics* 26 (1995): 177–99.

Norman, Elizabeth M. "The Victims Who Survived." *American Journal of Nursing* 82, no. 11 (1982): 1696–98.

Nunn, W. C. *Texas under the Carpetbaggers*. Austin: University of Texas Press, 1962.

Oates, Stephen B. "Supply for Confederate Cavalry in the Trans-Mississippi." *Military Affairs* 25, no. 2, Civil War issue (1961): 94–99.

Odintz, Mark. *Handbook of Texas Online*, s.v. "Colorado County." Available at http://www.tsha.utexas.edu/handbook/online/articles/CC/hcc18.html (accessed September 20, 2006).

Osburn, Mary McMillan, ed. "The Atascosito Census of 1826." *Texans* 1, no. 4 (1963).

Owsley, Frank L. *Plain Folk of the Old South* (Baton Rouge, 1949). In "Cows, Ticks, and Disease: A Medical Interpretation of the Southern Cattle Industry," by Tamara Miner Haygood. *Journal of Southern History* 52, no. 4 (1986): 551–64.

Page, Kathryn. Louisiana State Museum, New Orleans. Identification of McQuoid & Co. of New Orleans. E-mail to author, October 18, 2006.

Parent, Anthony S., Jr. *Foul Means: The Formation of a Slave Society in Virginia, 1660–1740*. Williamsburg, Va.: Omohundro Institute of Early American History and Culture published by the University of North Carolina Press, Chapel Hill, 2003.

Parks, Joseph H. "Review of *The Civil War in Louisiana*, by John D. Winters." *Journal of Southern History* 30, no. 1 (1964): 116–17.

Parrish, T. Michael. "Review of The Papers of Jefferson Davis, Vol. 9, January–September 1863, by Jefferson Davis, Lynda Lasswell Crist, Mary Seaton Dix, and Kenneth H. Williams." *Journal of Southern History* 64, no. 2 (1998): 370–71.

Partlow, Miriam. *Liberty, Liberty County, and the Atascosito District*. Austin: Pemberton Press, 1974.

Phleger, Fred B. "Patterns of Marsh Foraminifera, Galveston Bay, Texas." *Limnology and Oceanography* 10 (November 1965): 169–84.

Plummer, Mark. "Review of *The Siege of Charleston, 1861–1865*, by Milby Burton." *Journal of American History* 58, no. 1 (1971): 171–72.

Post, Lauren C. "The Rice Country of Southwestern Louisiana." *Geographical Review* 30, no. 4 (1940): 574–90.

Power, J. Tracy. "Review of . . . *the Real War Will Never Get in the Books: Selections from Writers during the Civil War,* by Louis P. Masur." *Journal of Southern History* 61, no. 1 (1995): 159–60.

Proctor, Ben H. *Handbook of Texas Online,* s.v. "John Henninger Reagan." Available at http://www.tsha.utexas.edu/handbook/online/articles/RR/fre2.html (accessed December 9, 2006).

Ragan, Cooper K., ed. "Notes and Documents: The Diary of Captain George W. O'Bryan [*sic*], 1863." *Southwestern Historical Quarterly* 67, nos. 1, 2, 3 (1963–64).

Ramos, Ralph. "Big Man on Texas Frontier." *Beaumont Enterprise-Journal,* February 23, 1975, Section C.

Ramsdell, Charles W. "General Robert E. Lee's Horse Supply, 1862–1865." *American Historical Review* 35, no. 4 (1930): 758–77.

———. "The Problem of Public Morale in the Southern Confederacy." In J. Cutler Andrews, "The Confederate Press and Public Morale." *Journal of Southern History* 32, no. 4 (1966): 445–65.

———. "Texas from the Fall of the Confederacy to the Beginning of Reconstruction." *Southwestern Historical Quarterly Online* 11, no. 3: 199–219. Available at http://www .tsha.utexas.edu/publications/journals/shq/online/v011/n3/article (accessed October 28, 2006).

Rao, S. L. N. "On Long-Term Mortality Trends in the United States, 1850–1968." *Demography* 10, no. 3 (1973): 405–19.

Rawley, James A. "The General Amnesty Act of 1872: A Note." *Mississippi Valley Historical Review* 47, no. 3 (1960): 480–84.

Reagan, John H., Fort Warren, Massachusetts to President Andrew Johnson, Washington, 28 May 1865. In J. T. Dorris. "Pardoning the Leaders of the Confederacy." *Mississippi Valley Historical Review* 15, no. 1 (1928): 5–6.

Reid, Joseph D., Jr. "Sharecropping as an Understandable Market Response: The Post-Bellum South." *Journal of Economic History* 33, no. 1 (1973): 106–30.

Richard, Jacob Fraise. *The Florence Nightingale of the Southern Army: Experiences of Mrs. Ella K. Newsom, Confederate Nurse in the Great War of 1861–65* (New York and Baltimore, 1914). In H. H. Cunningham, "Confederate General Hospitals: Establishment and Organization." *Journal of Southern History* 20, no. 3 (1954): 376–94.

Riegel, Robert E. "Trans-Mississippi Railroads during the Fifties." *Mississippi Valley Historical Review* 10, no. 2 (1923): 153–72.

Roberts, Randy, and James S. Olson. *A Line in the Sand.* New York: Touchstone/Simon and Schuster, 2002.

Robinson, Armstead L. "In the Shadow of Old John Brown: Insurrection Anxiety and Confederate Mobilization, 1861–1863." *Journal of Negro History* 65, no. 4 (1980): 279–97.

Roland, Charles P. *Albert Sidney Johnston, Soldier of Three Republics.* Austin: University of Texas Press, 1964.

Roman, Colonel Alfred, Assistant Inspector-General, Confederate Army, December 28, 1864. In Beauregard Papers (Division of Manuscripts, Library of Congress). In J. P.

Dyer, "Some Aspects of Cavalry Operations in the Army of Tennessee." *Journal of Southern History* 8, no. 2 (1942): 210–25.

Rothbard, Murray N. "The Panic of 1819: Contemporary Opinion and Policy." *Journal of Finance* 15, no. 3 (1960): 420–21.

"Sabine Pass II, Sept. 8, 1863." *CWSAC Battle Summaries.* The American Battlefield Protection Program, Heritage Preservation Services, National Park Services, U.S. Department of the Interior. Available at www.cr.nps.gov (accessed June 3, 2006).

Sabine River Authority of Texas, s.v. "Description of Sabine River Basin," Available at www.sra.dst.tx.us/basin/overview information (accessed on July 11, 2006).

Sackett, Frances Robertson. *Dick Dowling.* Houston: Gulf Publishing, 1937.

Scurlock, Ruth Garrison. "The Unsung Opelousas Trail." *Texas Gulf Historical and Biographical Record* 5, no. 1 (1969): 8–12.

Schlesselman, G. W. "The Gulf Coast Oyster Industry of the United States," *Geographical Review* 45, no. 4 (1955): 531–41.

Schoenfeld, Benjamin N. "The Psychological Characteristics of Leadership." *Social Forces* 26, no. 4 (1948): 391–96.

Schmitz, Neil. "Refiguring Lincoln: Speeches and Writings, 1852–1865." *American Literary History* 6, no. 1 (1994): 103–18.

Schultz, Jane E. "The Inhospitable Hospital: Gender and Professionalism in Civil War Medicine." *Signs* 17, no. 2 (1992): 363–92.

Scribner, John C. L. "Civil War." Texas Military Forces Museum (Austin: Camp Mabry). Available at www.texasmilitaryforcesmuseum.org (accessed April 7, 2006).

Sears, Stephen W. *Landscape Turned Red: The Battle of Antietam.* New York: Houghton Mifflin, 1983.

Sellers, James. L. "The Economic Incidence of the Civil War in the South." *Mississippi Valley Historical Review* 14, no. 2 (1927): 179–91.

Shyrock, Richard H. "A Medical Perspective on the Civil War." *American Quarterly* 14, no. 2, Part 1 (1962): 161–73.

———. "Review of *The Conquest of Cholera: America's Greatest Scourge,* by J. S. Chambers." *Mississippi Valley Historical Review* 26, no. 1 (1939): 91–92.

Siegel, Stanley E. Review of *Texas Divided: Loyalty and Dissent in the Lone Star State, 1856–1874,* by James Marten. *American Historical Review* 96, no. 3 (1991): 964.

Smyrl, Vivian Elizabeth. *Handbook of Texas Online,* s.v. "Guadalupe County." Available at http://www.tsha.utexas.edu/handbook/online/articles/GG/hcg12.html (accessed September 20, 2006).

Sonstegard, Lois, Neva Hansen, Linda Zillman, and Mary K. Johnston. "The Grieving Nurse." *American Journal of Nursing* 76, no. 9 (1976): 1490–92.

Southwestern Historical Quarterly Online. Vol. 1, no. 1, July 1897. Available at http://www.tsha.utexas.edu/publications/journals/shq/online/v001/n1/issue.html (accessed December 9, 2006).

Stavisky, Leonard Price. "Negro Craftsmanship in Early America." *American Historical Review* 54, no. 2 (1949): 315–25.

Stephenson, N. W. "A Theory of Jefferson Davis." *American Historical Review* 21, no. 1 (1915): 73–90.

Still, William N., Jr. "Facilities for the Construction of War Vessels in the Confederacy." *Journal of Southern History* 31, no. 3 (1965): 285–304.

"Stirling's Plantation, September 29, 1863." *CWSAC Battle Summaries*, The American Battlefield Protection Program, Heritage Preservation Services, National Park Services, U.S. Department of the Interior. Available at www.cr.nps.gov (accessed October 19, 2006).

Stuart, Reginald C. "Cavalry Raids in the West: Case Studies of Civil War Cavalry Raids." *Tennessee Historical Quarterly* 30 (1971).

Surdam, David G. "Northern Naval Superiority and the Economics of the American Civil War." *Journal of Economic History* 56, no. 2 (1996): 473–75.

Swanberg, W. A. *First Blood: The Story of Fort Sumter.* New York: Charles Scribner's Sons, 1958.

Talley, Reggie. "Monroe County Champion Trees: Black Gum." *Arkansas Gardener* (January 2002).

Texas State Cemetery. "John Austin Wharton." Confederate Section, 909 Navasota Street, Austin, Texas 78702. Available at www.cemetery.state.tx.us (accessed September 16, 2006).

Tolbert, Frank X. *Dick Dowling at Sabine Pass.* New York: McGraw-Hill, 1962.

Tomkins, Shannon. "Trinity River Wildlife Refuge Sees a Growth Spurt." *Houston Chronicle,* May 19, 2006, C14.

Trelease, Allen W. "Who Were the Scalawags?" *Journal of Southern History* 29, no. 4 (1963): 445–68.

Trépanier, Cécyle. "The Cajunization of French Louisiana: Forging a Regional Identity." *Geographical Journal* 157, no. 2 (1991): 161–71.

"USDA Requires New Test for Tickborne Horse Disease." *Journal of the American Veterinary Medical Association* (June 1, 2003). Available at www.avma.org/onlnews/javma/jun (accessed September 16, 2006).

U.S. Department of the Interior. "Migration of Birds" (August 3, 2006). Northern Prairie Wildlife Research Center, U.S. Geological Survey. Available at www.npwrc.usgs.gov/resource/birds/migratio/patterns (accessed July 22, 2006).

U.S. Food and Drug Administration, www.cfsan.fda.gov (accessed June 7, 2006).

Vandiver, Frank E. "Review of *Prince John Magruder: His Life and Campaigns,* by Paul D. Casdorph." *Journal of American History* 85, no. 1 (1998): 248.

———. "Some Problems Involved in Writing Confederate History." *Journal of Southern History* 36, no. 3 (1970): 400–410.

Wagener, A. Pelzer. "Review of *Flight into Oblivion,* by Alfred Jackson Hanna." *William and Mary Quarterly* 2nd Ser., 20, no. 2 (1964): 330–32.

Walker, Charles R., M.D. *Spaight's Battalion, C.S.A.* Beaumont, Tex.: Texas Gulf Historical Society, 1972.

Walmsley, James Elliott. "The Last Meeting of the Confederate Cabinet." *Mississippi Valley Historical Review* 6, no. 3 (1919): 336–49.

"Washington, Gateway to the Southwest." Town of Washington, Louisiana, Historical Society. Available at www.townofwashingtonla.org/history (accessed June 28, 2006).

Weinert, Richard P. "The Confederate Regular Army." *Military Affairs* 26, no. 3 (1962): 97–107.

Wertenbaker, Thomas J. *Patrician and Plebian in Virginia* (Charlottesville, 1912). In Leonard Price Stavisky, "Negro Craftsmanship in Early America." *American Historical Review* 54, no. 2 (1949): 321.

Westley, W. A. "The Nature and Control of Hostile Crowds." *Canadian Journal of Economics and Political Science/Revue canadienne d'economique et de science politique* 23, no. 1 (1957): 33–41.

Wetta, Frank J. Review of *Acadian to Cajun: Transformation of a People, 1803–1877,* by Carl A. Brasseaux. *Journal of Southern History* 60, no. 3 (1994): 574–75.

Westwood, Howard C. "After Vicksburg, What of Mobile?" *Military Affairs* 48, no. 4 (1948): 169–73.

Wiley, Bell Irvin. "A Time of Greatness." *Journal of Southern History* 22, no. 1 (1956): 3–35.

———. *The Life of Johnny Reb: The Common Soldier of the Confederacy.* 2005 printing. Baton Rouge: Louisiana State University Press, 1943.

Williams, T. Harry. *Lincoln and His Generals.* New York: Alfred A. Knopf, 1952; reprint, New York: Gramercy Books, 2000.

Williamson, Samuel H. "Five Ways to Compute the Relative Value of a U.S. Dollar Amount, 1790–2007." Available at www.MeasuringWorth.com, 2008.

Wilson, Charles Reagan. "The Religion of the Lost Cause: Ritual and Organization of the Southern Civil Religion, 1865–1920." *Journal of Southern History* 46, no. 2 (1980): 219–38.

Windham, William T. "The Problem of Supply in the Trans-Mississippi Confederacy." *Journal of Southern History* 27, no. 2 (1961): 149–68.

Wooster, Ralph A. *Texas and Texans in the Civil War.* Austin: Eakin Press, 1995.

Wooster, Robert. *Handbook of Texas Online,* s.v. "Ashley W. Spaight." Available at http://www.tsha.utexas.edu/handbook/online/articles/SS/fsp1.html (accessed December 6, 2006).

———. *Handbook of Texas Online,* s.v. "Burr's Ferry." Available at http://www.tsha.utexas.edu/handbook/online/articles/BB/rtb2.html (accessed November 2, 2006).

———. *Handbook of Texas Online,* s.v. "Newton County." Available at http://www.tsha.utexas.edu/handbook/online/articles/NN/hcn3.html (accessed October 21, 2006).

Wooster, Robert, and Christine Moor Sanders. *Handbook of Texas Online,* s.v. "Spindletop Oilfield." Available at http://www.tsha.utexas.edu/handbook/online/articles/SS/dos3.html (accessed November 7, 2006).

Wyatt-Brown, Bertram. "Review of *The Edge of the Swamp: A Study in the Literature and Society of the Old South,* by Louis D. Rubin, Jr." *Journal of Southern History* 56, no. 4 (1990): 750–51.

Young, Kevin R. *To the Tyrants Never Yield: A Texas Civil War Sampler.* Plano, Tex.: Wordware Publishing, 1992.

Index

Also available in the Sam Rayburn Series on Rural Life: